ALSO BY NATE CHINEN

Myself Among Others: A Life in Music
(with George Wein)

PLAYING CHANGES

PLAYING CHANGES

Jazz for the New Century

NATE CHINEN

 PANTHEON BOOKS, NEW YORK

Published in the United States by Pantheon Books, a division
of Penguin Random House LLC, New York, and distributed in Canada
by Random House of Canada, a division
of Penguin Random House Canada Limited, Toronto.

Pantheon Books and colophon
are registered trademarks of Penguin Random House LLC.

www.pantheonbooks.com

Library of Congress Cataloging-in-Publication Data
Name: Chinen, Nate, author.
Title: Playing changes : jazz for the new century / Nate Chinen.
Description: First edition. New York : Pantheon Books, 2018.
Includes bibliographical references and index.
Identifiers: LCCN 2017058677. ISBN 9781101870341 (hardcover : alk. paper).
ISBN 9781101870358 (ebook)
Subjects: LCSH: Jazz—2001–2010—History and criticism.
Jazz—2011–2020—History and criticism.
Classification: LCC ML3506 .C54 2018. DDC 781.6509/05—dc23.
LC record available at lccn.loc.gov/2017058677

Jacket design by Kelly Blair

Printed in the United States of America
First Edition
2 4 6 8 9 7 5 3 1

for Ashley, Athena, and Rosalie

Contents

Foreword

"A secret, a secret, I've got a little secret." Cécile McLorin Salvant flashes a grin as she sings this playful taunt, the preamble to an old show tune, "If This Isn't Love." She's at the Village Vanguard, which has entered its ninth decade with an indisputable reputation as the most hallowed jazz club in the world. In a couple of days Salvant would release a double album largely recorded in this room. But she doesn't so much as mention it during the set. Her only partner onstage is the pianist Sullivan Fortner, and she seems determined to meet him in an elegant free fall, making adjustments and testing out methods on the fly.

The burden of jazz history lies in wait for a moment like this. Headlining the Vanguard to a sold-out crowd without a proven set list is a recipe for all manner of anxiety, not least the anxiety of influence. But over the course of her casually stunning performance, on a late-September evening in 2017, Salvant shows that she's neither wrestling with ghosts nor shouldering a weight of obligation. Instead, she carries herself like the beneficiary of a trust: she's got a little secret, and she's letting her audience in on the action.

She knows better than anyone in the club that "If This Isn't Love" was a calling card for the sublime jazz singer Sarah Vaughan, who recorded her definitive version in the 1950s. There's a hint of Vaughan in Salvant's bell-like tone and swooping inflection, but also abundant creative liberties in her phrasing. Rather than evoke the past from a stance of decorum or deference, Salvant is bent on stirring it up with sly intellectual rigor. Given how much effort has gone into the canonization of the jazz tradition, she's a stealth subversive, working within a recognizable framework in ways that feel ecstatic and unbound.

The emergence of a jazz artist as audacious, unconflicted, and grounded as Salvant, at this stage in the game, suggests both the fulfillment of a promise and the rejection of an idea. During the waning phase of the last century, jazz was enshrined in the popular imagination as a historical practice, a set of codes to be reenacted endlessly. Market forces—primed by a relentless campaign of reissues and compilations, tributes and emulations—had fed a common perception that the music reached its peak in a distant golden age. What could Salvant possibly be if not a throwback? The art form had already completed a full life cycle of creation, maturation, obsolescence, and revival.

Gary Giddins, the astute jazz critic, once delineated that trajectory in an essay with a cheeky title, "How Come Jazz Isn't Dead?" In it, he argues that the development of any musical form can be divided into four stages. The first is Native, followed by Sovereign. Then comes Recessionary. Finally, we arrive at Classical—when "Even the most adventurous young musicians are weighed down by the massive accomplishments of the past."

Most mainstream narratives of jazz over the last several decades followed the general contour of this model. Critics and historians, planting their surveying equipment on Classical bedrock, took their measure of the music along a timeline. So it was no surprise that the conventional framework suggested an inexorable march of progress. And it made sense that jazz, especially for those outside its orbit, meant something openly retrograde. When Giddins updated his four-stage paradigm in 2009 for *Jazz*, a sprawling history coauthored with the scholar Scott DeVeaux, he suggested that it might help to envision the music in a "post-historical" mode. That notion seems almost custom-fitted to Salvant, with her refusal to be typecast by precedent.

But she's just one figure in a vast new complex, the dimensions of which make the four-stage paradigm feel reductive. What the most recent jazz surveys and histories tend to ignore is an explosion of new techniques, accents, and protocols that define the state of the art in our time. Some of this happened in response to widespread upheaval. As the art form began to settle into its second century, its practitioners faced tougher conditions than any previous generation: a broken infrastructure, an uncertain course, a distracted, if not alienated, consumer base.

But more than one wave of improvising artists has confronted this tumult, seizing license to create freer and more self-reliant forms of art. Raised with unprecedented access to information, they scour jazz history not for a linear narrative but a network of possibilities. Their frame of reference is broad enough to encourage every form of hybridism. They understand jazz as something other than a stable category. And their work has evolved the music—insofar as harmonic color, dynamic flow, group interaction, and a complex yet streamlined expression of rhythm are concerned.

Jazz has always been a frontier of inquiry, with experimentation in multiple registers. That's as true now as it has ever been. But to a striking degree, avant-garde practice and formal invention have now insinuated themselves into the mainstream, shifting the music's aesthetic center. Not even a resurgent strain of hot-jazz antiquarianism—the province of out-and-proud nostalgists—can stem the current trend toward polyglot hypermodernism, toward unexpected composites and convergences.

This book begins with a reflection on the crisis of confidence that distorted jazz's ecology during the late phases of the twentieth century. Tracing a historicist agenda that actualized in the 1970s, mobilized in the 1980s, and all but tyrannized the 1990s, this narrative sets an important context for our present moment of abundance. As the music transitioned out of the last century, it became increasingly clear that a conscientious foothold in tradition could work in peaceful tandem with many approaches that fall outside a strict definition of jazz. The whole idea of a definition, in fact, was beginning to feel outmoded. Whatever you choose to call the music, "jazz" is as volatile and generative now as at any time since its beginnings. Instead of stark binaries and opposing factions, we face a blur of contingent alignments. Instead of a push for definition and one prevailing style, we have boundless permutations without fixed parameters. That multiplicity lies precisely at the heart of the new aesthetic—and is the engine of its greatest promise.

PLAYING CHANGES

1

Change of the Guard

Kamasi Washington stood tall on a lot of big stages during his Year of Ascendance. Swaying in tempo, pushing heavy gusts through his tenor saxophone, he exuded the regal composure of a conquering hero: dauntless, doubtless, ablaze with rugged purpose. His sound on the horn—rangy and intemperate, or clipped and urgent—suggested an almost tactile force, a physical fact. He cut an equally imposing visual presence, in an unkempt Afro, a thick beard, and a dashiki, its patterned fabric loosely draped over his burly frame. And as his band raged around him, the music's exultant sprawl enacted a ritual of transcendence. It was all rattling and ecstatic, maybe a little mystical. For many who bore witness, it was, brazenly, something to believe in.

These details formed a reliable constant throughout Washington's rocketlike path from local notoriety to global celebrity after the release of his debut album, *The Epic,* in 2015. A soft-spoken but resolute musician rooted in South Central Los Angeles, he emerged as jazz's most persuasive embodiment of new black pride at a moment when few forces in American culture felt more pressing.

Washington, whose image suggested a revival of Afrocentric ideals from the Black Arts Movement of the 1960s and '70s, encouraged this interpretation. He was a known affiliate of Kendrick Lamar, the ambitious, insurgent, politically engaged young rapper from Compton. And Washington spoke often, pointedly, about his experience as a young black man in America. For the penultimate track on *The Epic*, he offered "Malcolm's Theme," a solemn vocal feature with lyrics adapted from Ossie Davis's eulogy for Malcolm X. The album's valediction, "The Message," was an odd-metered funk raga in which Washington opened his solo with a quickening flurry of rhythmic punches, moved on to feverish incantation, and finally resorted to screaming through his horn.

The Epic sprawls across three discs, with a suggestively cosmic vibe and occasional blasts of choral voices and orchestral strings. It elicited breathless acclaim from an assortment of media outlets that ordinarily have little use for jazz. With it Washington won the inaugural American Music Prize for best debut album, beating a field that included major arrivals in pop, country, and R&B. He appeared on both of PBS's marquee talk shows at the time, *Tavis Smiley* and *Charlie Rose*, gamely responding to questions like the one Rose asked about jazz's position in the present musical climate.

"Well," Washington said, clearing his throat, "I think jazz has been trapped in a poor image." He went on:

> And I think that it has been trapped in this image of something that is a historic relic, or something that is made to serve some purpose other than to just enjoy. And I think it's a music that, it's the reverse. It's such an expressive music, and when you hear jazz, you really hear a commune of people who are expressing themselves together.[1]

He was speaking with vested interests, having embarked on his first headlining tour in late summer of 2015. With his band, the Next Step, he'd galloped across the United States and Europe and off to Australia, New Zealand, and Japan. They played the coolly discerning Big Ears Festival, in Knoxville, Tennessee. They played at the Bonnaroo Music and Arts Festival, attended that year by nearly seventy-five thousand freewheeling fans. They played to capacity crowds in New York—not only at the Blue Note Jazz Club, where the line stretched down West

Third Street, but also at Webster Hall, a cavernous rock room, and in Central Park, under a summer night sky. They played a triumphant stand at Coachella, the desert summit of California boho-chic, where Washington was interviewed by *Esquire*. The resulting article ran with a headline that captured the spirit of the moment: "Kamasi Washington on the Pressures of Being Called Jazz's Savior."[2]

When Washington referred to jazz's "poor image," he was in fact describing the opposite: a common understanding of the music as something rarefied and precious, and also a bit of a bore. Since the early 1980s, jazz had become synonymous with respectability, befitting the designation of "America's classical music." It was refined and safe, a signifier of adult sophistication suitable for coffeehouse ambience or the advertising of luxury goods. It was staunchly historical, endlessly concerned with recapturing the mood of 1959, or 1963. And it was the recipient of support from institutions like Jazz at Lincoln Center and the National Endowment for the Arts. When the average person thought about jazz, the image that came to mind was often something stylish but inert, as much a function of iconography as of music making.

   According to the most widely disseminated histories of the music—like *Jazz*, the 2001 documentary series by Ken Burns, watched by more than 30 million viewers on PBS—this was the natural due of a discipline that had reached maturity sometime around midcentury. Whatever happened after that point was to be framed in self-referential or nostalgic terms, as the retelling of a familiar story. If that meant placing jazz and its traditions under glass, sealed off from the messy roil of pop culture, so much the better. Didn't jazz deserve as much? Its heroes had fought valiantly, through the twentieth century, for this level of respect.

   For an artist like Washington, respect wasn't the issue at hand. What he was talking about, and attempting to address in his music, was jazz's grasping struggle for relevance. And it's possible to see how one campaign set the terms for the other: how jazz won a Pyrrhic victory when it secured highbrow stature as "the quintessential American art form." There had been unintended consequences, repercussions in the culture. Some of them were insidious and difficult to parse, and others were screamingly clear.

If your experience of the music came through institutional channels, you might reasonably assume that jazz stopped growing and changing a long time ago. There are scores of musicians whose work has proven otherwise, supporting the idea that jazz is actually in the throes of a brilliant new evolutionary phase. But the machinery of culture and commerce is far better primed to highlight historical achievements. Each of those present-day artists compete in the same marketplace as Miles Davis, John Coltrane, and Charlie Parker. And at a time when jazz album sales suggested a bleak Darwinian outcome—routinely accounting for less than 3 percent of the industry tally, and sometimes as little as 1.4 percent—many successes came with the assurance of time-honored quality. A five-CD boxed set titled *Ken Burns Jazz: The Story of America's Music* sold forty thousand copies before the first episode of the series had aired.[3]

All of which set the stage for Washington's emergence as a great new hope for the music. Whether he was qualified for such a task was beside the point. There's a powerful insecurity built into any call for a jazz savior: the very idea presupposes a vital deficiency in the art form. Washington was merely the latest embodiment of an idea, the details of which are dynamic and fluid, like atmospheric conditions. Whatever it is that jazz is understood to be sorely lacking at a given moment—that's what a savior is expected to deliver. Cultural esteem. Social currency. Historical connection. Contemporary agency. Institutional elevation. Street-level energy. Renewal. Definition. Freedom.

The music's foothold in popular culture bears a precise correlation to the reports of its health or decline. Whatever is actually happening with the state of the art, among the musicians who make up its constituency, exerts less influence there. So the injunction to "save jazz," as if the art form were a damsel trussed on the railroad tracks, came into widespread circulation in the 1960s, one of the most vibrantly creative decades in the music's history. Partly it was a reaction to the rise of a fast-moving avant-garde that seemed to call everything—form, fixed tonality, even rhythm—into question. The alto saxophonist Ornette Coleman was the era's main agent of change, throwing down a challenge that the more forward-thinking of his peers felt compelled to accept. The press and the public were under no such obligation: in 1961, when John Coltrane was leading a bravely expeditionary band with the Coleman contemporary Eric Dolphy, a critic for *DownBeat*—the leading jazz magazine—infamously assailed their music as "anti-jazz."

But the scarier threat came from the outside, as rock 'n' roll, which had coexisted uneasily but tenably with jazz in the 1950s, devoured the culture almost whole in the sixties. The Beatles, the Rolling Stones, Bob Dylan, Janis Joplin: their emergence as a bloc profoundly undermined jazz's hold on the public, especially among young audiences. A few jazz musicians in that demographic, like the vibraphonist Gary Burton, chose to lean into the curve, forming the earliest bands in the hybrid form that would come to be known as fusion. Others grimly persevered, or dug further and more intently into abstraction.

Still others, like the organist Jimmy Smith and the alto saxophonist Cannonball Adderley, strengthened their bonds with an African-American popular audience, working in the affirmative subgenre of soul jazz. Among the albums released by Adderley was a funky live-at-the-Troubadour set from 1971: *The Black Messiah,* named after a tune by his keyboardist, George Duke, who would have a prolific solo career of his own, merging jazz with funk, rock, and R&B.

A similar confluence of styles formed the aesthetic profile for CTI Records, founded in 1967 by the veteran producer Creed Taylor. With high production values that extended to Pete Turner's album-cover photographs, CTI created a new commercial lane for already-established jazz musicians; its early roster featured the likes of guitarist Wes Montgomery, trumpeter Freddie Hubbard, and flutist Herbie Mann. CTI's production and marketing openly courted a crossover audience, setting the terms for what would later be termed smooth jazz—and enacting what many jazz partisans considered a deviation from, rather than an extension of, the righteous evolutionary path.

Righteousness was easier to locate in the ruminative, beseeching music of Alice Coltrane, who carried on a spiritual quest after the death of her husband, John, in 1967. A pianist and harpist originally rooted in bebop, Alice had played in late editions of John Coltrane's bands, alongside powerful musicians like bassist Jimmy Garrison, drummer

Rashied Ali, and saxophonist Pharoah Sanders—all of whom appeared on her first solo album in 1968. Over roughly the next decade, Alice Coltrane personified a swirling current of astral consciousness in jazz before establishing an ashram in the Santa Monica Mountains. But the earnest asceticism of her approach made it easy for the jazz establishment to relinquish her to the hinterlands: she was marginalized in jazz history even as her music assumed totemic properties outside it. Decades later, the horizon-scanning spirituality of Kamasi Washington's music would be one sign that Alice Coltrane was receiving her posthumous due. (Another sign was the glowing response to a compilation of her ashram cassette recordings, *The Ecstatic Music of Alice Coltrane Turiyasangitananda*, released on the stylish world-music label Luaka Bop in 2017.)

But the shocking void left by John Coltrane's death couldn't adequately be filled by his widow, nor by even the most powerful disciples— like Sanders and saxophonist Archie Shepp—whose exertions, on Coltrane's old label Impulse, came branded as expressions of "the New Thing." For a more general populace, the audience still catching up with Coltrane's skyrocketing abstractions, there was an opening for someone speaking that dialect in a more reassuring key.

One such figure was the tenor saxophonist and flutist Charles Lloyd. Preserving an acoustic postbop palette but with some groovy adornments, he projected the simmering spirituality associated with Coltrane, not in a blush of opportunism so much as cosmic alignment. Like Coltrane, Lloyd had a powerfully intuitive quartet, one that surrounded him with possibility. It featured a brilliant and impetuous young pianist, Keith Jarrett, and an elastically groove-minded young drummer, Jack DeJohnette. (Cecil McBee was the band's first bassist, followed by Ron McClure.) The Charles Lloyd Quartet struck a nerve especially with rock audiences, for a host of reasons. "That group came together at a time when the socioeconomic and political environment of this country was opening up," reflected DeJohnette. "And we had a vibe. We could play grooves or we could play abstract. Nothing was ever done the same way twice."[4]

Lloyd's quartet had a hit album in *Forest Flower*, recorded at the Monterey Jazz Festival in 1966, and soon became a fixture at the Fillmore,

Bill Graham's hippie temple in San Francisco. Lloyd often shared a Fillmore concert bill with acts like Jefferson Airplane, and he recorded another live album there in '67, calling it *Love-In*. Later that year his quartet became the first jazz group to appear in the Soviet Union without sponsorship from the U.S. State Department. *DownBeat* anointed him "Jazzman of the Year."

Some interested observers mused hopefully that Lloyd's outreach to the flower-power crowd might signal a new blush of prosperity for jazz, a corrective for all of the crucial ground that had been lost to the counterculture. Martin Williams, a leading critic, was more skeptical. "Lloyd certainly puts on a show of sorts," he sniffed in *The New York Times*. "With wildly bushy hair, military jacket, and garishly striped bell bottoms, he looks like a kind of show-biz hippie. He usually sounds like a kind of show-biz John Coltrane."

The fixation on Lloyd's appearance, and the intimation that he was less a hopeful shaman than a cynical showman, found an echo almost half a century later in the conversation around Kamasi Washington. *The Epic* came in at number 4 on the 2015 NPR Music Jazz Critics Poll, but the veteran critic Francis Davis, in his official annotation of the results, waved a dismissive hand: "Strings, voices, cosmic graphics, Washington's dashiki and all, it's merely jazz like we haven't heard it in a while—an intentional throwback to those 'spiritual,' early '70s Impulse, Black Jazz and Strata-East LPs whose greatest appeal might be to listeners too young to remember the dead end for jazz this sort of thing led to back then."[5]

Beyond the generation-baiting tone of the critique, the parallels are striking: here we have an ardent, communicative, spirit-minded, post-Coltrane tenor saxophonist stirring up the passions of a youthful, politically activated audience, and reaching well outside of jazz while continuing to play it, with a fiery and cohesive band. "Will Charles Lloyd Save Jazz for the Masses?"[6]—that was the headline of Williams's review in the *Times* in 1968. It's sardonic, but on some level it's still an endorsement of the premise that jazz did, in fact, need to be saved.

This trope has been as durable as it is powerful: it served as a defining character trait and plot device in *La La Land*, the 2016 Damien Chazelle film. A star-crossed musical romance with a touch of Hollywood satire, *La La Land* dramatizes the emotional growth of Sebastian (Ryan Gosling), a journeyman jazz pianist with antiquarian tastes. His love interest, Mia (Emma Stone), is an aspiring actress who stuns him one afternoon—by saying she *hates jazz*. Affronted, he spirits her off to the Lighthouse Café to hear some jazz in person, proceeding to talk over the music.

"It's *dying*," he says after one tune draws to a close. "It's dying on the vine. And the world says, 'Let it die. It had its time.' Well, not on my watch."

If Sebastian stops short of uttering the actual phrase "save jazz," that's a technicality. When Ryan Gosling went on to host *Saturday Night Live* the next fall, his opening monologue hammered at the point. "You guys know I saved jazz, right?"

The joke landed partly because of the dopey cliché in Gosling's sentiment, which well predated the Technicolor fantasia of *La La Land*. Kamasi Washington had implied something analogous during interviews that invariably revolved around the issues plaguing jazz in our time. It bothered him that the power center of New York had marginalized places like South Central Los Angeles, where the music had a real bond and history with its community. He was frustrated that young audiences, particularly young black audiences, often saw jazz as impenetrable or pompous, stringent or arcane. He didn't see why the music had to succumb to cerebral interiority, alienated from the movement of bodies in rhythm. He believed that reverence for the past, rather than flickering in a votive, could light a torch for the tasks at hand.

His convictions carried weight because of his resonance with a popular audience, one that saw him as the most exciting jazz musician in ages. The uncommon intensity of that regard was sharpened by the desperation of a musical community aware of its own marginalization. All of which begins to explain how Washington, a musician only provisionally and warily accepted by jazz's body politic, could suddenly become its most visibly empowered spokesman. But how could *he* be the one to save jazz? Whom was he speaking for? What was it that he would save?

·   ·   ·

"Conservation" is another word for saving. And the idea of conservation first began to exert a powerful pull in jazz during the 1970s, a decade in which American interests at large seemed to mobilize around the idea. (The Environmental Protection Agency was established, by executive order, late in '70.) The music's elders and originators were shuffling off in greater numbers—Armstrong died in '71, Ellington a few years later—fueling a disquieting fear that the jazz tradition itself was now endangered, like the ozone layer or the Pacific harbor seal. This feeling thrived in some influential corners despite the continuing work of musicians in the jazz mainstream, like the pianist McCoy Tyner and the guitarist Jim Hall. It thrived despite the vitality of a post-sixties avant-garde, whose ranks included Ornette Coleman and others in his circle, like the cornetist Don Cherry; Cecil Taylor, a pianistic world unto himself; and the membership of the Association for the Advancement of Creative Musicians, a rigorous, freethinking collective more commonly known by its acronym, the AACM. The prolific, often daringly original efforts of these artists didn't provide a great deal of comfort to those fretting about the legacies of Louis Armstrong, Duke Ellington, or Benny Goodman.

Compounding this insecurity about jazz's aesthetic survival was the tidal wave of fusion, which swapped out a swinging and lyrical sensibility for something more bombastic and turbocharged. Older jazz musicians griped about fusion the way a neighborhood's longtime residents might talk about new freeway construction. But the single greatest catalyst for the mutant genre was, at least on some level, one of their own: Miles Davis, the combative yet tersely poetic trumpeter who had played bebop alongside Charlie Parker before delineating the cooler side of hard bop (in the fifties) and the bleeding edge of postbop (in the sixties). His groove-rich, darkly entrancing album *Bitches Brew*—recorded within a few days of Woodstock, the sprawling peace-and-love confab in the summer of '69—represents one of the small handful of decisive inflection points in jazz history. Musicians who played on the album would go on to form the defining juggernauts of fusion's first wave: Weather Report, Headhunters, Return to Forever, the Tony Williams Lifetime, the Mahavishnu Orchestra. *Après Bitches, le déluge.*

If "jazz" is to be understood as the music made by jazz musicians in their time, then fusion should have represented a new chapter of the jazz tradition, an evolution of style. And because bands like Weather Report reached a mass public, eventually playing to sold-out rock arenas, you might say it was one answer to jazz's audience problem. But nobody of prominence made this argument, because fusion was such an alien, steroidal variation on the jazz language, and so entangled with commercial motives. Most figures in the jazz establishment, like Martin Williams, regarded it as a mistake, if not an affront.

What response could there be to the indignities of the age? One answer was to double down on core values and marshal the troops. After an ugly surge of youth unruliness prematurely ended the 1971 Newport Jazz Festival, its producer, George Wein, moved the following year's edition to New York City, in a big-deal, big-tent production whose offerings sprawled from New Orleans brass bands to a symphonic new work by Coleman to a midnight jam session that sold out Radio City Music Hall. The critic Albert Goldman, in a report for *Life* magazine, drew on his impressions of this festival to stake a claim: "The comeback of jazz is clearly the top American music story of 1972."[7] (This in the year of Aretha Franklin's *Amazing Grace* and Al Green's *I'm Still in Love with You*—not to mention Neil Young's *Harvest* and the Rolling Stones' *Exile on Main Street*, which could be seen as American music stories despite some geopolitical technicalities.)

Goldman was on target insofar as "jazz" could be a marker of showbiz flair in pop culture, a kind of vogue. Clint Eastwood made his directorial debut with *Play Misty for Me* (1971), a psychological thriller partly shot at the Monterey Jazz Festival, where a band led by Cannonball Adderley made a cameo. (The film's title invokes "Misty," a standard by the pianist Erroll Garner, which provides a central plot device.) Diana Ross, the glamorous disco goddess, portrayed Billie Holiday in *Lady Sings the Blues* (1972), a biopic steeped in tragic lore. The choreographer and director Bob Fosse breezily flirted with jazz iconography in his film *Cabaret* (1972) and his Broadway musical *Chicago* (1975), each a smash hit; he later won Academy Awards and wide acclaim for an impressionistic autobiographical feature called *All That Jazz* (1979). A more golden-hued Jazz Age nostalgia pervaded the Hollywood movies *The Sting* (1973) and *The Great Gatsby* (1974), both starring Robert Redford.

Most of these popular entertainments exploited jazz imagery with jaunty insouciance, as a backdrop or a signifier. (In that sense, *La La Land* simply carried on a dubious tradition.) The self-appointed stewards of the jazz tradition might have found this more aggravating had they not been deep into their own conservation agenda. One consequential outcome of that agenda was the formal construction of a jazz canon, through initiatives like *The Smithsonian Collection of Classic Jazz,* a six-LP boxed set curated and annotated by Williams and issued in 1973. That same year saw the formation of the National Jazz Ensemble and the New York Jazz Repertory Company, organizations devoted to preserving and reviving the music's history in performance.

These repertory organizations were, like the Smithsonian, principally concerned with canonization. They often built their concerts around transcriptions of important records or landmark solos. The work was archival and academic as well as artistic, but it all flowed together: Dick Hyman, the musical director of the New York Jazz Repertory Company, was celebrated for his grasp of antiquated piano styles, including those of ragtime heroes like Scott Joplin and Eubie Blake. (When the producers of *Jazz: The Smithsonian Anthology* were deciding how to begin an updated compendium in 2011, they went with Joplin's "Maple Leaf Rag," which had also opened the original set. But they chose a jazz-repertory version recorded by Hyman in 1975, as if to endorse the idea of a post-historical age.)

The parallel between jazz repertory programs and the work of Western classical institutions was intentional, part of a push toward dignity for an African-American art form. The phrase "America's classical music" was coined around this time, in a doctoral dissertation by the veteran pianist Billy Taylor, who later carried it into wider circulation as a jazz educator, a correspondent for *CBS News Sunday Morning,* and the jazz director for the Kennedy Center. "It is both a way of spontaneously composing music and a repertoire," Taylor wrote, "which has resulted from the musical language developed by improvising artists. Though it is often fun to play, jazz is *very serious* music."[8]

The new jazz historicism rumbled throughout the ecology of the art form. Some members of the old guard, who had lived through epochal changes only to slip into one or another form of career purgatory, saw material returns. A stateside appearance by the tenor saxophonist and longtime expatriate Dexter Gordon became an irresistible human-interest story, as did the reemergence of Jabbo Smith, a trumpeter once said to have rivaled Armstrong.

Within the avant-garde, which in the sixties had been dominated by a rhetoric of newness and hurtling progress, traditionalism became a viable mode. The AACM, founded by musicians with a traditional foundation, produced notable statements along these lines. Among them was an album in two volumes actually bearing the title *In the Tradition*, by Anthony Braxton, a saxophonist known for his arcane compositional systems. Another powerful alto saxophonist with an avant-garde profile, Arthur Blythe, released his own album called *In the Tradition:* a program of Ellington, Coltrane, and Fats Waller made new by a band with Stanley Cowell on piano, Fred Hopkins on bass, and Steve McCall on drums.

Hopkins and McCall were two-thirds of the collective trio Air, along with Henry Threadgill on saxophones and flutes. That group won *DownBeat*'s coveted Album of the Year honor for *Air Lore*—a new spin on Joplin and Jelly Roll Morton, effectively an act of radical jazz repertory. Conservation didn't have to be conservative.

Even fusion coughed up a major contribution to the cause. Herbie Hancock, who had earned his first gold album with the street funk of Headhunters, formed V.S.O.P., an openly throwback acoustic postbop quintet. First assembled for a Hancock retrospective at the 1976 Newport Jazz Festival–New York, the band—its acronym evoked top-shelf cognac as well as the tagline "Very Special Onetime Performance"—was cast in the image of the peerless 1960s Miles Davis Quintet, in which Hancock had played. Notwithstanding Davis, who was in murky self-exile at the time, it brought the whole gang back together: Hancock, the saxophonist Wayne Shorter, the bassist Ron Carter, the drummer Tony Williams. Filling in on trumpet was a swashbuckling peer, Freddie Hubbard. Hancock later remembered the group's revived-yet-changed rapport in jazz-repertory terms: "It somehow made the past become new again."[9]

Less than a decade had passed since the dissolution of Davis's quintet, upheld then and now as one of the most advanced small groups in jazz history. The relentless upheavals of the period made it seem much longer than a decade. V.S.O.P. received such thunderous approval in New York that its one-time performance led to a world tour, where it met with equally clamoring enthusiasm. Even before releasing its debut in 1977, the group had appeared on the cover of *Newsweek* under the splashy headline "JAZZ Comes Back!"

That specific choice of language—an echo of Goldman's "comeback" line, and of *Homecoming,* the 1977 album that heralded Dexter Gordon's return—reflects a prevailing new narrative for the music. The implication was not just that jazz had rebounded, but also that some of its most gifted prodigals had returned to the fold. It was convenient to cast this turnabout as evidence of some kind of sober realization, a putting-away of childish things. The jazz-repertory movement, rooted in its noble conservation strategies, could claim credit for tilting the culture toward this baseline of historicism. Its advocates would claim that it saved the music's roots from obsolescence and extinction.

Still, working jazz musicians in the seventies were contending with difficult conditions: in the record industry, where rock and pop were the priority, and on the ground, where audiences weren't easy to rally. The economy was in a recession; New York City was on the brink of bankruptcy. Jazz clubs, of the sort that had sustained musicians in Manhattan for more than forty years, were dwindling in number and purpose. For the more intrepid artists, the action shifted to a confederation of lofts and other noncommercial, artist-operated spaces in Lower Manhattan, like Studio Rivbea and Ali's Alley. A shadow history of jazz in the 1970s could be set entirely in this milieu, among post-Coltrane/post-Coleman mavericks like Arthur Blythe, the tenor saxophonist David Murray, and the cellist Abdul Wadud. Some of these artists were members of the AACM; others, like the saxophonists Oliver Lake and Julius Hemphill, had come out of another collective, the Black Artists Group. They all shared a commitment to fierce originality and self-determination, along with a driving interest in new forms and approaches. They firmly belonged to the jazz tradition, but over time they were largely written out of its mainstream histories.

Partly this was because of a winner-take-all order circumscribed by the popular media. Partly it was the result of a conservative ideology that envisioned the jazz tradition as a stricter set of practices, a smaller circle. The influence of that constriction was pervasive enough to be almost invisible for a time, functioning as a new baseline reality. The saxophonist Branford Marsalis unintentionally illustrated the point in an interview for Ken Burns's *Jazz*.

Speaking of the music's situation in the 1970s, Marsalis said: "Jazz just kind of died. It just kind of went away for a while."[10] He went on to soften the point, noting that there had been outliers who kept the fires burning under adverse conditions. But when Burns's film was broadcast in 2001, it presented the quote without qualification, laying out the Death of Jazz as a concrete historical event, rather than an offhanded generalization. This left out a lot of context but served an irresistible narrative function for Burns and his team. For as Western orthodoxy has it, where there's a death, you can count on a resurrection—and naturally, a savior—arriving close at hand.

Wynton Marsalis was born in 1961, a little over a year after Branford. Because he hailed from New Orleans, the cradle of jazz, and brilliantly played the trumpet, its alpha horn, a certain notoriety was his natural due. He and Branford had played in funk and R&B bands with a halo of black pride—"For us, the dashiki-clad, big-Afro revolutionary was *it*,"[11] Wynton once recalled—but his identity was forged in a conscientious blaze of inheritance and generational respect. That and an intimidating level of self-confidence, backed by feats of bravura.

Jazz musicians of a certain age still describe Wynton's arrival in New York, as a first-year student at Juilliard, in terms befitting a rare meteorological event. Steven Bernstein, a trumpeter almost exactly the same age, encountered him immediately. On one of his first nights in town, Bernstein showed up to play with a rehearsal band led by the saxophonist Paul Jeffrey:

> Wynton and I were in the trumpet section. It's obvious we were kids, almost wearing out our high school clothes. He played lead on a song, and he played it perfectly. Then we did Coltrane's "Moment's Notice." He played a solo, just an incredible

solo. Then we did a blues, and everyone got a chorus. He did two choruses of eighth notes, circular breathing. I was just like, "*Fuck*. Whoa!" Then about a week later, someone called me to go to Giardinelli's trumpet shop, because Yamaha was showing new instruments after hours. I walk in and hear someone playing the Brandenburg Concerto on a piccolo trumpet. "Oh, shit!" It's him. Everyone's jaws dropped.[12]

Some version of this scenario was surely repeated in other settings. "Two weeks into it, everybody was saying, 'There's a kid in town,'" Bernstein remembered. "My trumpet teacher told me: 'You just can't worry about it. You could practice all your life and never be able to do that.'"

Marsalis's undeniable virtuosity, in multiple modes and traditions, would have been remarkable at any point in jazz's development. At this point in particular, it seemed like the answer to a plea that few had been bold enough to make. More than twenty years later, the *Atlantic* critic David Hajdu recalled that "Marsalis was ideally equipped to lead a cultural-aesthetic movement suited to the time, a renaissance that raised public esteem for and the popular appeal of jazz through a return to the music's traditional values: jazz for the Reagan revolution."[13]

That's a barbed appreciation, but it bears down helpfully on one factor critical to the young trumpeter's reception, which was timing. Within the jazz fold, Marsalis receives grateful credit and scathing criticism for the emergence of a neoclassical strain in the music, as if he were the sole author of the shift. In fact, he was neatly positioned to catch that wave just as it was cresting. He arrived in New York a few years into the repertory boom and its accompanying jazz-is-back ballyhoo, warmed up and ready to go. His clarion tone and unassailable technique were as striking as his youth and composure, but there was a larger story unfolding, one precisely primed for the rise of a diligent young hero like himself.

A key part of the narrative around jazz's resurgence was a passing of the torch from one generation to the next—another trope made tangible by Marsalis, whose father was a noted pianist, Ellis Marsalis. And in 1980, while still at Juilliard, he was hired by the redoubtable hard-bop drummer Art Blakey, who took pride in his mentorship of younger musicians. Marsalis went on tour with Blakey's ferocious band, the Jazz Messengers, quickly becoming its star attraction.

By 1981 Marsalis was also touring with Hancock, Carter, and Williams: the sterling V.S.O.P. rhythm team, and a direct link to the legacy of Miles Davis. One result of that association was *Quartet,* a Hancock album on Columbia in '82; another was Marsalis's self-titled debut, issued in the same year and on the same label (and with the same personnel, in parts).

Wynton Marsalis, produced by Hancock, wasn't a V.S.O.P. album by another name, despite the fact that it included one composition apiece by Hancock, Carter, and Williams. (One of these, Carter's "RJ," had appeared on Davis's *E.S.P.*) The album also introduced three pieces by Marsalis, including "Hesitation," a brisk tune designed to highlight some brotherly sparring between Wynton and Branford. A variation on George Gershwin's standard "I Got Rhythm" progression, "Hesitation" features a melody with an intriguingly off-balance tonality, patently influenced by Ornette Coleman's early quartet writing. (The brothers articulate a few notes in the line with a Colemanesque scoop reminiscent of chortling, or the musical equivalent of "Humph!" As in Coleman's band, there's no piano in sight.)

Elsewhere on the album, Marsalis steps out of the V.S.O.P. matrix to lead a rhythm section of his peers: Kenny Kirkland on piano, Jeff "Tain" Watts on drums, and either Charles Fambrough or Clarence Seay on bass. Their comportment suggests something other than a junior varsity crew. On the album's curtain raiser, a tune by Marsalis called "Father Time," they shift between cruising swing and a higher polyrhythmic gear, periodically modulating tempos in a way that the Davis Quintet helped invent. The audacity is impressive: on an album that otherwise features one of the superlative piano-bass-drums alignments in jazz, these youngbloods (only Fambrough was out of his twenties) proudly held their own.

The historicist tone of the age is one reason why Marsalis— recognized as a major acquisition by his label, Columbia—made his debut in the company of elders, who could lend experience and an implicit cosign. Another reason might have been simple expedience;

he had already established a rapport with V.S.O.P. But having proven that much, Marsalis didn't need to repeat any intergenerational gestures in 1983. His next jazz album, *Think of One*, featured Kirkland and Watts. And in what proved to be an effective bit of marketing, Columbia released it only a few months after Marsalis's classical debut, *Trumpet Concertos*, consisting of works by Haydn, Hummel, and Leopold Mozart, and recorded with the National Philharmonic Orchestra under Raymond Leppard.

In the decades since Marsalis's arrival, it has become all too easy to forget the magnitude of the impression left by his multivalent talent—by the notable fact that he was at once a virtuoso in the classical mold and a dashing young paragon of jazz. It's easy to forget because those two ideas aren't as incongruent or discordant as they used to be, which is one measure of his project's success.

What's striking now about the presentation of Marsalis back then is how shrewd and brand-conscious it seems. Consider for a moment the 26th Annual Grammy Awards, celebrating achievements in the record industry for 1983. Held at the Shrine Auditorium in Los Angeles on February 28, 1984, this edition of the Grammys is often remembered as Michael Jackson's night: still basking in the world-beating success of *Thriller*, he won a record eight awards. Partly as a function of Jackson's celebrity, the network broadcast reached 48.3 million viewers, the highest rating in Grammy history, not likely to be surpassed. This was a peak moment for the monoculture, that chimerical ideal of true popular consensus, reinforced by the image-making apparatus of a new and explosively successful music video channel, MTV. Jackson's video for "Billie Jean" was one of the first by a black artist to receive heavy rotation on the channel, after considerable pressure from his label. Instantly iconic, it helped cement MTV's place in modern life, and Jackson's stature as the King of Pop. The Grammys were effectively his coronation.

But more than one young potentate was anointed that evening. Marsalis, twenty-two, arrived with nominations in both jazz and classical categories, another unprecedented achievement in the awards history, and one that the show's producers amplified with clever pageantry. After a respectful introduction from John Denver, the evening's host, the young trumpeter appeared onstage in a dark tuxedo jacket, next to a studio chamber orchestra that, like the set design, was festooned in formal white. With extravagant ease and precision, Marsalis performed a selection from *Trumpet Concertos:* the Rondo from Hummel's Concerto for Trumpet and Orchestra in E Major.

He happened to play the same piece months later in a concert at Lincoln Center, where he was reviewed in *The New York Times.* "There was enough virtuosity for three concertos," wrote Will Crutchfield, singling out the Rondo. "Impeccable scales, faster than one would have thought possible; rapid-fire repeated notes; delicate echoes; dazzling arpeggios—there was something for everybody. Near the end came a rising chromatic chain of trills such as to leave the sourest critic with a silly grin of delight on his face."[14]

The impact was much the same at the Grammys, loud cheers mingling with the applause. Then Denver announced that Marsalis would show another side of his talent, performing "Knozz-Moe-King," the opening track from *Think of One.* Stepping to another part of the stage, Marsalis joined his young quintet, looking slightly and uncharacteristically nervous. After a tentative start, this, too, became a demonstration of prowess: a four-minute mile stamped by chromatic tensions, with an entirely different tempo set by each soloist.

Afterward, the band filed into the wings to await the announcement of Best Jazz Instrumental Performance, Soloist. When Marsalis was declared the winner (out of a nominee pool of his elders, including Blakey, on whose album he was featured), he walked to the podium and gave an off-the-cuff acceptance speech with a transparent subtext. First thanking his parents for enduring his many hours of practice, he then acknowledged the staff of CBS Records "for presenting my work with the quality that's necessary to get to the elite jazz audience." (He put a slight but discernible emphasis on the word "elite.") "And I would like to thank all of the guys in the band, because without the band I wouldn't be able to play anything; this music is very difficult."

There was more: "And last but certainly, certainly not least, I'd like to thank all of the great masters of American music: Charlie Parker,

Louis Armstrong, Thelonious Monk. All the guys who set a precedent in Western art, and gave an art form to the American people that cannot be limited by enforced trends or ... bad taste." The last two words came with a crooked grin, raised eyebrows and a little head waggle, as in the delivery of a punch line. It seemed clear that Marsalis had a target in mind—Hancock, who appeared on this same awards ceremony to perform his single "Rockit," the winner of Best R&B Instrumental Performance that year.

Hancock was forty-three, and while he had been serving as an advisor, bandmate, and producer to Marsalis in acoustic jazz settings, he was also riding his latest category-exploding pop smash. He'd made "Rockit" with Bill Laswell and Michael Beinhorn, whose vanguardist rock band Material was a staple of the downtown scene in New York. Along with Hancock's synthesizer hook, the signature element of the track was the rhythmic record scratching of a prominent DJ from the Bronx, GrandMixer D.ST.

"Rockit" was the breakout single from Hancock's album *Future Shock,* whose title perfectly conveyed the impression made at the Grammys. Hancock took the stage with a keytar slung over a black leather jacket and a reflective silver shirt. His band had synth drums and a stacked keyboard rig, with D.ST on a raised platform behind a set of Technics 1200s, in a wireless headset and blocky sunglasses. The stage design echoed the frenetic, posthuman surrealism of the song's music video, in heavy rotation on MTV. There were herky-jerky robots, including three pairs of disembodied legs kicking and flailing above the stage. (A few of the robots were revealed, in a climactic flourish, to be breakdancers in disguise.) The performance was a pop-culture milestone, often cited by future turntablists as transformative.

But it wasn't befitting the highbrow ideals so firmly articulated—and so effectively embodied—by Marsalis. The reproach that he issued from the podium was in line with a few other points he implied: that his own musical pursuit was advanced ("very difficult") and aspirational (for "the *elite* jazz audience"), with a seriousness of purpose worthy of its noble lineage ("a precedent in Western art"). Strongly implicit in Marsalis's appearance at the Grammys, too, was the conviction that jazz deserved a stature and cachet equivalent to classical music. This was an audacious proposition even in the mid-eighties: Dr. Billy Taylor and others were still waging what seemed like a long-odds campaign.

For the arbiters of high culture, only a young hero with the cultural literacy and aesthetic mobility of Marsalis—somebody capable of pirouetting through a concerto in one moment and improvising through an obstacle course the next—could make this argument in good faith. As for the unwashed rabble with no appreciation for such an accomplished art form, Marsalis could still communicate with sheer mastery and evident sophistication. He didn't receive the standing ovation that Hancock got for "Rockit," but he did reach those 48.3 million viewers with his message. To the extent that a single turn in the spotlight can set the terms for a movement, this was that turn. And anybody who missed the broadcast, or somehow missed the point, would soon find plenty of additional evidence to support Marsalis's serious-minded convictions, much of it emanating from the hand and horn of the man himself.

In 1985 he released the defining statement of his early period, *Black Codes (From the Underground),* an album that pressed advanced postbop techniques into the service of an expressive, volatile, and heroic music with ample precedent in the particulars but no exact precursor as a whole. Kirkland's pianism was biting, harmonically restive, and set at a forward tilt, suggesting a targeted update to the crashing modalities of McCoy Tyner. Watts created a bulldozer propulsion that had as much to do with rumbling seizures and unexpected crashes as with a swinging ride cymbal. The accord between Wynton and Branford was sharp and jostling, often voiced with tight dissonance, as on a sixties-Miles set of trapdoors titled "Delfeayo's Dilemma" (a nod to their younger brother, a trombonist). A superheated track called "Chambers of Tain" crystallized a proprietary band strategy called "burnout," whereby the musicians attacked a tune with plunging intensity in a prescribed key but with a contingent tempo and no set chord changes, conveying the adrenalized, precarious feeling of racing along a ridge line.

These were not conservative values. Nor was the political thrust of the album, a reference to the postbellum laws in Southern states that restricted African-American freedoms. But Marsalis presented his argument in a context of disciplined erudition: the cover depicts a young boy in a classroom, looking thoughtfully in the direction of the chalkboard, where the album's loaded title has been scrawled. The boy wears glasses, a tie, and a dress shirt with sleeves rolled up; it's a portrait of the artist as a young man. Also within the trajectory of his gaze is a trumpet, planted upright on the teacher's desk. And just beyond it, a globe.

Marsalis and his granite convictions had an almost immediate effect on the culture of jazz, the public perception of jazz and, consequently, the business of jazz. He and his peer group became identified as a cohort, the so-called Young Lions. Major-label record deals were handed out, tours and festival dates promptly booked. Along with Wynton, this early contingent included Terence Blanchard, a trumpeter who came up one year behind him in New Orleans, and Donald Harrison, an alto saxophonist from a Mardi Gras Indian family there. (It was no accident that Blanchard and Harrison, like the Marsalises before them, were also alumni of the Jazz Messengers.)

"The Young Lions of Jazz" had been the name of a concert in 1982 at the Kool Jazz Festival (formerly known as the Newport Jazz Festival–New York). The program was conceived by Nesuhi Ertegun and Bruce Lundvall, top executives at two leading major record labels, as a showcase of the youthful talent on their rosters. George Wein, the producer, came up with the "Young Lions" phrase, which for him was a reference to the World War II novel by Irwin Shaw. (Nesuhi, who like his younger brother, Ahmet, had been born in Istanbul, jokingly threatened to change the name to "the Young Turks.")[15] The concert's lineup was stylistically diverse, including Marsalis and the versatile guitarist Kevin Eubanks alongside avant-garde operators like Abdul Wadud, the baritone saxophonist Hamiet Bluiett, the flutist James Newton, and the pianist Anthony Davis.

The Young Lions had also been the name of a short-lived band that released one self-titled album in the early sixties, with Lee Morgan on trumpet and Wayne Shorter on tenor saxophone. An extension of Morgan and Shorter's smartly pugnacious hookup in the frontline of the Jazz Messengers, this band had long been a proud footnote in the hard-bop annals. Now, given Marsalis's affinities with Morgan and Shorter—

and his successive link to Blakey—its legacy found renewed purpose. An album culled from the Kool Jazz Festival concert was released on Lundvall's label Elektra Musician, and its wild abundance of personalities and approaches hardly made for a coherent whole. This could be one reason why *The Young Lions* proved less durable than "the Young Lions," as a marketing slogan and an update of hard bop's aesthetic ideal. Another reason was articulated by the critic Robert Palmer in the *Times*:

> The record producers, critics, and other nonmusicians who dub them Young Lions tend to be too committed to the eternal verities of jazz, to its traditional structural and rhythmic language, to be entirely comfortable with the frequently messy and sometimes anarchic work of the radicals.[16]

But the disdain for experimental practices outside certain parameters was vociferously shared by Marsalis, who declaimed the avant-garde as a harbor for those too lazy or incapable to seriously engage with technique. And fusion, as he saw it, was empty and crass.

Marsalis's rhetoric and example were alluring to a mass audience: *Time* magazine put him on its cover in 1990 beside a boldfaced headline proclaiming "The New Jazz Age." Among the tropes laid out uncritically therein was the claim that jazz "almost died in the 1970s," reinforcing the dubious prospect of resurrection.

What heralded this bright new age was a second pack of Lions, precocious torchbearers groomed by the record industry to fit a reassuring image and narrative. As a cover story in *The New York Times Magazine* put it, they were "Young, Gifted and Cool," equipped with major-label resources, including meticulous wardrobe and grooming consultation. Among those in this crew were the Hammond B-3 organist Joey DeFrancesco, the guitarist Mark Whitfield, the pianist Marcus Roberts, and the trumpeter Roy Hargrove.

A package called Jazz Futures, conceived by Wein around the same time, gathered a cadre of these hyped young players in one touring band; the roster included Hargrove, Whitfield, the pianist Benny Green, and the bassist Christian McBride. The group performed at the Newport Jazz Festival, released a live album on a major label, and seemed to formalize a consensus around the new cream of the crop. They mostly stuck to a grooving hard-bop mode, recalling the 1950s and early '60s, and barely touching the dissonance and rhythmic gamesmanship that Marsalis had explored on his first few albums.

With developments like these, a message was absorbed by the aspiring next generation of musicians: that there was a beaten path to a successful career in the jazz mainstream, and that it ran through the standard songbook, the bebop stylebook, and a regulation suit and tie. By the mid-nineties, a seasoned jazz critic (Francis Davis again) could reflect on this climate and come to a rueful conclusion: "The real story is the commodification of youth."[17] He didn't mention Jazz Futures, which was just as well: that might have been too on the nose, given the name's connotation of a busy trading floor.

The encouraging story told by the Young Lions' rise—from a certain angle, a perfect outcome for the crisis of continuity that the 1970s had seemed to pose—was dependent on the perception of jazz as a fixed set of values. Among them was a nobility of purpose that ran contrary to the shiny prerogatives of pop. But this led to a weird insularity from the rest of the culture, as the scholar Ronald Radano has observed: "It is as if jazz has survived as a protected gem of black creative wisdom, growing and changing yet miraculously unaffected by the overarching shifts in American life."[18]

Marsalis, for one, was determined to pull the culture along with him, carving out a space for jazz that was enlightened, enfranchised, and recognized as such. There were, of course, many other possibilities. Some followed a staunchly alternative path, and others ran in crooked parallel. A few eventually proceeded from the subversive premise that "Rockit" and "Knozz-Moe-King" weren't the diametric poles they'd been made out to be.

Kamasi Washington mostly toiled in a journeyman's anonymity before overnight success located him in his mid-thirties. Raised in the working-class African-American communities of South Central and Inglewood during the crack cocaine epidemic and its related spasms of gang violence, he was a product of West Coast hip-hop culture—but also like Marsalis the son of an underappreciated jazz musician, the saxophonist and flutist Rickey Washington. When he made *The Epic,* the younger Washington chose to open the album with a meaty, bobbing overture redolent of Young Lion dynamics, with a slick update in production values. He called it "Change of the Guard," which sounds like a proclamation of self-arrival. But Washington had different implications in mind, as he told Josef Woodard in an interview for *DownBeat:*

> It was written for my dad, for the generation of musicians who didn't necessarily make albums or get out there in a way that people would really know about them. It was almost like a generation lost, that generation of guys who graduated from high school in the '70s. The generation after them, with Wynton and those guys, got the spotlight. That's why I wrote "Change of the Guard"—for that generation of musicians in L.A. Usually, the whole world sees this passing of the baton, but nothing like that happened here.[19]

Washington decided to pursue jazz himself as a middle schooler, spurred in part by hearing records by Art Blakey's Jazz Messengers— quite possibly including the early-eighties edition that featured the Marsalis brothers. Blakey's music spoke to him culturally, not as a dispatch from some temple of high culture but as a word from the street: "West Coast hip-hop had that heavy sense of the beat, and Art Blakey played with that, too. It sounded like something that Dre would have sampled."[20]

Starting on alto saxophone, Washington soon graduated to his father's tenor, on which he began to find a voice. Among his mentors was a music teacher in Watts named Reggie Andrews, who had formed a Central LA magnet ensemble, the Multi School Jazz Band. The band was filled with other talented and industrious young players, like the brothers Stephen Bruner and Ronald Bruner Jr., virtuosos on, respectively, bass and drums; Ryan Porter, a trombonist; Miles Mosley, a bassist; and Cameron Graves, a pianist.

This familylike peer group of musicians, along with Tony Austin, a drummer of similar taste and ambition, would eventually form an artist collective called the West Coast Get Down, workshopping one another's music and playing in one another's bands, including what would become the Next Step.

First, though, they all freelanced for an array of pop and R&B artists. Washington had formative experience in a big band led by the venerable composer Gerald Wilson, but his earliest touring opportunity came with Snoop Dogg, the sly, drawling gangsta rapper. It arrived via a recommendation from another Multi School Jazz Band alum, Terrace Martin. Years later, Martin—an alto saxophonist with a honeyed, imploring tone, and a shrewd producer of hip-hop and R&B besides—would again bring Washington into the hazy stir of a hip-hop production. This time it was *To Pimp a Butterfly,* a magnum opus by Kendrick Lamar that was, by an alignment of critical acclamation and popular approval, 2015's album of the year.

Washington plays on just one track of *To Pimp a Butterfly,* a lacerating confessional titled "u." But he wrote all of the album's string arrangements, and because of the pervasive presence of his peers—notably Martin, on alto saxophone and production, and Stephen Bruner, aka Thundercat, on electric bass and ethereal vocal falsetto—his contribution felt larger and weightier. As a lone operator, Washington might have gone unheralded in the general public, like Eli Fontaine, the Motown saxophonist who played the bittersweet alto solo on Marvin Gaye's "What's Going On." But there was strength in solidarity, and of course in excellent timing. Few, if any, of those countless articles about Washington failed to mention his connection to Kendrick Lamar, often squarely in the headline. (*Esquire* again: "The Robe-Wearing, Kendrick-Collaborating Genius Who Might Just Save Jazz.")

Washington steered clear of hip-hop beats or electronic production on *The Epic,* favoring a style more in tune with Alice Coltrane's astral soul jazz. The cover art encouraged this interpretation, depicting the tenor saxophonist against a sci-fi backdrop of interplanetary alignment, a cosmic medallion resting on his chest. It was no wonder so many people mentioned him in the same breath as Coltrane, whose late-period music vibrated with a questing spirituality, and Sanders, who extended that agenda for the Aquarian age.

And *The Epic*—recorded during a marathon block of studio time that also yielded albums for the other members of the West Coast Get Down—recalls that lineage unabashedly. A manifesto of vaulting intensity and monumental scale, it crashes through an Afrocentric range of styles: surging hard-bop, steroidal jazz-funk, viscous soul. There are heavy, reverberating echoes of the black church, and not only on the tracks where Washington used a gospel choir and strings. There's tremendous vitality to the music, even in those moments when it feels like an eighteen-wheeler rig hurtling too fast down a two-lane highway—maybe in those moments most of all.

The album also has tedious ruts and draggy patches, themes that feel overstated or undercooked. Its sprawl and all-around muchness are an aesthetic choice, an effective one, but it can be hard to see through the muddle. As for the musicianship, it's a feast of imploring spirit and fervor, but less impressive when subjected to close scrutiny. Washington's own mix of lyrical cries, expressive overblowing, and machine-like patternwork doesn't actually much recall Coltrane or Sanders so much as a consortium of strong but lesser lights—like Ernie Watts, an LA session ace steeped in midcentury bebop and rhythm-and-blues, or Grover Washington Jr. (no relation), a soulful melodist who pointed the way to smooth jazz.

In any case, it would have been impossible to top *The Epic*—a fact that Washington tacitly acknowledged by making his next statement not in album form but rather at the 2017 Whitney Biennial. *Harmony of Difference,* as he called this piece, was a multimedia installation involving film as well as music. Music was accompanied by moving images on three walls of the gallery space: mainly slow, panning video depicting abstract paintings by Washington's sister Amani. The music itself, later released as an EP, adhered to the sound and personnel of *The Epic,* branching out at various points into slo-mo disco or heaving samba. The tunes bore evocative, ponderous one-word titles, like "Desire," "Humility," and "Knowledge."

The finale, "Truth," wove in elements from each of the five preceding tracks. In the installation it came paired with a fourteen-minute film conceived by Washington and directed by AG Rojas. The film—a stylish, dreamily lit procession of images shot in South Central and East Los Angeles—features a lot of ocean spray, flower petals, and interstellar nebula. Young black faces are caught in contemplative poses. And during the tenor solo that takes up the middle portion of the track, the camera lingers on an iconic still image: the Roy DeCarava photograph known as *Ellington Session Break, 1954*. In the picture, two musicians sit on folding chairs in a stark, high-ceilinged room (New York's Webster Hall). They're facing different directions, each immersed in a newspaper, while a coat rack hulks in the foreground, laden with topcoats and fedoras. Using digital tools and a trick of perspective, the video slowly moves in on the figure in the corner, the one with both feet resting on the lowest rung of a ladder. Just before a cutaway, he turns his head, as if aware of our creeping eye.

This Ellingtonian throwback was more than an arbitrary reference. On *Harmony of Difference* as on *The Epic*, Washington's tone, with its growly rasp, occasionally recalls Ben Webster, the irreplaceable tenor saxophonist in Ellington's bands from the mid-1930s to the early '40s. There's a famous DeCarava photograph of Webster and John Coltrane locked in an embrace, the younger saxophonist burying his head in the older's lapel. The image is tightly framed, ineffable, a blur of movement and emotion. But one thing it communicates clearly to a jazz viewer today is the generational chain of succession. Webster—in his early fifties in this photograph, older than Coltrane would ever live to be—seems to embody a kind of harboring reassurance. "It may look as if he is giving Coltrane his blessing, but it's impossible to tell whether we are witnessing a greeting or a leave-taking,"[21] the critic Geoff Dyer has observed.

For Washington, whose vocation dictates that he grapple with both Coltrane *and* Webster, jazz's deep legacy and iconography could probably feel at times like a hall of mirrors. His apparent solution was a pick-and-choose historical veneration, along with a canny sense of the weight that *he* displaces in his time. His innovations rest mainly in presentation and framing, and in the power of conviction that keeps the West Coast Get Down from spinning out into a dozen directions. What rattled some of his jazz detractors was the absence of a disciplined new voice. The usual attention-grabbing young jazz arrival comes with some thoughtful tweak to the conventions of the instrument. There was no question that Washington exerts a commanding presence with his horn, but he seemed to be the rare example of a major arrival in jazz who brings no new vocabulary or inflection to his instrument.

What he did bring was a robust, affirming narrative for a music plagued with uncertainties. He talked about the spirit of jazz in terms of communicative exchange and spiritual inquiry—what he took to be universal human truths, with the broadest possible appeal. And his attitude about the music's popularity was defiantly sanguine, the very picture of positive thinking. "I've never believed in the idea that jazz is dying and people don't like it," he said. "People who have taken the time to investigate jazz, they like it for their whole lives."[22]

By this light, Washington and his colleagues were doing the work of Johnny Appleseed across a sprawling topography. Whether the masses they reached could be converted into a new generation of aficionados was ultimately not his concern. The reigning class of jazz aficionados, after all, included a lot of people unimpressed by Washington's contribution to the methodology of the tenor, and even ambivalent about the fervent crush of his music.

It's possible to hold views like these and still recognize his importance as an emblem and a catalyst. Washington swept in with a combination of traits ideally suited to his moment, some inherent and others projected onto him. He wasn't the first to be anointed in this way. He surely won't be the last.

––––––––––

Arthur Blythe, *In the Tradition* (Columbia)
Herbie Hancock, *Future Shock* (Columbia)
Wynton Marsalis, *Black Codes (From the Underground)* (Columbia)
Wynton Marsalis, *Wynton Marsalis* (Columbia)
Kamasi Washington, *The Epic* (Brainfeeder)

2

From This Moment On

Introducing Brad Mehldau opens with a quick spray of staccato: *tap-tap-tap, tap-tap-tap*, like someone knocking impatiently at a door. It's the preface to Mehldau's arrangement of a show tune, "It Might As Well Be Spring," from the Rodgers and Hammerstein film musical *State Fair*. The song had long been a verifiable jazz standard, with dozens of canonical recordings: by singers like Sarah Vaughan, Frank Sinatra, Ella Fitzgerald, and Nina Simone, and by others ranging from the pianist Bill Evans to the trumpeter Clifford Brown.

Mehldau's version arrived in 1995, precisely half a century after the line "I am starry eyed and vaguely discontented" made its way into the popular lexicon. He and his trio had made a neat structural modification to the tune, tinkering with its pulse in a way that their syncopated prelude set in clear relief. Instead of the even 4/4 cadence known as common time, the track races along in 7/8, creating the impression of a rhythmic hiccup, or a sprint with a hitch in its stride.

Jazz musicians have been dabbling in irregular meters since well before Dave Brubeck's enormously popular 1959 album *Time Out*, which made them an exotic selling point. What's striking about Mehldau's performance is where he ventures after the opening vamp, phrasing the melody in a cool, flowing cadence even as his partners, the bassist Larry Grenadier and the drummer Jorge Rossy, busy themselves with percolating chatter behind him. In his articulation of the theme, and in a solo full of deft intricacies punctuated with breathlike pauses, Mehldau gives the song a sleek, appealing contour. His performance doesn't feel herky-jerky or cerebral. It feels natural, even inevitable.

With hindsight, in fact, it's almost too easy to see how this version of "It Might As Well Be Spring" became holy writ for a legion of subsequent jazz pianists, many of whom would never dream of playing the song in pedestrian 4/4. (When the ballyhooed piano prodigy Joey Alexander recorded *his* debut album in 2014, it featured a version of the tune in the same 7/8 meter—and with Grenadier on bass, for good measure.)

Like so much about Mehldau's career, "It Might As Well Be Spring" proposes a personal realignment of the jazz-piano continuum, a mode of playing rooted in the postbop tradition but reaching in earnest toward an identifiable new dialect. It was also the official shot across the bow by an artist who, by virtue of timing as much as temperament, would soon become jazz's version of a hyperliterate, half-reluctant generational symbol. An inward-seeking rhapsodist with a wary ambivalence about jazz's canon and conventions, Mehldau cut the figure of a late-twentieth-century existential hero, with a creative identity both restless and self-directed.

His virtuoso style—a confluence of silvery precision, ambidextrous ease, floating equilibrium, and courtly lyricism—has traveled widely since *Introducing Brad Mehldau*. You'll find traces of it among a remarkably diverse coalition of gifted younger pianists, from Fabian Almazan to Glenn Zaleski. (Sometimes you'll find more than traces.) A few inheritors, like Gerald Clayton, have openly acknowledged the debt, framing Mehldau's idiomatic signature as an essential link in the evolution of jazz piano. Mehldau was the first member of his peer group to exert this level of influence, and in that sense he's a bridge from jazz's late neoclassical era to its postmillennial mainstream. If you were an improvising pianist coming up at any point since the mid-1990s, he was as plainly unavoidable a point of reference as McCoy Tyner, Wynton Kelly, or Ahmad Jamal—a few of the essential figures in *his* heroes' gallery, back when he was getting started.

Mehldau developed his voice early and saw daylight soon afterward, which meant that to many observers, he seemed to drop out of the sky fully formed. But his early experience wasn't hermetic, or even all that exceptional; it was fairly typical of a precocious talent with access to a supportive community. Born in Jacksonville, Florida, he moved with his family to West Hartford, Connecticut, at age ten. (It was an upper-middle-class household; his father was a doctor.) Mehldau studied classical piano before a turn to jazz, becoming enamored of swinging midcentury rhythm-section paragons like Kelly and Tyner. "So jazz for me was this magical thing on all these records," he reflected. "My aesthetic when I was younger was really governed by this classic feeling for jazz as defined on these great recordings."[1]

Mehldau received rigorous classroom training at William H. Hall High School, home to a nationally recognized jazz band. He also had hands-on experience through a weekly gig at the 880 Club, a no-frills but well regarded haunt not far from his home. The gig, which he kept through high school, brought him into regular contact with local elders, like the drummer Larry DiNatale, and fellow aspirants, like the trombonist Steve Davis. He played his share of weddings and cocktail parties in the greater Hartford area, and formed a bond with the tenor saxophonist Joel Frahm, a classmate at Hall High.

Had Mehldau come of age just a decade earlier, his first national exposure would likely have come under the wing of a celebrated jazz mentor like Art Blakey. Because he emerged during the post–Marsalis Young Lions boom, things shook out a little differently. One heralded discovery of that era had been the alto saxophonist Christopher Hollyday, a lanky Connecticut native seven months Mehldau's senior, who caused a stir on the strength of a vinegary bebop style derived from Charlie Parker and Jackie McLean. Hollyday was fifteen when he landed his first review in *The New York Times.*[2] Six years later, in 1991, he asked Mehldau to join his band, an association that led to the pianist's first studio recording date and first European tour.

These experiences cut slightly into Mehldau's coursework at the New School for Jazz and Contemporary Music, where he was studying with older pianists like Junior Mance and Fred Hersch. The venerable hard-bop drummer Jimmy Cobb—one of the names Mehldau knew from albums like Miles Davis's *Kind of Blue*—was also at the New School, teaching an ensemble class that effectively functioned like a weekly rehearsal band. Cobb turned one edition of this class, which included Mehldau and the guitarist Peter Bernstein, into a working group, Cobb's Mob.[3]

But Mehldau's more pivotal sideman appointment came in 1994, with a member of his peer group: Joshua Redman, who was several albums into a contract with Warner Brothers. Redman had swept into the spotlight a few years earlier when he won the Thelonious Monk Institute of Jazz International Saxophone Competition, at twenty-two. He came with an alluring backstory: he was the son of a well-regarded but oft-overlooked jazz musician, the tenor saxophonist Dewey Redman. (Their relationship wasn't a model of stability; Joshua had been raised by his mother in Berkeley, California.) The younger Redman was also a recent Harvard graduate who had deferred entry to Yale Law School to pursue jazz in New York. The Monk Competition had only been around for a few years—its inaugural winner, in 1987, had been Marcus Roberts, the pianist in Wynton Marsalis's band—but it already served as something like the NFL scouting combine for the jazz record industry. Redman's unflappable performance, ratified by a multigenerational panel of judges, resulted in a major-label bidding war. And that Yale Law deferment quickly became an irresistible part of his narrative, repeated in dozens of articles in the mainstream press.

The details of Redman's backstory were exceptional, but his balance of talent and erudition made him the embodiment of a paradigm. The Young Lions boomlet to which he belonged had come of age in the thick of jazz's neoclassical era, and could be understood as the fulfillment of a prophecy made back then by Marsalis:

> We're entering a period now when there are young kids fourteen and fifteen years old all over the country who can really play. They'll all be emerging four or five years from now, and they'll insist on being heard. I don't think people are going to try to sound like me, but you are going to see young cats getting serious

about their music, and I definitely think I have something to do with that.[4]

The intensity of Redman's media spotlight meant that the release of *MoodSwing*—his third album, introducing a quartet with Mehldau on piano, Christian McBride on bass, and Brian Blade on drums— registered as an event. And so Mehldau, up to that point a promising name circulated among jazz insiders, found himself operating on a much larger stage.

He happened to have the perfect temperament for Redman's music, which prioritized an agenda of direct emotional clarity. Redman had taken it upon himself to push back against jazz's "rotten public image," as he put it in the album's liner notes—an overintellectualized, preciously ennobled, eat-your-vegetables idea of great American music. Left unspoken was the extent to which that image went hand in hand with the Marsalis agenda. The prototypical Young Lion album was pyrotechnically intense, an ostentatious gut punch. *MoodSwing* was medium cool, laid back, an arm draped over a shoulder. "There is much elegance and virility going on here," observed Greg Tate in his review for *Vibe*, "the kind of suave that creeps up on you rather than checking itself in the mirror every two minutes."[5]

And it didn't escape notice that Mehldau's unhurried erudition, as an accompanist and a soloist, was at the heart of the album's stylish nonchalance. This was as true on a bossa nova like "Alone in the Morning" as on a churchified swinger like "Rejoice." But the emblematic track on *MoodSwing*, certainly for Mehldau, was "Chill," which exudes the noir composure of a smoke-filled Herman Leonard photograph. The song's simple form involves a languid vamp in E-flat minor, with a salutary flip into the major key during an eight-bar bridge. Mehldau plays the first solo, continuing the vamp with his left hand, and leaving deliberative pockets of space between each obliquely bluesy phrase in his right. There's a bit of Wynton Kelly in his articulation, and in the way he hangs behind the beat. But the entire solo is touched by an insinuative ease that feels distinctive even now, and felt like a quiet manifesto at the time. Among the listeners who took notice was the guitarist Pat Metheny, who had appeared as an approving elder on Redman's previous album. Metheny first heard "Chill" on the radio while he was driving, and was so immediately struck by the piano solo that he pulled the car over to give it his full concentration.

"Brad's appearance on the scene was really significant to me," Metheny said a dozen years later, as he was preparing to embark on a concert tour with Mehldau's trio, "because I just recognized immediately so many of the ideals that I aspire to myself, rendered in a way that was unbelievably refreshing."[6] Among those ideals: strategic patience, a careful use of space, and a composerly command of harmonic resolution.

Most of these attributes are evident to some degree on *Introducing Brad Mehldau*—notably in a languorous stroll through "My Romance" and in the honey-drip saunter of "Prelude to a Kiss." The album includes a version of Cole Porter's "From This Moment On" that ratchets into breakneck double time, against which Mehldau improvises like a bird in flight. His solo wheels above the fray in one moment and lunges back in the next, culminating in a chorus or so of two-handed octave work à la the bebop wonder Phineas Newborn Jr. But Mehldau isn't reaching back with "From This Moment On." In his overall comportment, he reorients the song from a dreamy romantic pledge into a vow of artistic intent—staking a claim, here and now, that things are going to be different.

Mehldau was just beginning a decade-long run with Grenadier on bass and Rossy on drums, but he had earned early acclaim for his hookup with McBride and Blade in the Redman quartet. So his producer, Matt Pierson, split the album into two sides, with one half featuring Redman's sinewy rhythm section and the other effectively rolling out the new Brad Mehldau Trio. In that sense the album offers a glimpse of the pianist at a transitional moment, winding down one journey and embarking on another.

Even at the time, it was obvious which of the two groups pointed the way forward for him. Rossy, who hailed from Barcelona and had found his way to New York via the Berklee College of Music in Boston, was a drummer with an unusually delicate attack: agile and propulsive but also placid and sparse. Grenadier had a deep, luxurious sound on the bass, and a warmly authoritative way with harmony as well as rhythm. Their rapport with Mehldau had originally coalesced in group settings with other articulate peers, like the guitarist Kurt Rosenwinkel and the tenor saxophonist Mark Turner. They were all recent conservatory graduates honing their craft at Smalls, a comfortably low-stakes basement club in Greenwich Village. One of their defining early statements was *Yam Yam,* Turner's debut album, released in 1995. It featured a balletic quintet with Mehldau, Rosenwinkel, Grenadier, and Rossy, exuding a youthful style but an already well-developed chemistry.

Among the shared values in this peer group was a fondness for streamlined complexities delivered with a relaxed lightness of touch. They were inspired not only by the warrior kings of jazz history but also by some of its more outré and standoffish types, like the modernist cult composer and pianist Lennie Tristano. Within a prevailing musical culture that had recently tacked so heavily toward a combative and masculinist ideal, there was something subversive about this bookish field of interest. Mehldau, whose style was often likened to Tristano's, didn't identify as an acolyte of the Tristano school, but that was a label you easily could pin on some of his closest collaborators, notably Rossy.

And lateral influence, among musicians roughly the same age, was a matter of profound importance for Mehldau. "Actually I think that's the strongest form of influence," he said a decade into his solo career, at a time when the jazz culture's fixation on patrilineage was still earning him reflexive comparisons to his elders. "And one thing that does puzzle me a little bit is that there's very little discourse about how players of the younger generation, let's say forty and under, are influenced by their peers. They have to be tied to something that's already been in the vocabulary for so long, and it's reified and it's well-known."[7]

No artist likes to be reflexively compared to his precursors, but for Mehldau it seems to have been infuriating. As he once complained, notoriously, in print: "The constant comparison of this trio with the Bill Evans trio by critics has been a thorn in my side." He was referring to a common bit of reductionism at the time, which saw in Mehldau another sensitive white pianist with slouchy posture and a tendency to appear lost in reverie. Some jazz critics also couldn't help seeing another victim of substance abuse—a step too far for Mehldau, though he did speak openly at times about his battle with heroin addiction. (Evans, who had begun using heroin in the late 1950s and later gravitated to cocaine, died an ugly death in 1980, at fifty-one.) But what seemed to irritate Mehldau most was that the invocation of Evans forestalled any recognition of his trio's musical independence, to say nothing of its formal innovations. Analogies to Keith Jarrett would have been more insightful, but still a problem; Mehldau wanted to shrug off the smothering weight of precedent, and engage with the music on his own terms.

He was already concerned with some of these issues when he made his debut album, and the best evidence resides in his original compositions. *Introducing* contains four of them, including "Say Goodbye," a soulful reverie, and "London Blues," a sly take on the twelve-bar blues form, studded with major-seventh chords that seem to hint at an alternate key. Even more intriguing is a song called "Young Werther," which unfolds in a floating eighth-note pulse, neither swinging nor exactly straight, and has a melody openly indebted to Brahms. (It shares the same wistful intervallic motif as the first movement of the Capriccio in F-sharp Minor, op. 76.)

Mehldau was hardly coy about his classical interests, nor did he recoil from high literary allusion. The track's title evokes Goethe's *The Sorrows of Young Werther,* a foundational text for the German Romantic movement—and a portrait of the artistic temperament in voluptuous torment. As if to wave a banner of recognition, Mehldau had named his music-publishing company Werther Music. And as if to be absolutely clear about his frame of mind, he and Pierson sequenced the album's track list so that the first original in the lineup was an ethereal waltz with another loaded title, "Angst."

When David Foster Wallace, the brilliant regent of postmodern fiction, took his own life in 2008, one of the more soulful quick-fire appraisals of his art came from the critic A. O. Scott, in *The New York Times.* Describing Wallace's literary voice, Scott offered a list of attributes— "hyperarticulate, plaintive, self-mocking, diffident, overbearing, needy, ironical, almost pathologically self-aware"—that would seem to apply not only to one writer in particular but also to the cohort that claimed him. It would be wildly reductive to call Wallace a Generation X artist, but that's the category in which he's unavoidably filed. Still, among that demimonde he was a special case, as Scott observes:

None of his peers were preoccupied so explicitly with how it felt to arrive on the scene as a young, male American novelist dreaming of glory, late in the 20th century and haunted by a ridiculous, poignant question: what if it's too late? What am I supposed to do now?[8]

Mehldau grappled with precisely this conundrum, at least in the first decade of his solo career; replace the word "novelist" with "jazz musician" and you have an accurate depiction of his circumstances. And because he also saw himself as a writer—a public intellectual on the page as well as the piano bench—he did much of his agonizing in plain view. The album that followed his debut, in 1997, came bearing a self-important title, *The Art of the Trio Volume One.* That phrasing was the brand-conscious work of Pierson, and Mehldau later attempted to distance himself from it. But he was the one who, in lieu of liner notes, chose to include one of Rainer Maria Rilke's *Sonnets to Orpheus.*[9]

The following year, when he released *Live at the Village Vanguard: The Art of the Trio Volume Two,* Mehldau made up for any lost verbiage: his essay in the CD booklet amounted to a lengthy disquisition on irony, the Gen X über-subject, framed as a barroom dialectic. In a conversation between two imagined characters, proxies of his own subconscious, Mehldau lays out some of the insecurities and obsessions with which he felt so afflicted. "I can't help being overly cognizant of the fact that harmony exhausted itself, played itself out, as it were, at the turn of this century," he says. "Here we are on the crest of another millennium and I'm playing what? *Showtunes!*"[10]

Elsewhere in the essay Mehldau disparages the glorification of aesthetic lineage, along with the authority of any self-appointed spokesman for a tradition. (He doesn't need to name names; his crosshairs are obviously trained on Marsalis.) "When this kind of chauvinistic ideology and myth step into the foreground," he asserts, "there arises a tendency toward a sort of musical fascism, steeped in the conservative, with a sensibility inclined toward the downright reactionary."

If it was youthful idealism that had Mehldau determined to plant his flag on the right side of history, maybe it was youthful arrogance that led him to toss around words like "fascism" when peering over at the other side. In any case, he was painfully self-aware about the meager contribution he and his generation would be able to make within the given constraints of the art form. It's a point undercut slightly by the vitality of the music on *The Art of the Trio Volume Two*—especially a breathtaking version of "The Way You Look Tonight," at once quick and light, with a harmonic mercuriality made possible by hair-trigger interplay. Ethan Iverson, a pianist in Mehldau's circle, has described this track as "a thrilling moment for jazz," implying that the trio's place in history was secure.

Years later Mehldau looked back on his frustration from a more objective remove:

> What you have a lot when you talk about our generation—let's say Joshua Redman and me, Mark Turner, Brian Blade, Larry Grenadier—is an idea that there was this orthodoxy or this way to play. A lot of that came out of this thing that Wynton Marsalis was presenting, which was really cool in a lot of ways. But the down-side was, it gave us the idea that we had to play in this correct style. We're the generation of Quentin Tarantino and Beck and this mash-up of stuff: listening to Bird and Monk and Coltrane, but also being on the road and listening to Soundgarden and Alice in Chains, or going to a Sonic Youth concert.[11]

What changed from the mid-nineties on was both the impact of Mehldau's peer circle and the permissions around the state of the art. The two things are interlinked. *Songs: The Art of the Trio Volume Three*, the most fully realized of Mehldau's albums prior to the turn of the century, reveals the extent to which he and his trio stretched and personalized modern jazz conventions, dictating new terms without discarding the old. Partly it's a matter of how fully Mehldau has broken away from the established grid of bebop pianism, which relegates a player's left hand to chordal accompaniment while the right hand plays elaborative lines. Partly it's the translucent quality of the playing itself, with a pristine but unfussy touch, a pronounced Brahmsian bent, and a shrewdly digressive approach to harmony. Partly it's the trio's on-again, off-again relationship to swing, and its ability to make those straight eighth-note cadences glide and breathe.

Then there's the repertoire: *Songs* introduces several originals with a classically steeped yet poplike melancholy, beginning with "Song-Song," a sonorous waltz, and "Unrequited," a bittersweet ballad with a skittering rhythmic undercarriage. There are several achingly lyrical songbook standards, like "For All We Know." And in what would soon become a Mehldau trademark, there are intently thoughtful covers of rock tunes: "River Man," by Nick Drake, and "Exit Music (For a Film)," by Radiohead.

"River Man" is the more conventional of the two, despite the fact that it seems to hover, ghostlike, as Mehldau translates a hypnotic acoustic guitar part to the palette of a piano trio. Drake was an English singer-songwriter of depressive temperament (he committed suicide at twenty-six), but "River Man," released in 1969, was one of his prouder achievements: a mysterious ballad in 5/4 time, delivered with a self-assured quietude, like someone imparting a long-held secret and savoring the telling. There's folk wisdom in the song, and Mehldau locates that quality along with its tragic stoicism.

He does much the same thing with "Exit Music (For a Film)," another dirgelike ballad sung by a mopey Brit. But the particulars of this song ensured a more intense public reception. Radiohead had created "Exit Music" for the closing credits of Baz Luhrmann's *Romeo + Juliet,* in 1996. It resurfaced the following year as a track on the band's third studio album, *OK Computer*—the most acclaimed rock album of the day, a commercial and cultural as well as a critical success. Mehldau released his cover in 1998, less than a year after *OK Computer* arrived. He brought somber purpose to his arrangement, which teased out the song's affinities with Chopin's Prelude in E Minor, op. 28, no. 4. Using his left hand to trace arpeggios through the Romantic chord progression, Mehldau made the piece a tour de force of simmering grace and brooding calm. It was a distillation of his personal aesthetic, rooted but new.

And for a phalanx of musicians who made up the jazz generation just behind Mehldau's, it sounded something like a call to action. Re-imagined pop tunes have always been part of the dossier for jazz—since Louis Armstrong and "(Up a) Lazy River" in 1931, let alone John Coltrane and "My Favorite Things" thirty years later—but no artist of Mehldau's prominence had yet adapted material from the nineties alternative rock scene, not with such uncompromising élan. This wasn't a smooth-jazz musician flipping an R&B hit for commercial airplay. Mehldau had recorded "Exit Music" because it spoke so directly to his sensibilities, in personal as well as generational terms. He was born in 1970, within a year or two of Radiohead's front man and lyricist, Thom Yorke, and its lead guitarist, Jonny Greenwood. And just as Radiohead recalibrated the sonic profile for rock, embracing classical harmony and electronic texture, Mehldau found ways of personalizing the band's songs. He soon incorporated a dynamically astute interpretation of "Paranoid Android," another *OK Computer* track, into his solo recitals. His repertoire would eventually include songs from the Radiohead albums *Kid A, Amnesiac,* and *In Rainbows.* Many other musicians followed suit, to the point where it began to feel almost like a cliché: by 2004, *JazzTimes* could run a trend piece titled "Radiohead: The New Standard Bearers?"[12] and have it feel like settled fact.

But Mehldau's palette was broader than that: the arranging strategies he'd developed for "Exit Music" were easily applied to other material from the alt-rock and grunge milieu—"Gen X music," as he typified it in another liner-note essay, further explaining: "That music spoke to the way we all felt lost and untethered in the world."[13] His catalog came to include Nirvana, Alice in Chains, Soundgarden, Oasis, and Stone Temple Pilots. And he branched out to include more of what he called "interesting pop music"—mainly 1960s and '70s classics by the Beatles, Paul Simon, and Antônio Carlos Jobim. These were all selections made in earnest, with no trace of ironic distance. Mehldau was more inclined to embrace a mode of radical sincerity perhaps best articulated by Wallace, in an essay from 1993:

> Real rebels, as far as I can see, risk disapproval. The old postmodern insurgents risked the gasp and squeal: shock, disgust, outrage, censorship, accusations of socialism, anarchism, nihilism. Today's risks are different. The new rebels might be artists willing to risk the yawn, the rolled eyes, the cool smile, the nudged ribs, the parody of gifted ironists, the "Oh how banal." To risk accusations of sentimentality, melodrama. Of overcredulity. Of softness.

Mehldau's trio with Grenadier and Rossy lasted a single decade, developing a dialect that hasn't been precisely replicated since—not even by Mehldau and Grenadier, in the new trio they formed with an earthier, more emphatically percussive drummer, Jeff Ballard. The original trio's swan song played out over a pair of albums, recorded during the same two-day session but released in staggered fashion: *Anything Goes* (2004), a spruce menu of standards and covers, and *House on Hill* (2006), a sophisticated program of originals. Both albums capture the band at its most coolly refined, with Mehldau often spreading the melody evenly across hands and registers, while Grenadier forms a shifting pivot and Rossy levitates the beat. One original, "Happy Tune," in a bouncy 7/8 meter, even suggests a distant echo of "It Might As Well Be Spring." But by this point, spring has sprung: *House on Hill* is a posthumous statement as far as the trio is concerned. Its first track is a flowing, valedictory piece titled "August Ending," rife with chromatic dissonance but no more turbulent than a strong gust through a canopy of trees.

There's a garbled but intriguing video clip on the Internet titled "The Jon Brion Show—Feat. Elliott Smith/Brad Mehldau ('00)."[14] Apparently transferred from VHS tape, it's the raw footage of an ersatz variety show hosted by Jon Brion—the indie producer, multi-instrumentalist, and all-purpose pop savant, as well as a composer of film scores for Paul Thomas Anderson and others. The taping came about after VH1 passed on the pilot for a real *Jon Brion Show*, mixing musical segments with sketch comedy in a post-slacker vein. For reasons of solidarity or sympathy, P. T. Anderson arranged for Brion to have another crack at it, renting an Ocean Way Recording studio in Hollywood and rolling tape with no mandate beyond creative freedom. The footage, uploaded to Anderson's YouTube channel in 2013, suggests a shambling clubhouse vibe: a storehouse of instruments, cheap Christmas lights, faded Persian rugs.

Brion's first guest on this deconstruction of a talk show is his friend Elliott Smith, a singer-songwriter with a vulnerable air and an adoring following. They're playing songs from an album they worked on together, Smith's *XO*. For two of those songs—"Independence Day" and "Bottle Up and Explode!"—they welcome someone Brion identifies as "one of my favorite persons to make mistakes with, Brad Mehldau." The atmosphere is awkwardly tentative but the musicianship is on point, as Mehldau takes his place at the piano and Brion plays a pump organ and a glockenspiel. After the second tune, Mehldau shakes Smith's hand and makes a hasty getaway, rushing to catch a plane.

Mehldau briefly relocated from New York to Los Angeles in the mid-nineties, in search of a less hectic lifestyle and a healthy distance from the scene. Shortly after settling in there, he paid his first visit to Brion's weekly singer-songwriter residency at a club called Largo. The residency had earned a glowing underground reputation for its musicality and manic spontaneity. On any given night, Brion might be joined onstage by the singer-songwriters Fiona Apple or Aimee Mann, whose albums he had produced. He might start a set with a songbook standard, alone with parlor instruments and a looping pedal, and end it several hours later in a sweaty hard-rock duo with a drummer. Mehldau was instantly hooked, attending the residency as a fan for months before he began sitting in. The admiration turned out to be mutual: Brion had become a Mehldau admirer after hearing his cover of "Blackbird," the Beatles tune, on *The Art of the Trio Volume One.*

"Meeting Brad was thrilling for me, because I didn't like any new jazz musicians I was hearing," he later said. "I didn't *believe* in them. I was extremely disturbed that this music built on spontaneity should be so frighteningly unoriginal, that it had turned into people who had learned to play a series of notes over chord changes. And in Brad I saw the person I was waiting for."[15]

The first tangible by-product of their rapport was Mehldau's album *Largo,* in 2002. It featured his piano at the center of a stylized blur of chamber jazz and indie pop, with the airless punch of a commercial rock record from the seventies. Along with Mehldau's working trio, Brion had enlisted heavy lifters from his side of the fence, like the first-call studio drummers Jim Keltner and Matt Chamberlain. Some tracks featured French horns and trombone; the opening and closing tracks draped Mehldau's graceful melodies in a filmy curtain of oboes, flutes, clarinets, and bassoons.

By all accounts, the *Largo* sessions unfolded with a sort of junk-shop whimsy much like what's depicted on P. T. Anderson's fake *Jon Brion Show.* Mehldau would come into the studio and discover that Brion had prepared the piano with some new sonic treatment: putty for dampening the strings, or a guitar pickup fed through a Leslie amplifier and wah-wah distortion. Some tunes were conjured on the spot, jammed into being; others were fleshed out from a preparatory sketch. There were covers of "Paranoid Android" and "Dear Prudence." The entire album reflected a desire to reinvent the possibilities for jazz musicians in a studio setting, and to access the drive and attitude of rock without resorting to any known species of fusion.

Mehldau had already won over an aspiring jazz generation with his choice of material; *Largo* found him tinkering with his methodology. The album entered the world as a curio, but soon had extraordinary resonance with the wave of musicians coming up after Mehldau. Some, like the pianist Frank LoCrasto, adopted the album's lo-fi pop grandeur as a signature. The keyboardist Marco Benevento earnestly re-created its sound, going so far as to hire Chamberlain as his drummer. "I've seen people form bands based around individual tracks on that record," Brion said, a bit sardonically, about its reach.

The well-trammeled post-*Largo* landscape partly explains why Brion and Mehldau were both averse to a straightforward sequel when they reunited, at Ocean Way studios, in 2009. Another reason was the enlarging of Mehldau's vision as a composer. He had grown more invested in classical new music: in 2005 he premiered a Carnegie Hall commission, *Love Sublime,* for piano and voice (specifically, the soprano Renée Fleming). And shortly before the release of his new project with Brion, he was named to Carnegie Hall's Richard and Barbara Debs Composer's Chair, a position previously held by the classical composers Ellen Taaffe Zwilich, Pierre Boulez, John Adams, Thomas Adès, Elliott Carter, and Louis Andriessen.

Highway Rider, the album Mehldau made with Brion, reflected this new level of compositional ambition with an original score for a chamber orchestra. Mehldau's main template was *Metamorphosen,* a late work by Richard Strauss for twenty-three strings, with the unusual feature of a unique and independent part for each player. Borrowing that instrumentation and strategy, Mehldau added three French horns, a bassoon, and a contrabassoon, for heft. And against this dark Romantic swoon, he brought in Redman on tenor saxophone, as a gallant and spontaneous lead voice.

Redman also surfaces on a number of tracks with no complement of strings, including a sprightly tune called "Capriccio," featuring just piano, soprano saxophone, handclaps, and light percussion. It leads into the track that most recalls *Largo,* a ballad with a loping groove, a laid-back piano solo, and the mournful wheeze of a pump organ. Mehldau titled it "Sky Turning Grey (For Elliott Smith)."

The second Brad Mehldau Trio—formed in 2005, with Grenadier as the holdover and Ballard as the newcomer—revitalized the rhythmic traction in his music, and strengthened his anchoring tether to the postbop tradition. Mehldau had known Ballard since his conservatory years, and what drew them back together was something almost wistful. It hadn't escaped Mehldau's notice that Ballard, Grenadier, and Turner—three of his longest musical acquaintances—were making separate strides as a cooperative trio, Fly. He enlisted them all for a one-off quartet gig at the Village Vanguard, and then poached Ballard (with the blessing of all involved). The new Mehldau trio made its debut with a strong studio album, *Day Is Done* (2005), followed by a stronger double album, *Brad Mehldau Trio Live* (2008). At a certain point, with hardly anyone seeming to notice, it outlasted the tenure of the original trio.

What registered clearly was the omnivorous enthusiasm of the group, and the way in which a wildly divergent repertoire could be bound by the force of its cohesion. A 2012 album called *Where Do You Start,* after the ballad by Johnny Mandel, also featured material by Nick Drake and Elvis Costello, the indie-folk artist Sufjan Stevens, the alternative-rock band Alice in Chains, the Brazilian musicians Chico Buarque and Toninho Horta, and the modern jazz lodestars Sonny Rollins and Clifford Brown.

Meanwhile there were productive dalliances outside any trio framework. Mehldau recorded and toured with the new-groove drummer Mark Guiliana and the beyond-bluegrass mandolinist Chris Thile; with Metheny and another stylistically frisky jazz guitarist, John Scofield; with the mezzo-soprano Anne Sofie von Otter. A 2010 album titled *Modern Music* featured him and a contemporary, Kevin Hays, on two pianos at a crossroads of jazz and new music. He reunited with Redman for a series of duo tours that yielded a live album, *Nearness,* in 2016; among the reasons to hear it is a version of the Charlie Parker flag-waver "Ornithology," featuring some of the most luxuriant peeka-boo bebop phrasing of Mehldau's career.

Through every chapter, solo piano was the format in which Mehldau made the most dramatic growth in public. His first solo album, *Elegiac Cycle*, from 1999, was an exercise in style, a grief-stricken, album-length suite that he later described as a purging. Mehldau gradually moved toward a more song-oriented solo-recital ideal, following the exam-ple of his former teacher Fred Hersch. But there was also the loom-ing shadow of Jarrett, whose solo recitals have often delivered a grand rhapsodic sweep to go with their high emotional drama. This is one obvious reference point on a 2004 album called *Live in Tokyo*, which includes a version of "From This Moment On," the Cole Porter tune from *Introducing Brad Mehldau*. Here it unfolds in somber grandeur, an ornate cathedral built using the thematic materials of the song.

Mehldau's solo output found a suitably expansive frame in *10 Years Solo Live*, a 2015 boxed set initially pressed on eight LPs, and subse-quently issued on four CDs. Assembled from a decade's worth of Euro-pean concert recordings, it assumes a baronial sprawl more in line with a deluxe archival package than the work of an improviser at mid-career; one of its few precursors in that regard was Jarrett's *Sun Bear Concerts*, a ten-LP collection recorded in Japan and released on ECM in 1978.

Comparisons aside, *10 Years Solo Live* presented Mehldau at a new stage of maturity and self-reflection, extracting rich possibility from a deceptively simple formula: "Short, small songs that get stretched out into bigger vehicles with grand expressive gestures," as he writes in another extensive liner-note essay.

Throughout the set, Mehldau engages song form as a springboard rather than a road map. "I am no longer relying on the structure of the song for my improvisation, in the classic jazz manner of theme and variations," he explains, "but instead am using pieces of the melody as motific jumping-off points, and then allowing the harmony to fol-low in a freer manner." He did this no less probingly with Coltrane's "Countdown" than with Nirvana's "Smells Like Teen Spirit." And there may be no better example of his prismatic elaboration as a solo pianist than the final track in the collection: "God Only Knows," the

Beach Boys aria, extrapolated in a way that's shimmery, inquisitive, and grave. Over the course of a suspenseful sixteen minutes, Mehldau preserves the intervallic heart of the melody while shifting textures and tonal centers almost constantly. His spiritual frame of reference for the song includes not only Brian Wilson, its star-crossed composer, but also Wagner—in particular, the climactic finale of *Tristan und Isolde,* known as the "Liebestod" (Love-Death). From the first pale tremolo to the last seismic rumble, the performance is unmistakably Mehldau's handiwork, and a stunner.

Less jaw-dropping, but perhaps more telling, is one of the shortest tracks on the set: a brisk reading of "John Boy," the opening theme from *Highway Rider.* A song at once sun-dappled and touched by a lingering sadness, it's a tribute to several figures in Mehldau's personal pantheon: Jon Brion, for one, and John-Boy Walton, the writerly young character from *The Waltons,* a seventies television drama burned into Mehldau's pop-culture subconscious. "Last but not least," he notes, "'John Boy' is Johannes Brahms, the composer I have always felt so close to in my heart." (On the track list, it sits beside Brahms's Intermezzo in B-flat Major, op. 76, no. 4.)

"One reason that Brahms is such a model for me is the way he straddles two epochs," Mehldau once explained, in the essay accompanying *House on Hill.* The reasons why that straddling would appeal to him aren't laid out, exactly, but they don't need to be: they run throughout his music, which perpetually strives to balance the weight of jazz history against the possibilities of its exigent present.

Brad Mehldau, *Highway Rider* (Nonesuch)
Brad Mehldau, *Introducing Brad Mehldau* (Warner Bros.)
Brad Mehldau, *Songs: The Art of the Trio Volume Three* (Warner Bros.)
Joshua Redman, *MoodSwing* (Warner Bros.)
Mark Turner, *Yam Yam* (Criss Cross Jazz)

3

Uptown Downtown

John Zorn was in his battle uniform—camouflage cargo pants, hooded sweatshirt, high-top sneakers—as he paced the stage in the Rose Theater. He seemed lathered up and agitated, alto saxophone hanging from a strap around his neck. This in itself wasn't unusual. But the circumstances were: Zorn and his band Masada were about to perform their half of a double bill with the redoubtable pianist Cecil Taylor, under the auspices of Jazz at Lincoln Center. The concert, in March 2007, was the result of a first-time invitation for both Taylor and Zorn, each a galvanizing figure in the postwar American avant-garde. Given the setting, their presence suggested an incursion.

Zorn seemed to think so, anyway. "Let's hope this is the beginning of a trend of enlightened programming here!" he barked from the stage. "There are more young faces in the audience here than there have been since the inception of this place!"[1]

He was taking aim at Jazz at Lincoln Center, which in less than twenty years had amassed an imposing cultural stature and tremendous resources—along with a conservative reputation in line with the image of its artistic director and public face, Wynton Marsalis.

As Zorn made his proclamation, he was standing in the largest of three performance spaces in Frederick P. Rose Hall, Jazz at Lincoln Center's home on the fifth floor of the Time Warner Center at Columbus Circle. This facility, the first of its kind for jazz, had been completed a few years earlier at a cost of almost $130 million. The grandeur of the complex fed a suspicion in some circles that Jazz at Lincoln Center was a behemoth, gobbling up philanthropic resources for jazz while sternly dictating its aesthetic boundaries. Marsalis had taken to calling it the House of Swing, an epithet intoned as a welcome to concert audiences—but also an implicit admonition that this was no kind of place for the unswinging. For reasons like these, devotees of experimental music saw Rose Hall as loosely analogous to the Imperial Death Star, while someone like Zorn—spontaneous, unruly, irrepressible—stood for the plucky Rebellion.

Another way to understand Zorn's appearance on the Rose Theater stage was as a tenuous alignment of cohabiting forces. Jazz at Lincoln Center embodied one institutional model for jazz. The avant-garde was connected to others, most of them adaptive and informal. Zorn was the very picture of self-reliance, an artist who'd created his own support structure: he was the proprietor of a thriving independent record label, Tzadik, and a small but vital nonprofit performance space, The Stone. He received major commissions from the Guggenheim and the Metropolitan Museum of Art. He had built a dynamic network, at once intimate and global, around his work and the work of his peers.

A similar spirit of dauntless enterprise had kept Cecil Taylor going in the 1950s, when he developed some of the earliest free-improvisational techniques in spaces like the Five Spot, and the '60s, when he was involved in the founding of the artist-run Jazz Composers Guild. But Taylor also cultivated relationships with high-culture institutions like the Whitney Museum of American Art, where he performed a number of times over the years. He received a Guggenheim Fellowship in 1973. The MacArthur Foundation, whose fellowship amounts to a kind of knighthood in American culture, had selected Taylor for its honor in 1991. The same had happened for Zorn in 2006, six months before he stood on the Rose Theater stage.

There's a danger of false equivalency in the suggestion that Jazz at Lincoln Center, with an operating budget north of $40 million, could find any counterbalance in experimental artists creating their own infrastructure, through a piecemeal of gigs, composer grants, and foundation support. But framing the situation in stark David-and-Goliath terms oversimplifies the complex ecosystem to which all parties can't help belonging.

However you choose to see it, the institutionalization of jazz—through performance organizations, commissioning bodies, and educational programs—exerted profound influence on the music during the period that began in the late twentieth century. The effect was pervasive, touching the music's aesthetic development along with its audience and business models. Zorn has a part to play in that story as well as Marsalis, with neither as squarely opposed to the other as the popular history might have you believe.

Every Goliath has its David phase. The jazz world was in the throes of its so-called renaissance when, in the mid-1980s, the Lincoln Center for the Performing Arts—a citadel of high culture, home to the New York Philharmonic, the Metropolitan Opera, and the New York City Ballet—began to consider ways of diversifying its audience. Jazz was raised as an option, but only in the most provisional terms: when Lincoln Center's Committee for the Future issued an audience-development report in May 1986, its findings concluded, in part: "No compelling case can be made for adding a new constituent in an area like jazz."

Still, the organization made a pitch to Marsalis, who already had proven himself fluent in both jazz and a classical métier. In 1987, working with the Lincoln Center staff member Alina Bloomgarden, he programmed a three-concert series, "Classical Jazz," to run in late summer, when resident companies like the Philharmonic were away on tour.

Marsalis was asked to program another round of "Classical Jazz" in 1988. To promote it, he wrote an article for *The New York Times* that staked an aesthetic position. The piece bore the headline "What Jazz Is—and Isn't," and in it Marsalis articulated his core belief that the music has a determinative essence and can be understood within objective parameters, including swing. He also insisted that at this stage in its history, jazz had to choose between one of two existing models: classical and pop.

It was clear which of those options Marsalis endorsed. A classical

approach would emphasize a time-honored literature and an acceptable language, placing new work in a stable artistic context. A pop
approach meant dilution, bastardization, and debasement. "To many
people," Marsalis lamented, "any kind of popular music now can be
lumped with jazz." At the time of his writing, Kenny G, the pied piper of
smooth jazz, was finishing his fifth studio album, which would sell more
than four million copies in the United States. Against the backdrop of
such blatant heresies, Marsalis argued, a generation of musicians was
coming up without the rigors of history. He posed a loaded question:
"How can something new and substantial, not eccentric and fraudulent,
be developed when the meaning of what's old is not known?"[2]

Pop wasn't the only unwelcome paradigm for Marsalis; so was the
entire hemisphere of creative approaches aligned with what he considered a Eurocentric avant-garde. Abstraction, atonality, anything
that subverted formal practice—he saw these elements as the result of
misplaced priorities by the critical and academic establishment. When
Marsalis talked about classical music, he didn't mean twentieth-century
serialists and chance merchants like Pierre Boulez. As the composer,
trombonist, and scholar George Lewis has noted: "In a critical discursive shift, the term 'classical' became less a description of a musical
tradition than of an attitude—one of reverence and preservation."[3]

Lewis, a longtime member of the AACM, points out that one
exclusionary effect of this rhetoric was the erasure of composers like
Anthony Braxton and Anthony Davis, who had been working for years
with orchestral or operatic forms. Their work fell out of the critical discourse, he argues, because of "the promulgation of a revisionist canon
that emphasized a unitary, 'classic' tradition of jazz."

Marsalis had a powerful intellectual ally in Albert Murray, the cultural critic, novelist, and blues philosopher who saw jazz as the ultimate
expression of an African-American drive toward elegant purpose. In
Stomping the Blues, an influential essay collection published in 1976, Murray had argued that the blues found its highest expression in jazz, grant-
ing a ritualistic power to triumph over adverse conditions. The music,
as he put it, was "equipment for living."

Murray, along with Stanley Crouch, a former loft-scene drummer
who had become a prominent jazz critic, formed a brain trust against

which Marsalis could bounce ideas and test his moorings. Once, in a lengthy conversation that was documented and later published, Murray advised Marsalis to think of the avant-garde in military terms: "Avant-garde means shock troops, explorers, and whatnot. You can't be a pathfinder unless you have a turnpike or superhighway coming behind you."[4] By this light, Murray added, the one indisputably avant-garde musician in jazz had been Louis Armstrong.

The aesthetic framework that Marsalis developed, with input from Murray and Crouch, was essential in building the case for Jazz at Lincoln Center. Central to their thesis was the conviction that jazz embodies a model of democratic action, and a prism through which the American experiment can best be understood. It was a concept with tremendous appeal: beyond advocating for the conservation of a musical tradition, it proposed a grand vision of cultural heritage, one that rewrote even the national sins of slavery and racial injustice into a narrative of transcendent resilience. This understanding would eventually form the backbone of Ken Burns's *Jazz,* and a bedrock of education initiatives like Jazz in the Schools, sent to high schools across the country by the National Endowment for the Arts.

The concept was less broadly familiar in 1989, when Lincoln Center formed an exploratory jazz committee whose members included Murray, Marsalis, and Crouch. The committee—chaired by Gordon J. Davis, a key member of Lincoln Center's board—issued a report. "We rigged the conclusion so that Lincoln Center should create a permanent jazz program," Davis recalled. And the ideological engine behind the programming proved vital in sealing the deal:

It's like a good political campaign, in the sense that when you're trying to raise money for a candidate, you try to have a way of describing that candidate in terms of aspirations and ideas. And if you've got a good idea with some substance that you believe in, that is the best way to raise money. That is the thing that will open people's minds and get them to understand that you are not involved in something monosyllabic or single-layered. And from the first meetings in that committee, that was in the room. Because Albert was in the room, because Stanley was in the room, because Wynton was in the room.[5]

Lincoln Center began the process of forming a jazz department, and Davis, as chair of the jazz committee, assumed the responsibility of solidifying financial support. This proved daunting, given that there was scant philanthropic precedent for such an effort:

> There were people on the board of Lincoln Center who thought this was nuts! The odds were ninety to one that we had any chance at all. Raise money? Do you have any idea how hard it was to raise money for jazz in 1989? People looked at us like we were crazy![6]

But Jazz at Lincoln Center became an official department of Lincoln Center in 1991, hiring Rob Gibson, formerly with the Atlanta Jazz Festival, as its director. The news made the front page of *The New York Times*, which reported that the program's projected budget was $1 million. As if to underscore the scope of this coup, the article included a quote from Nat Leventhal, the president of Lincoln Center. "I had the same prejudices about jazz that opera lovers or ballet lovers might have," he said. "But I've learned a lot, and now I am a convert. There is as much richness and as much variety in Duke Ellington as there is in Mozart."[7]

The new organization's first season included a smattering of events around New York City, but its centerpiece was still Marsalis's "Classical Jazz" series at Alice Tully Hall. And along with a sense of arrival in the precincts of high culture, there came a greater and more pointed brand of scrutiny. Musicians complained about the collegial makeup of the Lincoln Center Jazz Orchestra, accusing Marsalis of nepotism; critics attacked the historicist programming, lobbing a charge of conservatism. Still others in the press took issue with the project's sociocultural foundation. Whitney Balliett, reviewing a "Classical Jazz" tribute to Ellington for *The New Yorker,* praised the musical execution but noted that a stark minority of performers in the series had been white. Raising the specter of reverse racism, Balliett cleared his throat: "Blacks invented jazz, but nobody owns it."[8]

Marsalis and his constituency were predisposed to view an argument like this as baseless from the start. And as Jazz at Lincoln Center weathered the controversies, its footprint and coffers only grew. By 1996 it had amassed enough support to secure full constituent status at Lincoln Center—joining the likes of the New York Philharmonic and the Metropolitan Opera and earning the right to form its own board.

"It deserves the place," Leventhal said at the time of the announcement, referring to the organization's seat at the table.[9] Marsalis noted with satisfaction that the news sent a message around the world about jazz's value as a fine art.

In 1987, the same year that Lincoln Center served its first helping of "Classical Jazz," an upstart young promoter named Michael Dorf was breaking in the Knitting Factory, four miles south, in a former Avon Products office near the Bowery. On some level this was a late reverberation of the loft scene, which had tapered off in the face of a recovering city economy and a new crop of commercial jazz clubs, including the Blue Note (est. 1981) and the new Birdland (est. 1985). But the Knitting Factory also came out of a do-it-yourself punk underground. Its ideology, to the extent that there was one, ran in opposition to aesthetic rules and definitions. In his first press release, Dorf made a point of declaring that "the Knitting Factory considers many things art and is open to suggestions."[10]

Thanks to the enterprising work of musicians like the keyboardist and composer Wayne Horvitz, the Knit quickly became a clubhouse for an experimental fringe drawn to the sorts of musical ideas that, to borrow Marsalis's phrase, might proudly be filed under "eccentric and fraudulent." One of the club's other early leaders was Zorn, whose performances could take the form of procedural game play, and whose frame of reference ran deliriously through surf music, roadhouse blues, free jazz, cartoon music, and extreme metal.

Already a creative cyclone with a decade's worth of documented provocations in New York, Zorn had broken through to a wider public with his 1986 album *The Big Gundown,* a postmodern spree through the movie themes of Ennio Morricone. In 1987 he released *Spillane,* his nod to the pulp mystery writer Mickey Spillane. A deck shuffle of musical styles made new by juxtaposition and panache, it featured a clutch of Zorn's contemporaries, including Bill Frisell on guitar, Anthony Coleman on piano, and Bobby Previte on drums. John Lurie, of the "fake jazz" band the Lounge Lizards, provided occasional voice-over on the twenty-five-minute title track, muttering the hardboiled thoughts of Mike Hammer, Spillane's franchise private eye.

Zorn wasn't averse to paying homages, provided they were on his own terms. His 1986 album *Voodoo* was a repertory tribute to the bop pianist Sonny Clark. And one of Zorn's most talked-about performances in the Knitting Factory's inaugural year was a joyously splenetic tribute to Ornette Coleman, featuring his fellow alto saxophonist and iconoclast Tim Berne. (The crowd spilled out onto Houston Street.)[11]

Berne was a second-generation by-product of the loft scene, though he might not have put it that way. Originally from Syracuse, New York, he had grown up with Stax and Motown soul, barely listening to jazz. He first picked up a saxophone in college, around the same time he heard the alto saxophonist Julius Hemphill, a member of the Black Artists Group. Berne was instantly riveted by *Dogon A.D.*, Hemphill's 1972 debut, which grounded experimental urges with Stax-like earthiness: a deep soul cry, a slow-cooker funk groove, Adbul Wadud's guitarlike cello growl. When Berne moved to New York City in 1974, he quickly found his way to Hemphill, becoming a disciple, an assistant, and a friend. Hemphill was in the process of releasing his own albums through a tiny independent label, Mbari, and Berne helped out. When it was time to begin putting out his own music, Berne followed Hemphill's lead and formed a shoestring label in 1979, giving it the tongue-in-cheek name Empire Records.

When Berne landed an unlikely deal with Columbia Records in the mid-eighties, it was more or less by happenstance: the guitarist Gary Lucas, an acquaintance from Syracuse, was writing ad copy at the label, and had put in a good word.[12] Berne made an album with Frisell, the cellist Hank Roberts, and the drummer Alex Cline, pursuing a scratchy-but-soulful ideal loosely related to Hemphill's, though its formal character was stubbornly original. Berne hadn't been signed to Columbia as an outright experimentalist—he later speculated that label executives, hearing a demo he'd made with Frisell, expected something more like new-age music—but his album, *Fulton Street Maul,* released in 1987, had a jagged fury that left no doubt. One track, "Unknown Disaster," opens with a lunging cello vamp in irregular meter, over which Frisell's electric guitar sprays wild and disorienting electronic effects.

Moments like these made *Fulton Street Maul* a conspicuous outlier on a label roster so heavily vested in the Marsalis business—even though Columbia during the eighties had also been home to Weather Report and the post-Ornette bluesman James Blood Ulmer. To the surprise of skeptics at the label, Berne's experiment met with spectacular acclaim. Jon Pareles began an appraisal in *The New York Times* by proclaiming: "It's only February, but one of the year's most important jazz albums has just been released."[13]

That language notably placed the convulsive designs of *Fulton Street Maul* at the forward flank of the jazz continuum, despite Berne's hedging ambivalence on the matter. "I'm trying to figure out how not to sound like a jazz band," he said in the same *Times* article. Describing his approach to "Unknown Disaster," he explained: "I didn't want a guitar solo over the vamp, I wanted a noise solo—total annihilation right at the start."[14] But because of the integral role of improvisation in his music, and the fact that Berne was a saxophonist indebted to Hemphill, it made sense to file *Fulton Street Maul* under jazz. It also reflected a growing critical dissatisfaction with jazz conservatism, and with the related idea that the music's mainstream was no longer straining against formal limits. There were enough raves for Berne's album that Columbia saw no choice but to let him make another one, *Sanctified Dreams.*

For all intents and purposes Berne was in the trenches with Zorn: they favored many of the same collaborators and were equally serious about carving out space as composers. In 1989 Elektra Musician released their Coleman tribute as a Zorn album, *Spy vs. Spy*—a battle royal in which the musicians wrestled Ornette's tunes to the mat with a brawny intensity inspired by hardcore punk.

Zorn brought similar panache to Naked City, a maniacally twitchy band with a fondness for pairing soundtrack atmospherics with a rude graffiti scrawl. (When Coleman's plaintive "Lonely Woman" cropped up in the Naked City book, it was played with feral commitment to the

melody but a bass riff copped from Roy Orbison's "Oh, Pretty Woman.")
Zorn's confreres in the band included Frisell, Horvitz, the bassist Fred
Frith, and the drummer Joey Baron. There was usually a vocalist of vol-
canic heat and terror: either Yamatsuka Eye, of the Japanese noise band
Boredoms, or Mike Patton, of the American alternative-metal bands
Mr. Bungle and Faith No More.

At a moment when jazz was beginning to seem buttoned-up and
dutifully self-conscious, the rash audacity of this music and its makers
struck many observers, especially in the rock and jazz press, as a desta-
bilizing retort. It hardly mattered that the artists themselves showed
little interest in the debates around the jazz tradition. Nor did it matter
that their work belonged to a far-reaching downtown landscape that
also housed so much else: performance artists like Laurie Anderson,
postpunk minimalists like Rhys Chatham, drone auteurs like Tony
Conrad and La Monte Young, rock experimentalists like Sonic Youth.
Many in the jazz commentariat latched onto Zorn's example, recognizing a prankish gravity congruent with beloved AACM flagships like the
Art Ensemble of Chicago. This sort of chatter was only amplified after
Zorn began making strides with Masada, in the mid-1990s.

An acoustic quartet with Dave Douglas on trumpet, Greg Cohen on
bass, and Joey Baron on drums, Masada represented the convergence
of two of Zorn's personal interests: the early small-group signature of
Coleman and a more recent obsession, his own heritage. "When the
Masada project started, I was forty," Zorn reflected. "You begin to think
about your roots, where you came from, who you are. You begin to turn
inward. Being Jewish became important to me."[15]

The music for Masada involved lyrically terse, coiled-spring
melodies—derived from modal Jewish scales (often the Phrygian dominant, also commonly found in thrash metal)—and a rhythmic motor
that could seize up and overheat but also swing straight down the center or simmer into a groove. Behind Masada's exotic veneer there was
an agile, sympathetic, and cohesive jazz quartet. In a slanted way, the
band was even an act of nostalgia: Coleman's main outlet by this time
was the delirious funk unit Prime Time, and he hadn't worked regu-
larly with this instrumentation for years. (The all-too-rare exceptions,
like a quartet reunion on the 1987 album *In All Languages*, were regarded

as events.) So along with a novel formulation of "klezmer free jazz," as it was inevitably described, Masada offered a rambunctious thrill that somehow felt connected to the historic jazz lineage. Alex Ross, reviewing an early concert in 1994, accurately noted in *The New York Times* that Masada amounted to "Zorn's most ingratiating work to date."[16]

The familiarity was partly cultural: those Jewish scales carried a specific resonance. And Zorn was hardly the first downtown artist to explore what he came to call "Radical Jewish Culture." The Klezmatics, formed in the East Village in the late eighties, had become a Knitting Factory favorite, releasing a well-received album called *Rhythm + Jews*. A number of other improvisers who had studied at the New England Conservatory in Boston, with the multi-instrumentalist and ethnomusicologist Hankus Netsky, were just as conversant in these traditions.

Netsky had founded and led the Klezmer Conservatory Band, which brought a live spark to Yiddish musical traditions that had been all but lost. One of the band's founding members was Don Byron, a commanding, stylistically voracious clarinetist originally from the Bronx, and an unusual fit for klezmer in that he was neither Jewish nor white. (The dreadlocks he wore had nothing to do with Hebrew *payot.*) Byron fell in love with klezmer's wild, gulping exuberance, and with the fact that it was the rare strain of music that unabashedly gave the clarinet a starring role.

He grew fixated on Mickey Katz, a virtuoso clarinetist and bandleader who had worked in a comic Yiddish-novelty vein from the 1930s into the '60s. So after working for seven years with the Klezmer Conservatory Band, and then beginning to make his reputation in New York, Byron formed a repertory tribute to Katz, sparing not an ounce of shtick; it debuted at the Knit in 1987, causing an immediate stir. And while Byron tacked in a less idiomatic direction for his debut album—*Tuskegee Experiments,* on the Elektra/Nonesuch label in 1991, was an adventurous postbop outing whose intergenerational lineup included the former Coltrane bassist Reggie Workman, the Young Lion drummer Ralph Peterson Jr., and Frisell—he followed it two years later with *Don Byron Plays the Music of Mickey Katz.*

Taking a cue from Katz, whose bands had featured first-call musicians, Byron stocked the album not with klezmer specialists but rather with a cadre of multi-literate peers like the pianist Uri Caine, the violinist Mark Feldman, and the guitarist Brandon Ross. On trumpet, frequently playing lead with a matador's bravura, was Douglas, who would later do the same in Masada.

Douglas was no more Jewish than Byron. The son of an IBM executive, he went to Sunday school at a Presbyterian church as a small child, and later attended Phillips Exeter Academy, the New Hampshire boarding school. He studied jazz at the conservatory level, first in Boston and then in New York, and landed his first major gig in 1987, with the venerable hard-bop pianist and composer Horace Silver. From a certain angle Douglas might have seemed like a Young Lion in waiting: proficient, apprenticed, literate in the jazz tradition.

But he had a restless intellect, and was naturally drawn to a wider scope of music than what "the jazz tradition" was then understood to mean. His heroes on the trumpet included not only postbop paragons like Woody Shaw but also trailblazing oddballs like Don Cherry and Lester Bowie. When he returned to New York from a tour of Europe with Silver's band, Douglas found himself caught between two scenes that had become polarized not only in the press but also at ground level, socially as well as musically.

In that sense, *Parallel Worlds* was a good title for his debut album, released on the Italian label Soul Note in 1993. Featuring an unusual contingent of instruments—Douglas's trumpet alongside Feldman's violin, Erik Friedlander's cello, Mark Dresser's bass, and Michael Sarin's drums—the album interspersed playfully prickly originals with themes by Ellington, Stravinsky, Webern, and Weill. (Ironically, given that composer lineup, no one thought to call it a neoclassical album.) The chamber thrust and experimental twitch of *Parallel Worlds*, along with its high-minded selection of covers, proved a challenge for the record industry at the time.

"It took six years to convince somebody to let me do that album," Douglas said. "I had offers to make straight-ahead jazz-type records, playing standards, and I felt like it was worth waiting to define things my own way. I was sort of shocked by the way those divisions existed."[17]

But the divisions were endorsed by musicians and promoters as well as the media, which was constitutionally drawn to paradigms of crude opposition. This proved vividly true in the discourse around the Knitting Factory's first festival in New York. Dorf, emboldened and inspired by the club's scrappy success, decided to start his own summer fête in 1988.

It was understood as an alternative not to Lincoln Center's fledgling jazz program but rather to the JVC Jazz Festival–New York, produced by George Wein. JVC was a smoothly run commercial affair whose headliners were expected to fill major concert halls; that year's lineup featured Ella Fitzgerald at Carnegie Hall on the same night that Miles Davis was at Avery Fisher Hall. Sarah Vaughan and Carmen McRae each had her own headlining concert at Carnegie. One double bill at Avery Fisher put Marsalis's band opposite the great swing-era vibraphonist Lionel Hampton; another featured the guitarist Stanley Jordan alongside Kenny G.

These marquee names represented a level of popular success beyond the known experience of most jazz musicians in New York—major figures as well as up-and-comers. So while Dorf hadn't set out to create a jazz stronghold with the Knit, he recognized a niche to be filled. The first Knitting Factory Jazz Festival procured a small-time sponsor (Vinylmania, a West Village record shop) but received glowing press. The lineup included living embodiments of the historic avantgarde, including Cecil Taylor, the Sun Ra Arkestra, the trumpeter Bill Dixon, and the pianist Andrew Hill. There were emissaries from the loft scene, including David Murray. And there were stalwarts of the Knit's own emergent community, like Zorn, Horvitz, and the guitarist Elliott Sharp. Some concerts proposed a dialogue between experimental waves, like a double bill featuring the tenor saxophonist Dewey Redman, of Colemanesque free-jazz pedigree, and the alto saxophonist Steve Coleman, who was working with his more contemporary synthesis of bebop phraseology and pointillist funk.

The festival put the Knit on the cultural map, and not just in New York. Dutch promoters reached out to express interest in a collaboration, which led to a Knitting Factory Festival in Groningen, Holland, and subsequent European tours. The news coverage reached as far as

Japan, where jazz magazines and the national television network ran stories. (One evening as Dorf was taking tickets at the door of the club, a busload of Japanese tourists rolled up, eager to hear the latest in jazz. He struggled in vain to warn them that the lineup for the night consisted of a hardcore punk band.)[18]

Had there not been such demand for an upstart challenge to jazz's status quo, the Knitting Factory might have been understood in less idiomatic terms: as a downtown catchall, a laboratory and rugged outpost perched beyond the borders of genre. That's really what it was, in practical terms. But by 1994, when the club outgrew its original space and moved into a three-story building in Tribeca, the Knit was largely understood as a jazz room, albeit one whose idea of jazz allowed for all manner of downtown liberties. Much to the annoyance of Wein—and, for different reasons, Marsalis—the jazz press welcomed the Knitting Factory as an important new anchor of the scene. Dorf continued presenting a range of acts, always with growth in mind: he was an early advocate of live-streaming shows on the Internet (too early, as it turned out), and he started a label, Knitting Factory Works, to document the myriad voices on the scene.

In 1996, the What Is Jazz? Festival, as Dorf had slyly renamed the Knit's summer shebang, secured its first full corporate sponsor, a major beer company. That year's festival ran almost two weeks in the club's three spaces, with a total of more than 150 shows. (There were also bookings in Town Hall.) And for all the talk of contested traditions, the festival staked out a lot of middle ground. The jazz imprints of several major labels, including Columbia and Verve, helped underwrite showcases during the festival, which featured artists as prominent as the singer Abbey Lincoln and the bassist Charlie Haden. The press began to run stories that placed the What Is Jazz? and JVC festivals side by side as competing equals.

The momentum in the jazz underground, meanwhile, yielded further alternatives—notably the Vision Festival, which from its first edition in 1996 upheld an ideal more earnest and utopian than Dorf's. Founded by the dancer Patricia Nicholson Parker, whose husband, the bassist William Parker, had been a stalwart of the loft scene, the Vision Festival circled the wagons around a self-reliant but perpetually endangered avant-garde, a nonconformist and noncommercial music. Among the primary heroes in its ranks were free-jazz warriors like the tenor saxophonist David S. Ware, in whose band Parker played.

Ware was also a Knitting Factory regular, but he more precisely embodied Vision Festival ideals: he was a total improviser in the post-Coltrane, post–Albert Ayler mold, a heroically powerful force on his instrument and a persuasive conduit for spiritual inquisition. Along with Parker, the David S. Ware Quartet, formed in 1989, featured the dynamically fluid pianist Matthew Shipp and a succession of excellent drummers: first Marc Edwards, then Whit Dickey, then Susie Ibarra, and finally Guillermo E. Brown.

The accumulated energies in jazz and other improvisational musics in Lower Manhattan—encompassing Zorn as well as Ware, and so much else besides—proved an irresistible counterweight to what was happening in the vicinity of Jazz at Lincoln Center. Musicians as well as critics felt compelled to take sides in what became a rift colloquially known as the Jazz Wars. As a shorthand, many coded the difference in terms of the urban grid: uptown (conservatism) vs. downtown (anarchic freedom, stylistic range, rugged independence). There had already been official buy-in to this self-consciously divisive terminology. When the JVC Jazz Festival carved out a provisional space for its young rival in 1989, the concert series was advertised as "Knitting Factory Goes Uptown." And every jazz critic seemed to have a specific cohort in mind when he or she wrote, with admiration or judgment, about "the downtown scene."

Not many jazz musicians working in the mid-nineties moved credibly between downtown and uptown. (Frisell would have been a prime candidate, but he'd moved to Seattle in 1988, opting out of the whole fraught equation.) Douglas, who'd been puzzled by the rift in the first place, made a serious go of it. After finally releasing *Parallel Worlds*, he opened a spigot: from '95 on, he put out no less than an album a year, often with a new angle and personnel.

His second was the 1994 self-titled debut by a band he called the Tiny Bell Trio, with the guitarist Brad Shepik (then spelled "Schoeppach") and the drummer Jim Black. They played tunes drawn from (or inspired by) the Balkan klezmer repertory, reveling in keening folk melodies and irregular dance rhythms. But they also took advantage of the trio's permissively sparse format, gleefully chasing solo digressions over hill and dale.

Black, who like Shepik originally hailed from Seattle, was a sound and sight to behold: he piloted his drum kit like a sputtering jalopy, with a rack tom cranked taut as a timbale and a kick drum loosened so much that it produced a splat. His wafer-thin cymbals had a fast decay, but he often didn't wait even that long, clenching them quiet with a darting hand. Black knew the accepted schools of modern jazz drumming, but seemed to forage farther back and off to the side, conjuring a clattering ancestor like Baby Dodds, and projecting that ghost image through the distorted lens of a rock drummer like Keith Moon.

One of the few drummers on the scene that Black vaguely called to mind was Baron, who worked in Masada and on the third album by Douglas, the one most in line with standard jazz conventions. That album—*In Our Lifetime*, released in 1995—featured an assertive postbop unit otherwise made up of Caine, Chris Speed on tenor saxophone and clarinet, James Genus on bass, and Josh Roseman on trombone. It was a tribute to Booker Little, a trumpeter of startlingly progressive harmonic ideas who had died of kidney failure at twenty-three.

Among the album's highlights were two tracks from Little's underrated 1961 masterwork, *Out Front*, and a fanfare called "Forward Flight," recorded for his final album that same year. But that was it for historic repertory: the rest of *In Our Lifetime* involved Douglas originals composed with Little's instrumental palette and chordal language in mind. The title track opens abruptly in bright polytonal swing, with the horns moving in at an unrelated tempo, like a storm front. Douglas's voicings for the ensemble evoke Little's, but more as a springboard than as a blueprint. And there are state-of-the-art intricacies built into the tune, like a tumbling 11/8 bass vamp in one middle section, stealthily presaged in solos by both Douglas and Speed.

So the album, for all of its repertory precision, came pre-inoculated against any notions of conservatism. But just to be sure, the CD booklet included an inscription from the liner notes to *Out Front*, words spoken more than thirty years earlier by Little:

My own feelings about the direction in which jazz should go are that there should be much less stress on technical exhibitionism and much more on emotional content, on what might be termed humanity in music and the freedom to say all that you want.

Douglas spent the next several years putting this mandate to the test, with another handful of albums by the Tiny Bell Trio; a few more with a chamber string ensemble; and another jazz-repertory tribute—*Stargazer,* for Wayne Shorter, in 1997. That same year he released *Sanctuary,* a brazenly experimental improv summit recorded live at the Knitting Factory, with a cadre including Yuka Honda and Anthony Coleman on live samplers. He also convened a band that knowingly scrambled downtown and uptown signals—a limber acoustic postbop quartet featuring Genus, the drummer Ben Perowsky, and the prominent Young Lion–ish tenor saxophonist Chris Potter.

Reviewing this new band at the Knit, Peter Watrous seized on the smartly jabbering frontline of Douglas and Potter, "two esteemed members of ostensibly different jazz scenes." The quartet, Watrous wrote in *The New York Times,* showed promise: "Its success suggested that the raiding of two supposedly opposing teams should continue."[19]

By this point, most jazz listeners of a left-leaning disposition were already paying close attention to Douglas, compelled both by his proliferation of ideas and by the formal rigor with which he explored them. But it was something else to hear him in the context of a swinging acoustic quartet, going toe-to-toe with one of the most technically sound saxophonists in a centrist modern-jazz vein. Douglas's prominence spiked right around the time that he began releasing albums by the quartet: *Magic Triangle,* in 1998, and then *Leap of Faith* in 2000.

By the time of the second quartet album, Douglas was signed to a major label, RCA. He began his tenure with *Soul on Soul,* a tribute to the pioneering pianist, composer, and bandleader Mary Lou Williams. The most "uptown" release of Douglas's career up to that point, it began with a jazz boogaloo called "Blue Heaven" and moved on to a clutch of other originals composed in respectful homage to Williams. (The title of the album came from Duke Ellington's appraisal of her in his autobiography.) And at the center of the track list was a trio of Williams themes—"Aries," from her progressive *Zodiac Suite* (1945); "Mary's

Idea," from the band book of Andy Kirk and His Twelve Clouds of Joy (1938); and "Waltz Boogie," a slinky theme song (1946)—arranged in a punchy, contemporary style.

Soul on Soul was an unqualified success in jazz terms, selling more than thirteen thousand copies and earning Douglas the stature of a leading figure in the music. He swept almost every eligible category in the 2000 DownBeat Critics Poll: Artist of the Year, Album of the Year, Trumpeter of the Year, and Composer of the Year. (As a measure of how quickly he had dashed from the margins to the center, he also won Talent Deserving Wider Recognition.) Some critics saw fit to champion Douglas as an alternative to Marsalis, who'd become even more of an establishment symbol since winning the Pulitzer Prize in 1997, for his epic jazz oratorio *Blood on the Fields.*

The comparisons provoked some raw tensions—especially after Crouch, still the most vocal Marsalis confrere, chose to call out Douglas as the beneficiary of a pernicious agenda. In a 2003 column for *Jazz-Times,* Crouch came out swinging: the piece, "Putting the White Man in Charge," took aim at the institutionalized biases of a white critical establishment that purportedly hailed the likes of Douglas in order to suppress more deserving African-American counterparts. Crouch lobbed a specific attack on the critic Francis Davis (who "unintentionally makes it clear that he is intimidated by Negroes and also quite jealous of them"), but he saved his choicest barbs for the trumpeter of the hour:

> Douglas, a graduate of Exeter and a dropout from the New Jersey upper middle class, is the perfect white man to lead the music "forward." Unlike these misled uptown Negroes who spend too much time messing around with stuff like the blues and swinging, Downtown Dave brings truly new stuff into jazz, like Balkan folk material that surely predates the 20th century in which blues and jazz were born.[20]

Crouch's argument naturally met with an outcry, and in what can only be described as an awkward turn, *JazzTimes* unceremoniously ended his column shortly thereafter. The reasons presented by the magazine's editors had little to do with "Putting the White Man in

Charge," revolving around the difficulty of working with Crouch. But given the timing, it was all too easy to assume that a black voice had been silenced for calling out the white superstructure of his field.

Shortly after the termination of his column, Crouch stoked this very perception, writing an op-ed for *Newsweek* titled "The Problem with Jazz Criticism." Writing from a stance of righteous indignation, he decried "a conspiracy of consensus based in modernist European ideas of avant gardism,"[21] and made it clear he believed he'd been punished for speaking truth to power. Many of his colleagues, including Gary Giddins and the veteran jazz writer Nat Hentoff, spoke out in Crouch's favor, without necessarily endorsing his view of the matter.

For Douglas, meanwhile, the brouhaha cemented an unfortunate perception of stark polarity between him and Marsalis. When he released his 2004 album *Strange Liberation,* the standard tactic in the press was to compare it with a contemporaneous new Marsalis release, *The Magic Hour.*

The *New Republic*'s David Hajdu made that contrast explicit, pitting Marsalis and Douglas against one another with a subtext of uptown vs. downtown.[22] Thomas Conrad began a joint review in *JazzTimes* by quoting the old English saw that "comparisons are odious"—before going on to stipulate that "when it comes to Dave Douglas and Wynton Marsalis, they are also unavoidable."[23]

The artists themselves had little to do with this dichotomy. Marsalis issued no denunciations of Douglas, and the respectful reticence was mutual. Still, surveying the prevailing rhetorical terrain, Crouch's apparent nemesis Francis Davis noted in *The Village Voice* that "in terms of how they're perceived, today's trumpeters come in two varieties, Wyntons and Daves."[24]

Raising big money for jazz, ostensibly a larkish pursuit in 1989, had become standard practice by the turn of the century. It grew ever more targeted and efficient as Jazz at Lincoln Center settled into its permanent home, and other organizations began borrowing from its playbook.

One of the more prominent examples in the United States was SFJAZZ, the nonprofit presenting organization behind the long-running San Francisco Jazz Festival. In 2004, this organization formed its own repertory ensemble, the SFJAZZ Collective. Rather than a big band like the Jazz at Lincoln Center Orchestra, it was an octet, led for the first few years by Joshua Redman, and devoted in its first season to the music of Ornette Coleman. The group made a point of interspersing repertory pieces with original music by its members—and its repertory scope was wide enough to eventually include Stevie Wonder and Michael Jackson as well as Wayne Shorter and Thelonious Monk. (For a couple of years, Douglas was its trumpeter.)

In another coastal parallel to Jazz at Lincoln Center, SFJAZZ moved into its own purpose-built home in 2013: a three-story, thirty-five-thousand-square-foot, $64 million building in the Hayes Valley neighborhood, one block away from Davies Symphony Hall. Funded both by foundation support and by private donations, including an anonymous lead gift of $20 million, the SFJAZZ Center opened with a season that reflected its big-tent vision of jazz. There were concerts programmed by five resident artists, including Frisell and the violinist Regina Carter. There were multi-night engagements by Mehldau, the tabla player Zakir Hussain, and the banjoist Béla Fleck. And during a gala opening, there was much conversation about what the achievement of the center might mean for jazz at large.

"Jazz at Lincoln Center has been incredibly successful," reflected Redman in a dressing room on the second floor, "and if SFJAZZ can be successful, maybe one of the legacies will be that in the foreseeable future, they won't be the only two. There'll be other venues, other buildings for jazz that can enter the discussion."[25]

As if to waste no time in fulfilling that prophecy, a small but state-of-the-art new jazz space opened the following year in St. Louis, Missouri. The Harold and Dorothy Steward Center for Jazz, a $10 million complex, was funded by a local African-American businessman with an abiding love of jazz. The centerpiece of the facility was the Ferring Jazz Bistro—formerly the Jazz Bistro, a beloved club, newly renovated and expanded. To break in the 220-seat space in the fall of 2014, some marquee guests were brought in from out of town: the Jazz at Lincoln Center Orchestra, featuring Wynton Marsalis.

The Knitting Factory closed its Tribeca anchor in 2009, opening a smaller space in Brooklyn with little if any attachment to jazz. (By then it had been bought by a company that opened satellite Knitting Factory clubs in Los Angeles, Spokane, and Boise. Dorf had parted ways with the organization in 2002.)

The Stone, which Zorn opened in 2005 in a former Chinese restaurant on Avenue C, saw a dozen years of resolute and uncompromising musical activity. For much of that time the space was programmed by a different artist curator each month—not just Zorn and his peers but also an expanding circle of improvisers and composers, from across a range of creative disciplines. Beginning in 2013, Zorn changed the programmatic format to a series of weeklong artist residencies, strongly encouraging his curators to present something different on each night of the run. The space functioned as a laboratory for new works, a gravitational center for the contemporary avant-garde, and a no-frills showcase with a high bar for artistic integrity. (No drinks were served at the Stone, and all door proceeds went directly to the musicians.)

Zorn announced the end of this iteration of the Stone at the end of 2016. He then made arrangements to reopen the space in partnership with a prominent institution, the New School. The Stone at the New School, as this venture was named, would present music five nights a week, in accordance with the artist-as-curator model. The New School agreed to share operating and administrative expenses, and allow the venue to operate rent-free in the Glass Box Theater, an aptly named space just off the lobby of Arnhold Hall, the New School's performing-arts hub, with one street-facing glass wall and another one that faces the interior lobby.

"It was fun and exciting to play on a dirty corner in the East Village," Zorn told me in the office of Richard Kessler, the New School's executive dean for performing arts. "Now I think this music really deserves to be seen in a different way."

Careful to note that the Stone had not been squeezed out by rising rents or zoning issues, as was the case with Tonic and some other New York venues, Zorn described his decision as a matter of outgrowing the present circumstances, and also of expanding the possibilities for audience engagement. "With the landscape that we now have politically, economically, socially, culturally—I think 'outreach' is a good word," he said. "Maybe it's time to take something that's really edgy, really honest, really imaginative, really creative, and take it out of some dark little marginalized corner space and into a place where people are going to see it. People that never even knew something like that existed are going to be exposed to it. We're one block from a major subway. We're really in the middle of the Village now. And we're at an institution that's been around for a hundred years, that has garnered great respect."[26]

Jazz at Lincoln Center crossed the threshold of its thirtieth anniversary at full steam, having preserved its aesthetic mission and its place in the cultural firmament. The organization's programming still often skewed historical, with tributes to figures like Ellington, Coltrane, and Monk. But there was also a good deal of original music premiered under the organization's auspices, composed by Marsalis and other members of the Jazz at Lincoln Center Orchestra, like the bassist Carlos Henriquez and the multireedist Ted Nash. As a composer, Marsalis remained keen as ever in his desire to situate jazz in a larger continuum, composing violin concertos, ballets, a *Blues Symphony*. His *Abyssinian Mass,* premiered in 2008, is a sweeping rollick custom-designed as a collaboration with the Abyssinian Baptist Church Gospel Choir. And a zippy, engaging suite premiered in 2016, called *Spaces,* put the Jazz at Lincoln Center Orchestra in dialogue with two brilliant young dancers, Lil Buck and Jared Grimes.

Marsalis made no revisions to his firm definition of jazz, as he quickly assured anyone with the gall to ask. But as artistic director of Jazz at Lincoln Center, he seemed to grow less interested in endlessly relitigating the issue. One concert in the Rose Theater in 2009 featured the Five Peace Band, a fusion supergroup with Chick Corea on synthesizers and piano and John McLaughlin on electric guitar. Later that year in the same hall, Ornette Coleman appeared with his quartet. There were enthusiastic collaborations between the Jazz at Lincoln Center Orchestra and friendly interlopers like Willie Nelson and Paul Simon.

And in the spring of 2017 there was an eye-catching weekend run in the Appel Room, the handsome, glass-faced amphitheater at the front of the Rose Hall complex. It featured Douglas leading New Sanctuary, an update of what had arguably been his least "uptown" project, steeped in strategies of noise, free improv, and electronic manipulation. The personnel included several prominent jazz avant-gardists well into their seventies: trumpeter Wadada Leo Smith, alto saxophonist Oliver Lake, and drummer Andrew Cyrille. "It's not every day you get to play with your heroes," Douglas said from the stage.

But his ensemble was also well stocked with peers who had at one time been associated with the downtown scene in general, and the Knitting Factory in particular: Marc Ribot on guitar, Myra Melford on piano, Mark Dresser on bass, and Susie Ibarra on drums. During each performance, the musicians worked in a shifting series of configurations, while the others sat on either side of the stage. This methodology faintly evoked faraway loft-scene protocols—even as the band stood against a gleaming cityscape, the noiseless drift of headlights and taillights along Central Park South.

The music was a far cry from jazz historicism, and a riotously odd fit for the House of Swing. But Douglas had no use for yelping provocations, choosing instead to thank Jazz at Lincoln Center for its commission. Late in the performance, before an all-hands-on-deck finale, he also alluded to the state of political discourse in the early phases of a new presidential administration—an implicit reminder that some divisions are more meaningful than others.

"We're all in this together," Douglas said, his voice quavering slightly. "We shall overcome."

Tim Berne, *Fulton Street Maul* (CBS)
Dave Douglas, *Parallel Worlds* (Soul Note)
Jazz at Lincoln Center Orchestra with Wynton Marsalis, *All Jazz Is Modern: 30 Years of Jazz at Lincoln Center, Volume 1* (Blue Engine)
John Zorn, *The Big Gundown* (Nonesuch)
John Zorn's Masada, *Live in Jerusalem 1994* (Tzadik)

4

Play the Mountain

To hear him tell it, Steve Coleman had his first bolt of inspiration one afternoon on the South Side of Chicago, circa 1977. He was practicing his alto saxophone in a city park when he noticed some bees scudding about nearby. And in that moment, he was transfixed by their flight patterns, which seemed governed by an elaborate and esoteric schema.

"It's totally unexpected that I would make any kind of musical connection to this at that time," he recalled, a little over two decades later. "The bees were really just bothering me as I was practicing. But as I watched the bees, something—kind of a flash—hit me, and that took years to work out."[1]

Some artists arrive at a mode of expression so intensely original that it's tempting to place their work outside any known continuum. Coleman has been one of the most independent-minded, intently focused, and impactful musicians in the jazz idiom since he began releasing his own albums, in the mid-eighties. His creative output since has been exceptional in both its conceptual daring and its driving sense of purpose. But over the years, that body of work has also been framed, more often than not, as an exotic peninsula jutting out from the mainland, with only a provisional connection to the mainstream jazz tradition.

Coleman might even put it that way himself, given his sharp ambivalence about the word "jazz," and all of the reductive or prescriptive ways it has been deployed.

At the same time, he has made an imposingly deep study of Charlie Parker and John Coltrane, among other recognizable figures. He considers himself a part of the same lineage, pursuing a similar process of transformation. With his flagship band, a changeable unit known as Five Elements, Coleman has put forward an audacious, insightful, and confluent style that lays claim to the broad sweep of jazz harmony and much else besides: cyclical rhythmic strategies adapted from West African and South Asian musics; numerological precepts inspired by ancient Egyptology and Yoruban orishas; the complex processes of human biological systems; the snap and trance of a James Brown funk groove.

A typical performance by Coleman and Five Elements, to the extent that you can responsibly envision such a thing, takes the form of a slithery, unbroken arc, with jazz-historical references popping up in a refractively cubist mode. You might hear the chord progression for a songbook standard like "Autumn Leaves," stretched over a loping, asymmetrical pulse. Or Thelonious Monk's "'Round Midnight," obliquely drawn in shadow and line. Or a deconstruction of Parker's "Confirmation," identifiable by a few scraps of melody, glinting like sea glass scattered along a shore. You'd surely also hear pieces of Coleman's own authorship, pugnacious, brisk, and taut.

Five Elements is a changeable proposition, and while there have been several long-term editions of the band, it's built to accommodate the occasional interloping acolyte. Because of this policy, Coleman's band has been an essential crucible for many leading jazz artists in the late twentieth and early twenty-first centuries. Some, like the tenor saxophonist Ravi Coltrane, would begin their own solo careers in a Colemanesque sonic matrix before branching out on their own paths. Others, like the trumpeter Ambrose Akinmusire and the drummer Tyshawn Sorey, would encounter Coleman at a formative stage, internalize his philosophy, and apply it to a far different-sounding range of music. Vijay Iyer, one of a handful of important pianists to claim Coleman as a mentor, once memorably placed his influence on a heroic scale: "To me, Steve's as important as Coltrane," Iyer told *JazzTimes.* "He has contributed an equal amount to the history of the music. He deserves to be placed in the pantheon of pioneering artists."[2]

The declarative panache of the quote is tempered only slightly by the qualifier. "To me ..." implies personal opinion, but Iyer is hardly speaking for himself alone. Through dauntless persistence, a horizon-less aesthetic, and a direct, far-reaching influence, Coleman has not only carved out a space along jazz's contemporary frontier but also altered its tone and trajectory in the early twenty-first century.

For his part, Coleman sees himself merely carrying out an objective, fulfilling the vision that first revealed itself in that Chicago park early in his training. Bees were only the start of it. "I wanted to be able to look at a mountain and play the mountain," he told a European interviewer in 2006. He went on:

> I used to tell my friends that, and just like you, they said, "What do you mean? You mean being inspired by the mountain?" I said, "No, not just inspired. Of course I'm inspired by it, but I want to play the mountain, literally, play the mountain." They said, "Well, what do you mean by that?" I said, "I want to look at the mountain and see something like notation and be able to play it." They thought I was crazy. They would just dismiss what I was saying. But I was serious. I wanted to be able to look at the flight pattern of a bee, the flight pattern of a bird, and play that. Or have that directly influence my music, so almost be able to look at nature as one big gesture. You can call it notation. I mean, what is notation? It's a bunch of symbols that tell you, don't do this, do this. But I wanted to be able to look at life with my eyes as well as with my ears and be able to translate that into sound. That was, and still is, one of my biggest things.[3]

The fact that Coleman came up in Chicago is critical. Then as now, the city was a home to restless experimentation as well as a living and breathing tradition. The blues exerted a powerful presence there. So did a strain of African-American aesthetic agency famously embodied by, but by no means limited to, the Association for the Advancement of Creative Musicians.

One evening in his late teens, Coleman and some friends went to a club to hear the legendary bebop terror Sonny Stitt, who was passing through town. The bill had been split with another saxophonist, Chicago veteran Von Freeman, who was born within a year of Stitt but had an altogether burlier, woolier, less linear style.

"We were actually pissed that Von was there," Coleman later recalled, with a laugh.

We wanted to see Stitt, and they've got this other guy up there. And I didn't like his playing at the time. But Von was real nice; he understood that we were ignorant. And he saw that we wanted to play. So he said, "I have this set on the South Side, you guys should bring your horns down and come play." He didn't say "Come listen to *us*." He knew what would attract us. I found out it was right around the corner from my house. So I would go to this place, and Von and all these older guys who were born around the same time, they would play first.[4]

Coleman and his peers would reluctantly sit through the old-timers' gig, itching to get their turn on the bandstand. But because he had a habit of taping his outings, Coleman sometimes went home with documentation of Freeman and the other seasoned heads. "It didn't take long, maybe three or four months, to realize that they were really, really playing," Coleman said. "And then it took a little bit longer and I realized: these guys are on a totally different level than where I'm at. It's not even close. What they were doing was much more sophisticated than what I could hear, at the time." He apprenticed himself to Freeman, an experience that had a profound effect on his cultivation as a jazz musician.

The ongoing practice of an informal, hands-on, intensive workshop, unaffiliated with any formal institution, has been vitally important for Coleman. Over the years he has led such residencies in Chicago, sometimes in collaboration with the artist and activist Theaster Gates, who turns urban revitalization into an act of radical engagement. Coleman has also set up workshops in New York and other American cities, and in locales abroad. Those residencies have often led to new musical affiliations as well as new music. "Almost everybody I'm playing with now, I met them in workshops," he said. Looking back on the legacy of Freeman, who died in 2012 at eighty-eight, Coleman drew an obvious connection with himself: "Von's thing on the South Side, letting guys sit in and everything, it was sort of like a residency that lasted forever."[5]

Coleman moved to New York in 1978 and quickly found himself straddling a divide. On the one hand, he fell in with established jazz elders like the trumpeter and composer Thad Jones, joining the pace-setting big band that Jones led with the drummer Mel Lewis. On the other hand, Coleman became a fixture at Studio Rivbea, the down-town loft run by the avant-garde saxophonist Sam Rivers with his wife, Beatrice. He also worked with both the magisterial singer-songwriter Abbey Lincoln and the iconoclastic pianist Cecil Taylor.

But one of the most fruitful associations Coleman formed at the time was with the bassist Dave Holland, another Studio Rivbea regular. Holland was only a decade older, and another straddler: an alumnus of Miles Davis's rockish late-sixties band, a former member of the tumultuous free-jazz collective Circle, and an anchor in the rough-and-tumble Sam Rivers Trio. His own albums—notably his momentous 1973 debut, *Conference of the Birds*, with Rivers and Anthony Braxton sharing a front line—had set a high bar for experimental maneuvers in a chamberlike and almost delicate setting.

On *Jumpin' In*, released on ECM in 1984, Holland introduced a new group with Coleman on alto saxophone and flute, Kenny Wheeler on trumpet, Julian Priester on trombone, and Steve Ellington on drums. Coleman thrived in this setting, blending with and brushing against the other horns, and pouncing on Holland's open-ended compositional forms. He also contributed the only non-Holland tune on *Jumpin' In*, a groove-meets-gnarl concoction titled "The Dragon and the Samurai." Coleman would bring more new music to two subsequent albums by the Dave Holland Quintet—*Seeds of Time* (1985) and *The Razor's Edge* (1987), both featuring the drummer Marvin "Smitty" Smith in place of Ellington, and both charting an ever-deeper band cohesion.

Coleman continued his work with Holland after the quintet disbanded, notably in a blue-chip trio featuring Jack DeJohnette on drums. Their sole album, *Triplicate*, was released under Holland's name in 1988. (Among other things, it's worth seeking out for Coleman's fluent yet divergent take on "Segment," the Charlie Parker tune.) *Extensions*, released in 1990, featured an intriguing and expressive new lineup with Holland, Coleman, Smith, and a virtuoso young guitarist, Kevin Eubanks.

By that time, Coleman was an established solo artist himself, decidedly past what you might call his journeyman phase but still very much embarked on a journey.

M-Base, a term of art that Coleman introduced near the start of his solo career, stands for "Macro-Basic Array of Structured Extemporizations." Beyond that, saying what it stands for can get a little complicated. A system of creative expression rooted in improvisation within a form, striving toward the goal of transmuting human experience into sound, M-Base could be described as the logical outcome of Coleman's long-standing preoccupations. But from the jump it also described the work of a cohort: the M-Base Collective, whose early members included the cornetist Graham Haynes, the alto saxophonist Greg Osby, and the pianist Geri Allen.

In the late 1980s and early '90s, these and a handful of other artists effectively made M-Base feel like a dawning movement. The extravagantly gifted singer Cassandra Wilson had her first notable recording credit on Coleman's debut album, *Motherland Pulse* (1985), and then featured him and other charter members on her own debut, *Point of View* (1986).

At a time when the larger jazz ecology was so concerned with an evocation of historical norms, M-Base suggested a dispatch from the young black vanguard: formally inventive, aesthetically progressive, culturally forward. There was plenty of off-kilter funk and looping structure in the music of this peer group, which led many observers to associate M-Base with a particular sound. Coleman bristled against such essentialism, but the music was fairly easy to typecast at the time. A 1993 album called *Anatomy of a Groove* (DIW), credited to the M-Base

Collective, was presented as a mission statement—and like most of the other work in Coleman's camp, it featured jangly harmonic angularities over elliptical but in-the-pocket rhythm. Some critics pegged this approach as an intelligent and principled alternative to fusion, while others compared it to the harmolodic ecstasies of Ornette Coleman's Prime Time. Almost everyone began to use M-Base as a shorthand, as much for the music as for its musicians.

Coleman eventually clarified his intentions with M-Base, which have nothing to do with the proprietary refinement of a style. "One of the main ideas in M-Base is growth through creativity," reads an explainer on the official website, m-base.com. "As we learn through our experiences then the music will change and grow to reflect that. The idea is not to develop some musical style and to play that forever."

Perhaps the best indication of Coleman's struggle to resist outside misperceptions is a bulleted list on the same page of the website, which amusingly resembles an exasperated variation on "Frequently Asked Questions," otherwise known as FAQs.

WHAT M-BASE IS NOT:

- An acronym for some kind of computer language or computer talk.
- A musical style.
- A name made up to fool critics into writing about musicians who claim to "play" M-Base.
- A card carrying society with members who pay dues.
- An excuse to claim that you are different than other musicians.
- A name that you can call your music in order to get more gigs.
- An excuse to play odd time signatures.
- An indication that you do not like the music of Wynton Marsalis or musicians associated with Wynton.
- An excuse to ignore chords or to think of chord progressions as irrelevant.

Coleman's resistance to the idea of musical style, in particular, reflects a general skepticism about aesthetic labels. "Charlie Parker and

Dizzy Gillespie and those guys, when they found it useful to jump on the bebop bandwagon and talk about bebop from the standpoint of getting work and getting attention, they did it," he said. "But if you talk to the musicians, and if you look at interviews and things that they did, it becomes clear that Bird did not think what he was doing was bebop or jazz or whatever. It's clear that he was just looking at it as music."[6]

On some level, Coleman's articulation of an alternative was a show of self-determination, analogous to the impulse that led the early members of the AACM to drop "jazz" for the less rigid term "creative music." Early in Iyer's experience as an acolyte in Coleman's circle, during the mid-1990s, he published an essay placing both movements within an African-American creative tradition of collectivism. Reflecting on the meaning of M-Base, Iyer proposed that instead of a "style," it should be regarded as "a 'stance'—an approach to creativity."[7]

For some in the fold, that approach would remain a core conviction even after they were no longer producing music that fit any M-Base profile. Cassandra Wilson, to name the most prominent example, peeled off in the early nineties when she signed to Blue Note Records. "She had in mind to do something with her M-Base-type band," Bruce Lundvall, Blue Note's president at the time, later recalled. "I had sort of a disagreement with her and said, 'Why don't you make an acoustic record? Your downtown band is good, but we're not looking for musical democracy; I really signed you as a solo artist and want to be able to hear you.' I had seen her a couple nights before this meeting and didn't feel that it was the best situation for her."

The result of Lundvall's intervention was *Blue Light 'Til Dawn* (1993), the acoustic mélange that, together with a follow-up, *New Moon Daughter* (1995), was Wilson's commercial breakthrough. With a smoky blend of pop fare (U2's "Love Is Blindness") and roots-music touchstones (Robert Johnson's "Come on in My Kitchen," Hank Williams's "I'm So Lonesome I Could Cry"), the albums became cultural events of a sort. Both reached the top spot on *Billboard*'s Jazz Albums chart. The latter penetrated the Billboard 200 and won a Grammy for Best Jazz Vocal Album.

This enormous success ratified a notion, radical only in the context of the neoclassical nineties, that jazz repertory could come from the byways of American folk music (both the rustic and confessional varieties) as well as the standard songbook. A decade later, it was almost a given that any serious contemporary jazz singer might delve into rustic folk, world music, or adult pop and soul. It was also no longer so strange to hear a jazz singer backed by stringed instruments in addition to piano, bass, and drums. (When Blue Note ushered in its affiliation with Norah Jones, another Lundvall signing, in 2002, the unspoken in-house precedent was *Blue Light 'Til Dawn*.)

From the outside, then, it would seem that Wilson had left M-Base behind. This was maybe even true, to the extent that you fixated on the parameters of her sound. But Wilson had made clear that she shared Coleman's conceptual basis, free of stylistic identifiers. "More and more I find it's a way of life," she wrote of M-Base, in the liner notes for *Anatomy of a Groove*. "It's a way of living truth at the crossroads. A means by which we can develop our musical capabilities to their fullest, thereby expanding, redefining and propelling the music into the 21st century and beyond." Well after she had become one of the most prominent jazz singers of her generation, Wilson was still a member in good standing of the M-Base Collective.

In 2007, she reunited with Coleman for a single night at the Stone, in an ensemble that also included the drummer Dafnis Prieto, the saxophonist Yosvany Terry, and the pianist Jason Moran. Rather than dusting off old music, the group had settled on a conceptual framework inspired by the Yoruban divination system known as *Ifa*. Next to the stage was a posterboard diagram depicting the system's sixteen principal *Odu*, or stations of the human condition; Wilson announced that the group had conceived music for four of them. The ensuing performance was an intoxicating haze of gluey polyrhythm, with Wilson's voice palpitating in the mix, not in the mode of a lead singer so much as that of an instigator, or a shaman.

The idea that Wilson's career is an M-Base success story, and not some prodigal parable, reflects the musically permissive dimensions of "the stance." Other artists put that permissiveness to the test too, perhaps none more doggedly than Coleman himself.

Steve Coleman and Five Elements made their major-label debut in 1992, on the Novus imprint of BMG, with the momentously titled *Rhythm People (The Resurrection of Creative Black Civilization)*. The album cover featured a drawn illustration, by Malachi "Mike" Basden, that depicted figures from the past and the future—one in a zoot suit, another in a space suit—against a backdrop of urban surrealism, mixing street art with Salvador Dalí. The music enacted a similar temporal and textural whorl, with Coleman's alto darting through the machinery. On "No Conscience" he even ventured some rapping, with complex flow patterns and internal rhyme: "Signs of an empire in decline / Stressing the bottom line / Without regard to time / Or the limits of mankind / Paying no attention to the laws / Of cause and effect / Advance and decline / The way of ancient biorhythmic science / No conscience." But the synthesizers and electric slap-bass on the album would fix *Rhythm People* as an artifact of its era, valuable mainly as a status report from the center of a fast-charging artistic campaign.

That same year, Coleman released another, strikingly different album with "rhythm" in the title, as if to show another side of the coin. *Rhythm in Mind* was the by-product of a concert he'd put together for the centennial of Carnegie Hall. The loose premise was a generational exchange: Coleman featured his mentor, Von Freeman, along with the venerable pianist Tommy Flanagan and the masterly, free-thinking New Orleans drummer Ed Blackwell. The repertoire included another nod to the older jazz tradition, in the form of two compositions by Thad Jones.

Coleman also found a place on *Rhythm in Mind* for members of his peer group: Holland, Wheeler, Eubanks, Smitty Smith. And with his own compositions on the album, he mapped an M-Base trajectory more in line with the *sound* of jazz as it was already widely understood. A loping, coolly furtive theme called "Left of Center" captures the full potential of this tactic, with the two drummers laying down a wide swing beat. The solos are bracing across the board, culminating in an inspired round of friendly sparring between Eubanks and Coleman.

Through the remainder of the 1990s, Coleman broadened his scope and deepened his inquiry, bringing more musicians and concepts into his orbit. M-Base, as a social unit, gradually dissolved around the edges: by the mid-nineties it was best understood as a radial extension of

Coleman's output rather than a true colloquy in which other charter members, like Allen or Osby, could have equal say.

One area of intense focus during this time was hip-hop—notably in a project called Metrics, which amounted to Five Elements augmented with rappers. Coleman was especially taken with the hip-hop convention of the cipher, a circular confab of rappers, beatboxers, and break-dancers locked in a freestyle battle of wits. (The improvisational essence of a cipher was one obvious part of the appeal for him; another probably had to do with the name, and its implications of code and encryption.) After an EP called *Tale of 3 Cities,* which featured rappers like Sub-Zero and Black Thought of the Roots, Coleman and Metrics released one emblematic album, *The Way of the Cipher: Live in Paris.* This arrived in 1995 as the second volume in a trilogy, the other two being *Curves of Life,* documenting a Five Elements performance, and *Myths, Modes and Means,* featuring the worldly ensemble called the Mystic Rhythm Society, which included Iyer on keyboards, Miya Masaoka on Japanese koto, and Ramesh Shotham on Indian hand percussion.

The album trilogy—which was released on BMG as a boxed set titled *Live at the Hot Brass,* and reissued for a twentieth-anniversary edition as *Steve Coleman's Music Live in Paris*—caught up with Coleman at a key moment of multidimensional expansion. As always, he was self-conscious about it, and eager to situate his growth on a cultural-historical axis: *Curves of Life* opened with a piece called "Multiplicity of Approaches (The African Way of Knowing)."

As he expanded his purview, Coleman was rendering obsolete some of the old presumptions about his music: that it amounted to a metaphysical upgrade of jazz-funk, for instance. His work began to take on a more polyglot, chamberlike quality with an edition of Five Elements that featured the brilliant vocalist Jen Shyu, the precise, inquisitive trumpeter Jonathan Finlayson, and the subtly expressive drummer Marcus Gilmore. This group released its first scintillating album, *Harvesting Semblances and Affinities,* on Pi Recordings in 2010. At the time, it was Coleman's first release on an American label in almost a decade.

His incorporation of non-Western musical influence had come rooted in firsthand research, as he devoted an increasing proportion of his time and energy to traveling around the world: places including Ghana, Senegal, Egypt, India, Cuba, and Brazil.[8] He formalized his exploration into a regular sabbatical—usually a month long, and unrelated to any bookings or professional obligations. This custom of international travel, neither for vacation nor for business purposes, served a different purpose altogether: a peripatetic artist retreat, a freeform research trip, a recharging of the creative batteries. As Coleman explained:

> Why I do sabbaticals every year is I'm trying to force myself to spend a certain part of the year where I concentrate almost completely on creative things. And keep the other shit at bay. You're trying to keep all this other stuff that's encroaching, keep it back. This is why composers go away to compose. All the noise—they're trying to block that away. So I try to do that every year, and I just have one simple thing. Because it's really hard to judge your own progress. It's really difficult. You can't go by press, you can't go by what people are saying about you, awards. All this kind of stuff, it means nothing. Absolutely nothing. There's no award that ever created any music. The only thing that means anything, to me, is: What do I know this year that's different than what I knew two years ago? And am I *doing* something about it? Not just as trivia, but as information that I'm actually working with.

Coleman lives in Allentown, Pennsylvania, an hour's drive from Philadelphia and under two hours from New York. He moved there in 1991, after Eubanks extolled its virtues as a place with enough space to create, while still within range of the city. Coleman fully embraced the prospect of peace and quiet: he hadn't given a single public performance in the Lehigh Valley before 2016, when he headlined a concert at the Allentown JazzFest.[9]

One afternoon the previous spring, I met him in Philadelphia to discuss an upcoming project and a recent cavalcade of honors. After decades of influential yet scrappy work on the margins, acclaim was finally catching up to him: he'd become a MacArthur Fellow, joining some exalted company, including just a handful of jazz artists—several of whom considered him a mentor—over the roughly three-decade history of the award. He had also received a fellowship from the Guggenheim Foundation and two awards from the Doris Duke Charitable

Foundation. The month that we spoke, he was on the cover of *DownBeat* magazine.

We convened at Bartram's Garden, a botanical garden established in the eighteenth century, near the southernmost bend of the Schuylkill River. Coleman was contemplating a pair of concerts commissioned by the avant-garde presenting organization Ars Nova Workshop, to be held outdoors on the summer solstice and the fall equinox. He was dressed in what amounted to a uniform: backwards ball cap and an open robe resembling a karate gi, over a T-shirt from the Oakland metaphysical supply store Ancient Ways. During a stroll through the grounds, scouting locations for his performances, he seemed relaxed yet alert. "If you just look around, and look deep inside yourself, there's endless inspiration," he said, after pausing to admire North America's oldest ginkgo tree. "So I don't have to force that. The things that I'm interested in, they're all around me."[10]

Coleman's creative process had always been concept-driven, but he was refining his thematic approach into ever more graspable units. A 2013 album with Five Elements, *Functional Arrhythmias*, had been inspired by irregularities of the human heartbeat. He made his 2015 release, *Synovial Joints*, with the Council of Balance, which brought together a colloquy of percussion, woodwinds, and strings. At the heart of that album is a four-part suite of the same name, its inner dynamics meant to evoke the flexion and extension of joints—saddle, pivot, ball and socket—in the human body. Coleman's subsequent album, *Morphogenesis*, released in 2017, would explore a variation on the same idea: most of its pieces, including "Shoulder Roll" and "Dancing and Jabbing," were musical translations of boxing maneuvers, for a chamber ensemble called Natal Eclipse, with Shyu, Finlayson, and others, including a violinist and a clarinetist.

During our two-hour conversation in the Bartram's Garden administrative offices, Coleman characterized his obsessive research—in Egyptology, astrophysics, the *I Ching*, whatever else—not as phases that come and go but rather as part of a larger path of discovery. He compared his accumulation of information to geological strata, with the topmost layer representing just the most recent and readily accessible. *Synovial Joints* was a case in point, containing fresh ideas but also echoes of previous work, on recordings like *The Sonic Language of Myth*, from 1999.

One track on *Synovial Joints*, "Eye of Haru," features a technique he called "camouflage orchestration," inspired by his experience with the dimensions of natural sound in the Amazon rain forest. A section of the piece involving two woodwinds and a piccolo trumpet was his effort to evoke the wild chatter and commotion of monkeys raiding a bird's nest in the arboreal canopy. "If you look up in the trees, it's dense but not solid," he said. "So to me, there's kind of an opaqueness. I tried to create textures like that."

Just then he stopped talking and pointed to an open window.

"So this bee just flew in here," he said. "That was the first original idea I ever had, was about bees, and the motion of bees flying around. So you have all these kind of things that inspire different kind of movements, different kind of textures, different kind of motions, and things like this. If you're successful, even if somebody doesn't know the inspiration, they can still feel these things."[11]

The intensity of Coleman's focus, self-evident in so much of his music, has always rendered his circumstances—institutional or critical acclaim, ballooning stature, material gains, even the prospect of his influence among grateful younger musicians—more or less irrelevant to him. Maybe a better way to put it would be to say that he's careful to maintain a big perspective.

"I went through some bad years right before this recent spate of good stuff," he said. "I went through one of the worst periods, in terms of surviving. It wasn't so bad that I couldn't eat, but there was definitely a dip in activity. So, okay, fine. When that happens, you just increase the study end. You take that opportunity to study."[12]

Geri Allen, *Open on All Sides in the Middle* (Minor Music)
Steve Coleman and the Council of Balance, *Synovial Joints* (Pi)
Steve Coleman and Five Elements, *Harvesting Semblances and Affinities* (Pi)
Dave Holland Quintet, *Jumpin' In* (ECM)
Cassandra Wilson, *Blue Light 'Til Dawn* (Blue Note)

5

The New Elders

Danilo Pérez was thirty-five, a well-regarded Panamanian jazz pianist on the verge of a popular breakthrough as a bandleader, when he
decided instead to open Door Number 2. The choice came in the form
of a coveted invitation: he was asked by Wayne Shorter, the eminent
saxophonist and composer, to join a new quartet alongside the bassist
John Patitucci and the drummer Brian Blade. There was no question
that the group would be received with rapt attention, given Shorter's
luminous stature and the fact that he hadn't led a working band fitting
this description—an acoustic quartet, as in his storied postbop output
of the sixties—at any point in recent memory.

Still, Pérez had to give the matter some thought. This was in 2000,
just as his own career was hitting a beautiful stride. He'd released several acclaimed albums in the nineties, including *The Journey,* a brilliant
Latin-jazz tapestry, and *Panamonk,* a clever dalliance with Thelonious
Monk. But his heroically ambitious new album, *Motherland,* represented a major leap forward. Offering an audacious, sophisticated vision
of pan-American musical dialogue, it featured no fewer than seventeen contributors in the mix—most of whom joined Pérez for a statement booking at the Bowery Ballroom that fall, which registered on
every level as a triumph. Sharpening the issue, the album was widely

acclaimed, appearing at the top of a year-end list in *The New York Times*. For Pérez and many of the musicians in his circle, there was nothing but promise in the notion of taking *Motherland* farther, expanding its footprint in the world. The road looked wide and inviting, the destination clear.

And besides, Pérez had already put in the apprenticeship time that would seem necessary for his development as a jazz musician. During his early twenties, he'd worked extensively with the bebop patriarch Dizzy Gillespie—first in his United Nation Orchestra, and then in the smaller combos with which the trumpeter made his final recordings. Gillespie was a humanist with a message of cultural oneness, which Pérez took to heart. But he was also, to a large degree, a mentor and role model of the old school, intent on passing on guildlike knowledge of a practical sort.

Pérez had more recently come into contact with other important survivors of the bebop era: he and Patitucci made up two-thirds of the Roy Haynes Trio, whose indefatigable leader was a drummer of Gillespie's generation and stature. A live album by this band was released on Verve only months before *Motherland,* and hailed as both a power move for Haynes and a vibrant example of intergenerational exchange. But as far as Pérez was concerned, it was more of a blowing session than a body-and-mind immersion, not on the order of commitment that the Shorter gig would require.

So the decision to join the Wayne Shorter Quartet, as Pérez later described it, represented a crossroads. And once he headed down that path, reassurances were slow in coming despite the bond he had with Patitucci and Blade, who'd both appeared on *Motherland*. The concept that Shorter had for his quartet was related to the language of free improvisation but not entirely aligned with its objectives. The band would take well-known compositions from Shorter's back catalog, like "Footprints" and "JuJu," and often abstract them almost to the point of unrecognizability through a process of hair-trigger interplay. Nothing about a given piece could be taken for granted; with every footfall there was a chance of stepping on quicksand. Tempos and tonal centers were endlessly subject to flux, and discursive volatility was the rule.

Pérez initially felt thrown into the deep end, as he recalled a decade into his tenure with the band:

It was scary, to be honest, to live out all these new ideas. And it was a shock, because with *Motherland* I remember the standing ovations, and the three encores. Then to put myself into a situation where I had no idea what was happening. It felt like a dictation and ear-training class; I couldn't really judge it. Even when I listened back to a recording, I felt like an outsider: "What is that? What key are we in?"[1]

Shorter's affinity for elliptical whimsy was genuine, and Pérez quickly realized that his usual practice regimen no longer made much sense. He took down a list of movies Shorter had recommended, some of them terrible sci-fi entertainments that he'd endure for the sake of one throwaway moment in a single scene. Pérez also came up with his own version of Wayne Shorter wilderness training, gathering a stack of old *Tom and Jerry* cartoons and playing them in his study with the sound muted. He'd improvise to the antics onscreen, like a silent-movie accompanist, for two or three hours at a stretch. The idea was to learn how to twitch and pounce while still making sense at the piano, connecting one spasm of movement, with graceful haste, to the next.

The band's first album was released in 2002, to clamorous acclaim. But the album—*Footprints Live!*—was a highlight reel, weaving together material from three different concerts the previous summer. In real-time performance, the band could be a bit more of a gamble. It held to a rigorously thorough standard of discovery, welcoming not only flashes of inspiration but also irresolute pauses, stubborn quandaries, and heady longueurs. At its best the band made this process feel intuitive, creating cycles of action and implication; at other times, it could seem like a plane circling endlessly overhead, waiting for a landing signal from air traffic control.

There was a learning curve for audiences as well as for the members of the band. One of the quartet's first concerts, at the Spoleto Festival in Italy, met with a conspicuous dearth of applause. Shaken by the response, Pérez brought it up with Shorter after the show. "Well, that used to happen with Miles," the boss replied brightly. "I take it as a good sign."

.   .   .

Jazz has always relied, more than many other forms of music, on the wisdom of its elders. To put a finer point on it, the art form thrives best when there's a healthy line of communication across established and oncoming generations. The reasons are manifold, but for one thing, this is a tradition with just over a century of precedent, imperfectly captured on record and poorly served by written notation. Its lifeblood is the direct transmission of a vast, intangible body of knowledge, and so the influence of mentor-bandleaders has always been key.

For a long time, the situation adhered to conventional models of authority. A bandleader hired a younger musician for his developing potential, for his fire, for his availability and willingness to work—but also for the ability to conform to the band's metabolism. If the younger musician brought new information to the table, as Shorter did during his tenure with Art Blakey's Jazz Messengers, it was usually expected to sound like an extension, rather than a reinvention, of an existing sound. Such was the case with Gillespie, up to and during the years when Pérez came under his wing.

Shorter presented a different breed of jazz elder. Rather than reinforcing roles (or rules), he urged his bandmates to engage in an unpredictable process. Instead of trusting musical verities, he encouraged a condition of blank-slate unknowingness. And he held few fixed ideas about what shape his art should take, or to which aesthetic parameters it belonged.

When he invoked an experience with Miles, he was referring of course to his time with Miles Davis, and in particular the mid-1960s quintet with Shorter, Ron Carter on bass, Herbie Hancock on piano, and Tony Williams on drums. (That personnel had taken a while to solidify; Shorter's chair was originally held by George Coleman, then Sam Rivers.) By all accounts Davis, who was just entering his forties at the time, upheld a standard of terse and indirect guidance, pushing for constant discovery. He was also driven by the advances his younger bandmates were making on his watch, devising a slippery, open-ended approach to harmony and a magically elastic way with rhythm.

There's a boxed set of unexpurgated studio recordings the band made from 1966 to 1968, including the complete session reels for the album *Miles Smiles*. The box, *Freedom Jazz Dance: The Bootleg Series Vol. 5,*

offers a fly-on-the-wall glimpse into Davis's method in the studio, testing out approaches and issuing instructions. He knew how far to push
because he knew the capabilities of the band, which was pushing him
in turn.

Hancock characterized the interpersonal dynamic in the group well:

> Miles never said much about our playing. He just wasn't the kind
> of leader who gave notes or made suggestions unless we asked
> him to. Even then, he usually responded with cryptic comments,
> almost like little puzzles we had to solve. And Miles never talked
> about the mechanics of music, the notes and keys and chords of it.
> He was more likely to talk about a color or a shape he wanted to
> create. Once, when he saw a woman stumble while walking down
> the street, he pointed at her and told us, "Play that."[2]

That impressionistic dictum, and the set of sly practices behind it,
form a recurring theme in the recollections of Davis's sidemen. Shorter
and Hancock assumed chief stewardship of this mystique (it jibes with
their Buddhist practice), but the Miles Davis alumni society includes
many other influential artists besides: the pianists Chick Corea, Keith
Jarrett, and Joe Zawinul; the drummers Jack DeJohnette, Al Foster, and
Billy Hart; the bassists Dave Holland and Marcus Miller; the guitarists John McLaughlin, Pete Cosey, and John Scofield; the saxophonists
Gary Bartz, Dave Liebman, and Kenny Garrett.

All of these musicians—and more; that list is hardly exhaustive—
moved through Davis's bands at some point during his wolfman trans-
mogrification from a modern-jazz paragon to a gnarly funk shaman.
Some of them formed important electric bands of their own, populating
the first and second waves of what would come to be known as fusion.
As a bloc, their understanding of jazz was untethered from "the tradition" as it's often enshrined. That didn't mean they had little respect for
jazz history, just that they held to a broader holistic idea, with no real
investment in a rhetoric of purity.

During the 1980s and '90s, as the tide officially turned toward jazz
conservation, these views faced a backlash. In 1986 Stanley Crouch
wrote a scathing and widely read polemic, "On the Corner: The Sell-

out of Miles Davis," that decried the trumpeter's corruptive influence: "His pernicious effect on the music scene since he went rapaciously commercial reveals a great deal about the perdurability of Zip Coon and Jasper Jack in the worlds of jazz and rock, in the worlds of jazz and rock criticism, in Afro-American culture itself."[3]

Almost a decade later but along similar lines, the *New York Times* jazz critic Peter Watrous took the occasion of a new album by Shorter—*High Life*, produced by Marcus Miller, with a chamber orchestra and a funk-fusion rhythm section—to publish an essay titled "A Jazz Generation and the Miles Davis Curse." His pitch was simple: by following Davis down a fusion path (for crass commercial reasons, because what other motivation could there have been?), artists like Shorter, Hancock, and Corea had abdicated their place in the jazz pantheon, creating the vacuum that Wynton Marsalis had rushed in to fill. Watrous painted these musicians as pitiable prodigals, no longer possessed of even the ability to pick up where they left off. Shorter's *High Life* was, he carped, "a pastel failure and a waste of his enormous talent; it is as if Picasso had given up painting to design greeting cards."[4]

The wrongheadedness of Watrous's argument was borne out by subsequent events. *High Life* would be embraced and lionized by admirers who could see past the synthesizer patches, recognizing an ambitious display of insight and orchestration. Holland, who had played alongside Shorter in a transitional late-sixties Davis quintet, called the album "an absolute masterpiece of compositional construction,"[5] a milestone in the saxophonist's body of work.

Holland is one of at least a dozen Milesian alumni who put the lie to any charge of squandered talent and opportunity. A bassist and composer with a sterling track record—starting with his first album, the avant-garde classic *Conference of the Birds*, in 1972—he established his own lane in the modern jazz mainstream, becoming one of the most trusted bandleaders on the scene. The Dave Holland Quintet, active from the late nineties through the mid-aughts, worked in a chamber-esque but often swinging mode, with a contrapuntal front line of Robin Eubanks on trombone and Chris Potter on saxophones. (The band's smartly explosive double album *Extended Play: Live at Birdland*, recorded in 2001 and released in 2003, is an essential document of the era.)

Others in Shorter and Holland's peer group kept leading bands and releasing albums that burnished their stature. Hancock, Corea, and Jarrett loomed as a trifecta of piano exemplars. DeJohnette acquired a reigning preeminence as a drummer, second to none. And so it went; as hexes go, the Miles Davis Curse seemed in retrospect like a pretty good deal.

The Wayne Shorter Quartet was the best case in point, though it wasn't as if Shorter had anything to prove. His repertoire for the band put so-called classic material, like "Footprints," on an equal plane with his fusion inventions. One of the group's signature tunes was "Masqualero," which he'd played with Davis in both acoustic and jazz-funk iterations. Also in the mix were reclaimed Shorter compositions from the Weather Report book, and a couple from *Joy Ryder*, the even more flagrantly synth-heavy album that preceded *High Life*.

The band released only three albums in its first dozen years: *Footprints Live!* in 2002 and *Beyond the Sound Barrier* in 2005, followed in 2013 by *Without a Net*. But each of these albums, distilled from concert performances, received close and fervent attention. And when Shorter served as artist in residence at the 2017 Detroit Jazz Festival, at eighty-four, his performance with the band was predictably a marvel, brimming with kinetic mystique.

It hardly seems a coincidence that in the fifteen years after the emergence of the quartet, the aesthetic center of jazz moved perceptibly in the direction of a more collectivist, band-driven, exploratory ideal. "It really is something special that they've developed," attested Chris Potter. "And I think that's been an influence on a lot of us."[6] Younger players, just entering the conservatory, often cite the working Shorter quartet as a touchstone, having either seen it in action or pored over the recorded evidence.

So in addition to Shorter's most celebrated body of work—his brisk and insinuative compositions, which have been closely studied by jazz musicians for decades—the newer generation has also had the opportunity to grapple with his elusive philosophy of play.

"This kind of stuff I'm talking about is a challenge to play onstage," Shorter said in 2012, before citing a favorite source. "When Miles would hear someone talking about something philosophical, he would say,

'Well, why don't you go out there and play that?' One thing we talk about is that to 'play that,' we have to maybe play music that doesn't sound like music."[7]

Keith Jarrett became the most celebrated improvising solo pianist in the world largely on the basis of a single album, *The Köln Concert.* Recorded and released in 1975, it's a document of unfolding rapture and willful transcendence, and in that sense true to the artist involved. His spontaneous concert performances—often voluptuous with melody but mercurial in their flow, as he "read" the mood and psychic energy of a room like a sensitive instrument—became a source of wonderment for audiences across a spectrum, from jazz and classical connoisseurs to the post-Woodstock enlightenment seekers you might customarily associate with new age.

Jarrett cultivated a separate, less heralded profile as a consummate small-group bandleader. His 1967 debut album, *Life Between the Exit Signs,* introduced a profoundly intuitive trio with the bassist Charlie Haden and the drummer Paul Motian. He reconvened that rhythm section a few years later, after leaving Miles Davis. Then the trio became a quartet with the addition of saxophonist Dewey Redman, who had made his name with Ornette Coleman.

The Keith Jarrett Quartet had a serious run in the seventies, releasing a succession of earthy, spiritually searching, temperamentally unruly albums on major labels. Decades later, Jarrett remembered the band, with wry fondness, as "this absolutely raw commodity,"[8] perpetually on the verge of self-combustion. Among the band's more unconventional practices was a fondness for branching beyond the musicians' primary instruments: Jarrett often played soprano saxophone in the group, and at any moment there might be an interlude made up entirely of the clangor of steel drums or the rustle of shakers and bells.

There was nothing about the backward-glancing turn in mainstream jazz during the 1980s that would have happily accommodated the Keith Jarrett Quartet. That wasn't necessary, in any case: the band had dissolved by then, and Jarrett focused his energies on a new alignment with Gary Peacock on bass and Jack DeJohnette on drums. After the release of its first three albums in 1983—*Standards, Vol. 1, Changes,* and *Standards, Vol. 2*—this group became known as the Standards Trio. It would be Jarrett's principal outlet, both prolific and lucrative, for the next thirty years. And in some popular narratives of jazz, the earlier Keith Jarrett Quartet fell to the status of a historical footnote, or at least a secondary achievement.

The band found vindication in the afterlife, thanks to a jazz generation that revered its fearless ambition and boundless style. Branford Marsalis, introduced to the band's glories by his pianist Kenny Kirkland, went on the record as an admirer. (The impressionistic Jarrett ballad "Rose Petals," from a 1976 quartet session, appears on Marsalis's 1990 album *Crazy People Music.*) But the more powerful endorsement came from musicians a decade younger than Marsalis, notably the members of an acoustic piano power trio called the Bad Plus.

Made up of three independent-minded musicians from the upper Midwest—the bassist Reid Anderson, the pianist Ethan Iverson, and the drummer Dave King—the Bad Plus formed in 2000, releasing a self-titled album on the Fresh Sound New Talent label. That album opened with a wry version of "Knowing Me, Knowing You," by ABBA, and included a raging cover of "Smells Like Teen Spirit," by Nirvana. But there were also memorable original compositions on the album, and an overall spirit of rugged indivisibility that felt like a necessary tonic. I first heard the band in the same one-off Village Vanguard booking that secured their signing to Columbia Records. Like the A&R executive in the room, I was sold.

The resulting major-label debut, *These Are the Vistas,* appeared in 2003 to a mixed clamor of approval and umbrage. What was controversial about the band, for some, began with the opportunity it had been granted: this was in the midst of constrictions and cutbacks in the jazz record industry (neither the first nor the last of those), and there was consternation that a trio of irreverent white rabble-rousers had, in effect, skipped the line. There were all kinds of problems with this critique, among them the fact that it missed the point of the band's extraordinary sound, which was difficult to describe without pulling apart the strands of its DNA. Iverson used his piano as an instrument of orchestral dimensions, equally prone to grandiloquent outbursts, cubist outlines, and intimate music-box patter. Anderson was deft and full-toned as a bassist, a master of supple undercurrent. King was working with a razor's-edge flexibility, a steamroller's barreling momentum, and a big jolt of wicked humor. Altogether the trio conveyed an impressive, elastic sort of unity, forged of quick reflexes and dramatic flair.

One part of the shared social fabric for the Bad Plus was generational: its members had come of age in the 1970s and '80s, and hit the scene in the early '90s. But another part, not to be downplayed, was a collective reverence for the Keith Jarrett Quartet. This reverence was well stated by Iverson in a blog post published in 2006. The premise was a personal canon of essential jazz recordings from just after the Vietnam War through the early Young Lions era. "To begin with," Iverson wrote, planting a flag, "I believe the courageous, outlandish, down and dirty music played together by Keith Jarrett, Dewey Redman, Charlie Haden, and Paul Motian to be shamefully underrated and misunderstood."

He went on: "Reid Anderson and David King also consider this to be one of the great jazz groups, right up there with the Coltrane quartet, assorted Miles Davis bands, Ornette bands, Duke Ellington bands, Basie bands, Monk bands, and whatever else."[9] The implication, at the time, was that this statement could be seen as mildly heretical at worst, and overheated at best.

The Bad Plus had other guiding heroes: one high-water moment in their ascendance was a 2005 concert opening for Ornette Coleman, whose composition "Street Woman" had become a reliable show-stopper for the band. (About a decade later, an expanded version of the Bad Plus, with Tim Berne and Sam Newsome on saxophones and Ron Miles on cornet, would pay touring tribute to Coleman's 1972 album *Science Fiction*, a touchstone for all involved.)

In practical terms, another elder who loomed just as large for the band was Motian, who had followed his tenure in Jarrett's bands with an agenda of stubborn and revelatory independence. A musician defined by the sly, suggestive economy of his drumming and the stark, deceptive ease of his compositions, Motian was a master of terseness, of the unfinished gesture that turns out to be complete in itself. His compositions have the pliant, patient certainty of folk songs. And his influence on the two or three generations after him was deep and quietly profound.

He was fifty in 1981, when he recorded *Psalm,* featuring a band made up of Joe Lovano and Billy Drewes on tenor saxophones, Ed Schuller on bass, and Bill Frisell on guitar. According to jazz's actuarial standard, fifty doesn't clear the threshold for a jazz elder—but the musicians in Motian's band, especially Frisell, saw his validation as life-sustaining. The personnel shifted in the next few years, with Jim Pepper rotating in for Drewes. Then Motian pared down to a trio with Lovano and Frisell, marking this band's arrival with an album called *It Should've Happened a Long Time Ago.* Released in 1985 on ECM, it's a sleeper masterpiece: an experiment in abstracted song form and trilateral accord, with a dogged pursuance of revelation.

Motian already had a claim to jazz history outside of Jarrett's orbit: he was a member of the most influential iteration of the Bill Evans Trio, the one with bassist Scott LaFaro, captured in 1961 on the venerated album *Sunday at the Village Vanguard.* Motian had also worked with Mose Allison, the modern-jazz pianist and southern blues bard, among many others. But the music made by the Paul Motian Trio—later stylized as Paul Motian/Joe Lovano/Bill Frisell—might stand as his crowning achievement. For a certain kind of listener, its regular booking at the Vanguard became an important signpost on the jazz calendar in New York. Lovano would sometimes look out and see the same faces at the foot of the stage every night for two weeks.[10]

But Motian's stature as a mentor grew exponentially after he made the firm decision, around 2006, to stop traveling altogether. Rather than traverse Europe several times a year, which he'd done for most of his life, he set a new working perimeter that evoked the vantage of Saul Steinberg's most famous *New Yorker* cover: he no longer left Manhattan. The effect of this policy had something other than a restrictive effect. Some of Motian's groups—like the one he semi-accurately called the Electric Bebop Band, which had seen young musicians like Kurt Rosenwinkel and Chris Potter move through its ranks—began playing more dates in town. At the same time, Motian was circulating more as an eminent sideman with artists who had grown up studying him on record, like the guitarist Ben Monder, the tenor saxophonists Bill McHenry and Tony Malaby, and the pianists Anat Fort and Dan Tepfer.

After Motian died in 2011, at eighty, the scope of his influence could be felt in the form of a void, expressed by a great variety of musicians worldwide, but especially in New York. "In my whole life I probably spent more time with him than anyone other than my wife," Frisell told me a couple of years later, explaining that he still hadn't gotten over the loss.[11]

But Frisell had been able to pay tribute on a few notable occasions, including the 2012 Newport Jazz Festival, when he appeared as a featured guest with the Bad Plus. Their set opened with one Motian composition and moved on to another. And after a sublime reading of "It Should've Happened a Long Time Ago," Reid Anderson stepped to the microphone.

"We are going to play one more song," he said. "It's another Paul Motian song, because we love Paul so much, and his music means so much to us."

The pianist, composer, educator, and organizer Muhal Richard Abrams was eighty-seven when he died, in 2017. The Association for the Advancement of Creative Musicians, which he cofounded on the South Side of Chicago, had more than half a century of enlightened provocations in its rearview at that point, and untold others ahead.

Abrams was a brilliant, mostly self-taught pianist who combined a strong foundation in the blues with keen attunement to the shadow art of vibration and overtone. While he came up in a hard-swinging jazz context, and created some of his early work in that style, he was serious about a nonidiomatic approach to improvisation. This, along with a determination to explore his own compositional ideas, was what led him to form his Experimental Band in the early 1960s, with musicians like the saxophonists Joseph Jarman and Roscoe Mitchell.

"I needed a place to experiment with the things I wanted to do with music," Abrams told me in 2008. "So I organized the Experimental Band, the forerunner of the AACM. And I fortunately attracted musicians who were interested in that. It included quite a few of the musicians that you know today that are very accomplished in what they do. The reason they could accomplish what they did is that they found a workshop where they could experiment and learn and test themselves as to what could be done with things they find out, in terms of research and study."[12]

One of the great engines of experimental art in postwar America, the AACM had long enjoyed considerable support from the critical establishment, and the devotion of a small but vocal circle of followers. And Abrams had enjoyed the garlands of an elder statesman in his time, past the point of active oversight in AACM governance. In 2013 he joined Mitchell, the multireedist Henry Threadgill, and Jack DeJohnette for a special concert at the Chicago Jazz Festival, released under DeJohnette's name on ECM in time for the AACM's fiftieth anniversary. In that commemorative year, 2015, the all-star ensemble reconvened for a handful of dates, including a performance at Newport that was magnificent in its spontaneous formal coherence.

By then, something larger was happening with respect to the AACM's foothold in jazz. It wasn't just about the continuing advances of first-wave members like Threadgill, though that was a genuine source of awe. It was also that the organization's aesthetic value system—among other things, a multidimensional view of culture and time, and a focus on spontaneous colloquy—had slowly infiltrated the music's mainstream. The pianist Craig Taborn, who had turned on to the AACM as a teenager in the 1980s, remembers a period when jazz musicians of his generation were largely oblivious to its message. Talking about a musician like Threadgill, in certain circles, could feel like offering a secret handshake. "Now I can reference these people, and find a lot of young musicians who know what I'm talking about," he said in 2015. "That definitely wasn't happening in the nineties."[13]

What *was* happening in the nineties, among other things, was a stealth expansion of AACM ideals. Taborn recorded and toured with the Roscoe Mitchell Note Factory, alongside other free-thinking improvisers like the pianists Matthew Shipp and Vijay Iyer (in separate editions of the band). The Art Ensemble of Chicago was still an active concern. Lester Bowie was leading both Brass Fantasy and the New York Organ Ensemble, each a boisterous, audience-facing proposition. The multi-reedist Anthony Braxton was creating a flood of music—in concert, on paper, and on record—while holding court from a tenured faculty position at Wesleyan.

Threadgill, who had already exploded all preconceptions with Air in the seventies and his Sextett in the eighties, spent most of the 1990s at the helm of a band aptly named Very Very Circus. Featuring musicians like Marcus Rojas on tuba, Brandon Ross on guitar, and Gene Lake on drums, it was an ensemble of riotous polyphony over infectious funk rhythm. Its mad, exultant albums—none more so than *Too Much Sugar for a Dime*, in 1993—were critical darlings with a not insignificant commercial reach. (Two of those albums appeared on Columbia.)

All of which set the table for the early 2000s, when Threadgill formed Zooid, a band featuring sharp younger players like Liberty Ellman, on acoustic guitar, and Jose Davila, on tuba and trombone. This group was a laboratory for Threadgill's latest intervallic and rhythmic systems, as well as a real-time dynamo. The hiccuping syncopations and chromatic tensions in the music were difficult to parse but easy to enjoy, provided your guard was down. And as the band plunged deeper into the Threadgill matrix, its reach broadened. A Zooid album, *In for a Penny, In for a Pound*, won the Pulitzer Prize for Music in 2016, making Threadgill only the third jazz musician to receive that honor, after Wynton Marsalis and Ornette Coleman.

Several years earlier, the shortlist in that category had included the AACM trumpeter and composer Wadada Leo Smith, for an album called *Ten Freedom Summers*, inspired by key moments in the civil rights movement. Smith continued to create large-scale works addressing graspable themes, like the political meaning of the national parks system. He was another elder to emulate, as much for the self-reliant integrity of his approach as for the intrepid sonic dimensions of his art.

George Lewis, a trombonist, composer, and pioneering electronic musician belonging to the AACM's second wave, published a definitive account of the organization in 2008: *A Power Stronger Than Itself: The AACM and American Experimental Music*. Lewis's commanding show of scholarship—part musicological, part sociohistorical, part theoretical—framed the organization's contributions in a way that made it far easier to comprehend from the outside. Meanwhile, he was working on the inside—as tenured faculty in the music department at Columbia University, where his doctoral protégés in composition included category-exploding composer-improvisers like the alto saxophonist Steve Lehman and the drummer Tyshawn Sorey.

While not technically members of the AACM, these musicians were indelibly shaped by its methodologies. It was impossible to disentangle the association's influence on an album like *Travail, Transformation and Flow,* which Lehman created for an octet anchored by Sorey, using compositional techniques that put a premium on microtonal shadow and spectral overtone. That album, which Lehman released on Pi Recordings, sounded both familiar and alien, like a warped transmission from a solar nebula; it was one of the most forward-thinking jazz albums of 2009.

The landscape is crowded with other prominent examples of musicians inspired and mentored by a free-thinking constituency of artists, hardly restricted to the AACM. Your survey could begin with Craig Taborn, a conjuror of deep acoustical epiphanies, responsible for one of the revelatory solo piano recitals of our age, *Avenging Angel,* and one of the defining piano trio albums, *Chants.* Or Nicole Mitchell, a flutist and composer putting improvisation in focused dialogue with dystopian science fiction, nonwestern folk music, and postmodern dance. Or Mike Reed, a drummer and composer with a taste for postbop polyphony as well as a free-form textural scrawl. Or Kris Davis, a pianist with a judicious yet probing attack and a three-dimensional approach to free improvisation.

In this way, the ascendance of a class of jazz elders like Shorter, like Threadgill, like Motian—not guardians of a language so much as explorers in sound and space—rippled outward, redrawing the state of the art. Those coming up behind them could see myriad examples of artists working across dialect, genre, and medium, while still belonging to the fold.

––––––––––

Jack DeJohnette, *Made in Chicago* (ECM)
Paul Motian, *I Have the Room Above Her* (ECM)
Wayne Shorter, *Footprints Live!* (Verve)
Wadada Leo Smith, *Ten Freedom Summers* (Cuneiform)
Henry Threadgill's Zooid, *In for a Penny, In for a Pound* (Pi)

6

Gangsterism on a Loop

Jason Moran took an unorthodox route to his gig at the Three Deuces. His coordinates were off by about seventy years and more than four thousand miles.

In its original incarnation, the Three Deuces was an anchor of Swing Street, the famously bustling nightlife corridor on Fifty-Second Street, between Fifth and Seventh Avenues in Manhattan. An epicenter for swing and bebop in the 1930s and '40s, the street holds an enduring place in jazz lore, on record and in film. One iconic photograph by William P. Gottlieb, titled *Automobiles Parked on a Rainy Night on 52nd Street, New York City*, depicts a beckoning tableau of brownstone awnings and bold signage, neon letters ablaze in the dark.

Gottlieb also shot action portraits of many important musicians in the clubs on Fifty-Second Street, including more than a few at the Three Deuces, where the stage was bracketed by a folding set of tufted panels. A photograph from 1947 shows the drummer Max Roach wedged into a closetlike corner of that stage: His lips are slightly parted in a grin, and his eyes roll up slightly toward the pressed-tin ceiling. The drumstick in his right hand is caught in mid-stroke, a blur.

Moran had seen this image. Something about it stuck with him—

the way that Roach, one of the most politically outspoken artists of his time, seemed literally shoved into that space, flanked by padded walls designed to muffle his sound. "I saw the photograph of Max with those grommets behind him," Moran said, "and I just stared at it. What is this corner? *What is this fucking corner?*"[1]

A pianist-composer with an inquisitive streak and a compulsion for drawing connections across style and medium, Moran was more than casually interested in the implications here. Around the time that he fixated on Gottlieb's photograph, he was already forming some thoughts about the physical spaces that had helped shape jazz history—spaces that, over time, often fade into an intangible abstraction. "Usually when I'm listening to old music, I'm listening to the music," he said. "I'm not listening to the room. They don't exist anymore, so how can you uncover some of the answers that might be in that music by trying to unearth the stage that it happened on?"[2]

This line of speculation led Moran to conceive *STAGED*, an installation and performance piece included in the 2015 Venice Biennale. Officially Moran's first solo foray into the contemporary art world, this prestigious commission echoed his longtime track record as a collaborator with visual artists like Glenn Ligon, Stan Douglas, and Lorna Simpson. His other commitment at that year's Biennale was with his closest partner from that milieu, the venerable performance artist Joan Jonas, who presented a large-scale multimedia installation at the American Pavilion.

Moran created *STAGED* at the urging of the Nigerian-born curator Okwui Enwezor, for the Biennale's 56th International Art Exhibition. At its core, the work was a mythical evocation of the Three Deuces and another storied jazz room, the Savoy Ballroom in Harlem. Moran pored over archival photographs and historical documents, and then enlisted fabricators to create two sculptural reconstructions: a golden-hued, curvaceous Savoy bandstand and a boxy, upholstered Three Deuces stage. He placed the two hulking sets some distance apart in a vast gallery space, like strangers at a party.

But he also made sure they "spoke" to each other, by way of an ambient soundtrack playing from both locales, at regular intervals. Moran had composed one part of this sonic loop, "He Cares," as a minor-key piano reverie spiked with samples, like the clank and heave of a prison chain gang—a haunting, disembodied meditation on the African-American work song. Another sonic element involved a Steinway Spirio digital player piano programmed to play "All Hammers and Chains," a startling étude that revolves around a hard rumble of glissandi up and down the keys. In this sense Moran's touch and temperament were physically present in the exhibition even when he wasn't.

Months after the Venice Biennale, Moran brought *STAGED* to Luhring Augustine Bushwick, the Brooklyn outpost of the contemporary gallery that represents him. The installation was on display during the summer of 2016, making it possible for visitors of any background to stroll in and pore over the details in the work, like an African-meets-art-deco pattern on the backdrop for the Savoy sculpture. (Moran had sourced the pattern from a vendor selling fabrics from Holland. "So it's got that tension on it," he said, chuckling. "African textiles from the colonial mother."[3])

Along the perimeter of the gallery, Moran had displayed a few smaller recent works he had made, including *The Temple (for Terry Adkins)*, a found-art sculpture made of weathered temple blocks, and *Basin Street 1* and *2*, two charcoal-on-paper pieces that evoked both stride piano rolls and ancient biblical scrolls. In the gallery's reception area, Moran had stocked a glass vitrine with artifacts for sale: old sheet music, salvaged drink menus, rickety hat stands. Luhring Augustine was also selling the first copies of *LOOP*, a limited-edition art zine he had edited, with contributions from a number of his musical peers and two mentors, Steve Coleman and Cassandra Wilson.

Several times during the exhibition, Moran performed live in the gallery, leading the Bandwagon, his longtime trio with Tarus Mateen on bass and Nasheet Waits on drums. At one of these special appearances, on a Saturday afternoon in July, the musicians climbed onto the Three Deuces bandstand as if reporting for duty. Waits sat behind a vintage drum kit, stocked with woodblocks and wafer-thin cymbals. Mateen picked up the double bass that had been lying on its side, part of the scenery. The musicians were in contemporary attire; Moran wore a polka-dot dress shirt, sneakers, and a baseball cap.

Their performance began with a long improvisation in dialogue with one of Moran's spliced samples, of a female voice singing a gospel moan. They made this into a prayerful dirge, rustling quiet in a ceremonial free tempo, and then building a fervent arc. The remainder of the forty-five-minute set suggested a digest of themes from across Moran's career, as well as a reflection on the endless renewal of the jazz tradition.

So the trio played "Body and Soul," a standard ballad no doubt performed thousands of times on the actual Three Deuces stage. Moran's arrangement of the song, a staple of his set lists, assumed a gluey R&B cadence, making a vamp out of one ascending phrase ("I'm all for you") and the resolution that always brings it home ("Body and soul").

Next up was "Wig Wise," a sharp-cornered tune by Duke Ellington, from the early-sixties album *Money Jungle,* which featured Roach and the bassist Charles Mingus. The Bandwagon played it with the same antic sputter as on Moran's second album, *Facing Left*—before giving the tune a rattling Afrobeat cadence. This in turn provided the segue into a pair of 1920s standards associated with Fats Waller ("Sheik of Araby" and "I Found a New Baby") followed by the staccato Monk theme "Thelonious."

The closing number began with "Wind," a somber new original conceived for a large-scale commission. Moran morphed its melody into another of his recent inventions, "Study No. 6," fixating at one point on a single note, and letting its overtones hang in the air. The trio hovered in this zone for a while, before Moran shifted yet again, into the pointillist agitation of "Reanimation," a piece he'd written for Jonas.

Throughout the set, most of the audience sat on the concrete floor. A small child giggled as she scampered about the room. The Bandwagon made no obvious nod or concession to the idea of the Three Deuces as a historical locus; because of the enormous effort that had gone into creating the artwork itself, those implications were self-evident. So the musicians were free. They didn't need to sound like anything other than themselves, letting the past flow through just as it always does.

Moran grew up in ideal circumstances for a jazz musician of interdisciplinary ambitions. He was born and raised in Houston, Texas, specifically the vibrant African-American neighborhood called Pleasantville. This was in the Third Ward, southeast of downtown, which would later be celebrated as a cradle of influence (among other things) for the Knowles sisters, Beyoncé and Solange.

By anyone's standard, the Morans were serious about culture. Jason's father, an investment banker, had a collection of some ten thousand albums, spanning rock, pop, and soul as well as jazz. Jason's mother was an amateur cellist who taught deaf and at-risk children before opening a bakery; she enrolled him for piano lessons at age six, and often stood over his shoulder as an enforcer while he practiced his Suzuki method, scribbling notes. Because there was art everywhere in the house, Moran would always have something interesting in his field of vision as he played—he remembers one hyper-detailed image by the muralist John T. Biggers,[4] who had been founding chairman of the art department at Houston's Texas State University for Negroes (later renamed Texas Southern University). His family frequented art museums, the symphony, and the ballet. (They were also into recreational sports: golf, tennis, basketball. And Moran, like his two brothers, spent some adolescent years fairly obsessed with skateboarding.)

Not every jazz musician has a conversion story, a road-to-Damascus moment that later becomes a cornerstone of his or her narrative. Moran does. He was thirteen, going through a phase where the piano, with all of its classical baggage, had come to embody pure drudgery. He walked into a room in his house to find his parents watching news footage of a plane crash. They knew someone who'd been on the plane. The television was muted, and the only sound in the room was coming over the stereo: Thelonious Monk's " 'Round Midnight." Moran had what he would later call an epiphany. "It was all the commentary they seemed to need," he said, "the sound of loss and despair."[5]

It's telling that this recollection plays out as a dramatic moment with an expressive soundtrack—a scene from a film, in effect. But there was also something inherent in the music that suddenly clicked for him. " 'Round Midnight" is a ballad whose ubiquity in the jazz literature can make it hard to see properly. Its solemn severity, a function of chordal architecture, is also integral to the emotional content of the song. At the hands of Monk, who had a plangent attack at the piano, articulate

in ways that mostly fell outside classical orthodoxy, the song can communicate a devastating stoicism. Something about the attitude in the
playing also struck Moran as contemporary, in secret dialogue with the
hip-hop he was absorbing while away from the piano.

Moran became a Monk obsessive, pulling albums from his father's
collection and amassing others. His audition for the High School for
the Performing and Visual Arts—a magnet known for turning out
talent of all types (again, Beyoncé)—revolved around a Monk tune,
"Ruby, My Dear."

Over the next few years, Moran thrived at HSPVA, under the guidance of a legendary jazz educator, Dr. Robert Morgan. The perpetual
abundance of talent at the school made it a competitive environment:
during his first year, Moran didn't even play in a school ensemble,
because there were too many good pianists in the pool. But Moran
formed natural alliances with a handful of advanced peers, notably the
drummer Eric Harland, who would later play on his first album and
draft him into Charles Lloyd's New Quartet.

By his senior year, Moran was student director of the elite school
combo. He graduated in 1993, moving to New York for conservatory
training. More to the point, he matriculated at the Manhattan School
of Music for the express purpose of studying with Jaki Byard, a pianist
of abundant wit, brash dexterity, and a broad, nonideological grasp of
jazz history. Byard had worked prominently with Mingus, in a role that
showcased both his fluency with the codes of bebop and his adroit-
ness with 1930s stride piano. Moran was one of his many students who
absorbed a deep reverence for stride, along with the conviction that its
ebullient intricacies needn't be something trapped in amber.

The cloistered nature of the academy didn't agree with Moran's
sensibilities, so he sought stimulation elsewhere. One day, early in the
first semester of his second year, he trekked down to SoHo for a site-
specific performance by Cecil Taylor. It had been commissioned by the
Guggenheim Museum, and Taylor's collaborator for the occasion was
the Japanese dancer Min Tanaka, who'd expanded his formal palette
from a strict foundation in Butoh. A block of Mercer Street had been
closed to traffic, and Taylor and Tanaka performed to an audience of
several hundred people, who crowded the sidewalk. Moran stood on a
fire hydrant to watch.[6] As aesthetic practice, this moment was an eye-

opener, a model for how to engage with sound and space in new and unrestricted ways. (When Taylor performed again with Tanaka in 2016, as part of a residency at the Whitney Museum of American Art, Moran was once again in the audience.)

Word always gets around in New York jazz circles, and before Moran was out of school he had been hired by the alto saxophonist Greg Osby, one of the leading postbop modernists on the scene. Osby's quartet quickly became one of the must-hear new bands in New York, and Moran, whose playing radiated both spikiness and soul, was a big reason for that. There's a great, unfiltered document of the band made by Osby himself, using a minidisc recorder placed on a table near the stage, at the Greenwich Village club Sweet Basil in 1997.

This recording opens with one original, a noir aria called "13th Floor," and from there it ducks seamlessly through a series of jazz standards, like "Pent-Up House," by Sonny Rollins, and "Big Foot," by Charlie Parker. Osby liked this material so much—as an honest dispatch from the band's latest coordinates—that he insisted it be released on Blue Note, despite the bootleggish sound quality and the fact that his previous studio album had been released only a few months prior. He worked out an angle: the label titled the album *Banned in New York,* and sold it at a discount price. The cover art and insert were hand-drawn like a DIY punk flyer, and the credits disclosed only that music had been recorded at "an undisclosed New York City entertainment establishment."

The Osby-Moran alliance branched into other areas, like New Directions, a special-edition band that Blue Note put together in '99. Part of a brand extension for the label, it featured Osby as the scout leader of a group of serious younger players, including the vibraphonist Stefon Harris, Moran's roommate in Harlem at the time. The group mostly played retooled classics from the Blue Note catalog. Moran was responsible for four arrangements, including one of Horace Silver's "Song for My Father," which tinkered not only with the shape of the melody but also with the iconic vamp, familiar to both jazz insiders and fans of seventies FM rock (via "Rikki Don't Lose That Number," by Steely Dan). In Moran's update, the buoyancy of the vamp was intact, but it gently assumed oblong phrase lengths, leaving the impression of someone tiptoeing gingerly into a darkened room.

But it was an original, "Commentary on Electrical Switches," that most directly augured Moran's path to come. He dedicated this impressionistic ballad to Byard, who had died under mysterious circumstances just as New Directions was hitting the road. The song, which finds Moran in compassionate triologue with Waits and Mateen, is a fascinating document in retrospect—the earliest premonition of the Bandwagon, as it were. And even here, on a track that's over in less than three minutes, they already sound quite a bit like a band.

Speaking by phone while on the tour at the time, Moran praised Waits and Mateen for their knack, as a unit, for keeping him on his toes. And he took a particular pride in the band's way of spinning a nightclub set into a continuous fabric, a strategy that Osby had introduced. "We'll finish a piece and start to fade away, and then somebody will take over and play a solo to lead us into the next tune," he said. "It's very slick. It's like somebody with two turntables, mixing in the next song."

Moran, then twenty-four, hadn't yet released his debut album. But he knew that the wind was in his sails, and expressed a clear determination to honor the example of some of his heroes: Monk and Byard, and two other pianists he'd studied with privately, Muhal Richard Abrams and Andrew Hill. These were composer-improvisers whose common denominator was an artistic independence rooted in originality. They were also the kinds of musical thinkers who refused to stay put in whatever box had been drawn around them.

"You can listen to Andrew Hill and tell he's been listening to a whole bunch of crazy stuff," Moran said. "He listens to Hungarian chants and all types of stuff every day. There was a time when he didn't listen to music for about a year. So those people are obviously open to way more concepts and ways of thinking than the average musician. And I don't want to be the average musician. I want to be the man who, fifty, sixty, a hundred years from now, you're like: 'Man, he was really on another level. He was trying to come at it from a different perspective.'"[7]

Soundtrack to Human Motion was released one month after that conversation, in April 1999. It opens with a sinuous postbop waltz that owes a slight, superficial resemblance to Hill's music. But this impression may have something to do with the instrumentation: as in New Directions, Moran works on the album with Osby and Harris, in a format that recalls some of Hill's work on Blue Note. The melancholy sound of the tune was a matter of both atmosphere and melodic contour, and Moran had given it an intriguing title: "Gangsterism on Canvas."

This was an allusion to the downtown artist Jean-Michel Basquiat, whose 1983 painting *Hollywood Africans* includes the word "GANGSTERISM."—all caps, with a period—near the lower edge of the frame. The painting gathers an accumulation of old African-American stereotypes in the movies, along with a dash of autobiography: Basquiat inserted caricatures of himself and two creative peers, in a stick-figure shorthand. The text on the canvas evokes both Cy Twombly and urban street writing, a point that Moran later underscores. Another track on his album bears the title "JAMO Meets SAMO"—a convergence of Moran's nickname and a Basquiat-affiliated graffiti tag.

There were other signifiers in Moran's track listing, including an allusion to kung fu fighting technique; part of a Ravel piano suite; and "Retrograde," a tune he'd devised by playing a recording of Hill's "Smokestack" backwards on a turntable. Then of course there was the larger idea presented by the album's title: a soundtrack, but one with kinetic intentions. (You could track this idea through the titles of two other pieces on the album: "Still Moving" and "Kinesics.") The end result, in any case, garnered high praise: in *The New York Times,* Ben Ratliff selected it as his album of the year.

Moran was just getting started. *Facing Left,* in 2000, featured Mateen and Waits, formally putting the trio's rubbery, push-pull eloquence on display. That album's track listing is also telling, calculatedly so. "Wig Wise" and another Ellington composition, "Later," appear along with an art-pop ballad by Björk ("Jöga") and pieces of film scores (including the main theme to Akira Kurosawa's *Yojimbo*). There's also a tune by Byard, and a reprise of sorts: the album closes with "Gangsterism on Wood," a cousin to "Gangsterism on Canvas," rendered as a chiming solo piano rumination in largely free tempo.

This was the first indication of a leitmotif: Moran would include some variation on the "Gangsterism" theme on more than half a dozen albums, tweaking the titles as well as the arrangements. The piece functioned as a dynamic through line, a reminder that for all the relentless forward motion in his music, Moran was embarked on a project whose mission had been articulated from the jump.

"Gangsterism on a River," for instance, from the 2001 album *Black Stars*, spread out the theme in slow, dirgelike common time. That title neatly communicated a sense of drift, but it was also a play on words— "River" as in Sam Rivers, the august tenor saxophonist and flutist whose presence gave the album its *raison d'être*. A gruffly exuberant searcher who had made some important albums in the sixties, and been a linchpin of the loft scene thereafter, Rivers represented a bridge to a previous avant-garde generation. The success of the meeting reflected well on both the elder statesman and the young turk, serving notice that the language was alive and in trustworthy hands.

Moran made this point even more explicit on his first solo piano album, *Modernistic*, released the following year. While largely a collection of original compositions, it opens with a James P. Johnson stride number, "You've Got to Be Modernistic," whose title doubles in context as a manifesto. As if to answer that call, Moran goes on to introduce his slow-jam remake of "Body and Soul" and a smart, clattering evocation of an early hip-hop touchstone, Afrika Bambaataa's "Planet Rock"—the latter with a beat hammered out on a prepared piano, and a melodic transcription of the song's rapped cadences. There was more: a streamlined Schumann lied; an invention by Muhal Richard Abrams; "Gangsterism on Irons" and "Gangsterism on a Lunchtable," two more in a series; a sort of lullaby to close, called "Gentle Shifts South."

If there had been any question about Moran's drive to broaden the framework for jazz performance—in terms of materials, historical purview, and personal expression—*Modernistic* settled the issue decisively. Gary Giddins spoke for the emerging consensus when he declared it "one of the most rigorously unpredictable and rewarding solo piano albums in years."[8]

The Bandwagon, meanwhile, was growing into its stride, becoming at once a more turbulent and more fluent proposition. Their set lists would bounce from Brahms to Byard to Bambaataa without judgment or pause. This was a strategy far from standard in jazz at the time, and less of a commonplace than it would soon become, with the ubiquity of digital playlists and streaming services. What it suggested at the time was the precedent of hip-hop, and in particular the moves of a crate-digging deejay with an urge to mix it up. Hip-hop was a lingua franca for Moran and his bandmates, notably Mateen, who had close affiliations with the Atlanta rap royalty Outkast and Goodie Mob. So it made as much sense for the Bandwagon to "sample" a piece like "Planet Rock" (which was in turn built on a sample, of Kraftwerk's "Trans-Europe Express") as it did to refurbish a 1930s Ellington tune.

Around the time that Moran made *Modernistic,* he put together a minidisc recording that functioned as the Bandwagon's introduction, a jump-cut collage of sampled sounds. A Bartók chorus collided with a Robert Johnson blues, which in turn led to spoken-word fragments by, among others, the actor John Gielgud and Minister Elijah Muhammad. (Also in the mix were Moran, Waits, and Mateen themselves, in heated exchange.) The track concluded with a flourish: the Queens rapper Cormega, in his 2002 track "The Legacy," spitting "the bandwagon," spliced on repeat.

This was the triumphant overture for the Bandwagon's inaugural booking at the Village Vanguard, Thanksgiving week of 2002. As often happens with a Vanguard debut, an air of reverence was almost palpable on opening night, as Moran, in an overcoat and fedora, strode onstage. ("I'm not fronting; I'm cold," he said, chuckling, in reference to his attire. "It's chilly up here.") Then the group was off, racing into a tune called "Another One" with a precipitous and choppy propulsion. Later, attacking the Byard anthem "Out Front," Moran and crew began in a stride cadence and then went crashing through a series of tempos, starting and stopping, restlessly shifting gears. It was a powerful demonstration of swing rhythm that never settles; there was a feeling of on-the-edge displacement even during the toe-tapping portions of the tune.

Elsewhere in the set, something happened that I've seen at a handful of Moran performances over the years: his tactics startled the audience, and it seemed for a moment as if he might elude them. The source of this mystification was a piece called "Ringing My Phone (Straight Outta Istanbul)," which featured a sampled phone conversation between two women in Turkish. What was so disorienting about the sample, beyond its incomprehensibility to non-Turkish speakers, was the fact that Moran had harnessed the material not as an accent or supplement, but rather a compositional blueprint: the trio matched the cadence and tonality of the conversation, essentially note for note. The resulting performance was serpentine and syntactically complex—but also somehow free-flowing and organic, tied as it was to human speech. During its unveiling, the piece met with a sharp, collective intake of breath, but ultimately provoked an exhilarated round of applause.

"Ringing My Phone (Straight Outta Istanbul)" appears on *The Bandwagon*, an album culled from recordings of that first Vanguard engagement. (Another track, "Infospace," applies a similar conceit to a Chinese stock report.) The album also documents some of the staples of Moran's set list at the time, like a full-band version of "Gentle Shifts South" featuring snippets of conversational reflection by his grandparents.

Months after the gig, and not long before the release of the album, I visited Moran at the Harlem apartment he shared with his future wife and creative collaborator, the mezzo-soprano Alicia Hall. (They had gotten engaged during the Vanguard run, on Thanksgiving.) Sinking into a black leather Arne Jacobsen chair, Moran described the evolution of the Bandwagon's internal combustion. "It's gotten stronger, but at the same time stayed real loose," he said. "Once we really started to play together, we realized how much we could do with dynamics, how much we could do with time, how much we could do with cues within the music. And how much we could do with repertoire, as far as changing what the jazz repertoire is. We had a lot to say about that, because we all listen to so much different music that it would be silly to keep ourselves confined to playing Thelonious Monk's music or Tommy Flanagan's arrangements. We wanted to take it where we thought it could go."[9]

Where it went would naturally morph and mutate a number of times in the ensuing years. *Same Mother*, a vibrant album from 2005, signaled Moran's head-first engagement with Delta blues: the Bandwagon briefly became a four-piece with the addition of Marvin Sewell, a versatile guitarist he'd gotten to know years earlier, in Cassandra Wilson's band.

By the time the Bandwagon released *Ten*—the marker of a decade's work, in 2010—the album landed as a kind of event. A product of sturdy intelligence and untroubled confidence, it put the band's interplay in a center spotlight, as a model of lithe collectivism. Moran's piano, as always, forms the core of the album, but its sound is inconceivable without Mateen's nimble, nubby bass guitar playing, or the earthy mutability of Waits's way with rhythm. There are pieces on the album by each of Moran's major totems of pianism: Monk ("Crepuscule with Nellie"), Byard ("To Bob Vatel of Paris"), and Hill ("Play to Live," a co-creation). There's also an interrogation of a player-piano piece by Conlon Nancarrow, and a piece composed by Leonard Bernstein for the Jerome Robbins ballet *Fancy Free*.

The album also features a ballet theme of Moran's own invention: "Pas de Deux—Lines Ballet," a sternly gleaming ballad for solo piano. Elsewhere there are pieces commissioned by a jazz festival and an art museum, and one conceived as the soundtrack to a documentary film. Each feels shaped by the practices of the trio rather than imposed from the outside, with a style governed by the full sweep of the jazz tradition, and by hip-hop, blues, and gospel besides. The radiant, authentic sweep of the album was such that it almost seemed a premonition: later that year, Moran became a MacArthur Fellow, at thirty-five.

The far-ranging interests that set Moran in a class apart, at least among his jazz peers, hardly represented a stretch for him. As far back as 2003 he was talking about an idea he had for a grant proposal for the Bandwagon: a durational piece called "Storefront," in which he would lease a space for a month and occupy it, as a place of business, every day. "So we go hang out there, and whether we play music or watch TV, there will be seats set up so people can come in. And maybe a couple of nights out of the week there will be free concerts. And artists will be welcome to come in and interact."

Part installation, part community outreach, and part performance art, the idea jibed perfectly with Moran's creative conception. Yet he was matter-of-fact about it: "I just think this is a way to bring the art out," he said. "It's always about exposing the art, and creating it at the same time."[10]

"Storefront" didn't come to fruition in that exact form, but it had a strong parallel in *BLEED*—a five-day museum residency that he and Alicia Hall Moran organized in 2012, as part of that year's Whitney

Biennial. It featured dozens of collaborators, including the guitarist
Bill Frisell, the choreographer Rashida Bumbray, and, searingly, the
artist Kara Walker, in a sort of performance drag as "Karaoke Walkrrr."
The residency put into formal terms a sort of intuitive process that the
Morans had situated at the center of their creative life: community and
family, interdisciplinary collaboration, the transformation of materials
and environment.

In time Moran would find ways of bringing this feeling even to more
normative jazz settings—like the Village Vanguard, whose eightieth
birthday celebration he curated in 2015. Those weeklong festivities
included an evening of solo piano, featuring Moran alongside a peer,
Ethan Iverson, and several elders: Kenny Barron, Stanley Cowell, and
Fred Hersch. The Bandwagon served one night as accompaniment for
contemporary poets (Elizabeth Alexander and Yusef Komunyakaa) and
the next as a backdrop to comedians (Marina Franklin, David Alan
Grier, Keith Robinson). On another evening, Moran and company presented a commission inspired by the quilt makers of Gee's Bend, Ala-
bama, with Hall Moran on vocals and Frisell on guitar. The week ended
with a rare club appearance by the Charles Lloyd New Quartet, and
Lloyd, who hadn't played the Vanguard in nearly forty years, sounded
radiant and right at home.

Some of the generosity and connectedness inherent in Moran's
approach to art-making could be sussed out in an album he released
in 2006, titled *Artist in Residence*. Made up of selections from several
large commissioned works, it was the first organized statement to frame
Moran as not only a pianist and composer but also a fluent traveler
in the realm of contemporary art. The centerpiece of the album, in
many ways, is a track called "Artists Ought to Be Writing," which hinges
on remarks by the artist, conceptualist, and philosopher Adrian Piper.
The text, from a documentary film called *Other Than Art's Sake 1973–74*,
appears in a sampled and lightly spliced form:

Artists ought to be writing about what they do, and what kinds of
procedures they go through to realize a work, what their presup-

positions in making the work are, and related things. If artists' intentions and ideas were more accessible to the general public I think it might break down some of the barriers of misunderstanding between the art world and artists and the general public. I think it would become clear the extent to which artists are just as much a product of their society as anyone else, as in any other kinds of vocation.

Moran's scoring of this text inserts pauses and imposes cadences, but it respects the integrity of Piper's speech patterns. His most meaningful underlining occurs around the words "break down," which he imbues with a synchronized chordal fillip. If you've been listening to the album in sequence, you experience a blush of recognition: *Artist in Residence* opens with a track called "Break Down," which samples those two words, in Piper's voice, as a repetitive hook. There's more than one kind of break to be broken down here. And Moran, in reframing the comments in a stylish contemporary casing, seems to be doing some of the very work that Piper prescribes, if only from a kind of side door.

For a large-scale piece called *In My Mind: Monk at Town Hall, 1959,* commissioned by Duke University, Moran researched Monk's birthplace in North Carolina, making ambient field recordings at the plantation where the composer's great-grandfather had been a slave. The performance featured this found audio footage along with related footage by a video artist. Thanks to the research of Sam Stephenson, then a scholar at Duke, Moran also had access to fly-on-the-wall recordings of Monk and the arranger Hall Overton rehearsing a big band for the original concert at Town Hall. The sound of Monk's footfalls on the floorboards became a structural element: his clomping dance step, like a shuffling Clydesdale, leads into an arrangement of "Little Rootie Tootie," setting the pace for a stuttering recast of the tune.

In 2011 Moran became an artistic advisor for jazz at the Kennedy Center in Washington DC, and within a few years, he took full ownership as artistic director for jazz. The significance of his assuming this post—originated by Dr. Billy Taylor, of "America's Classical Music" decree—probably can't be overstated. Moran wasn't necessarily opposed to programming with a traditionalist bent, but from the start he generated a kaleidoscopic range of programming, testing out at the institutional level an aesthetic ideal that had already proven compelling in his own work.

So he presented Anthony Braxton. He hosted a seventy-fifth-anniversary celebration for Blue Note Records, pairing Wayne Shorter with Norah Jones in an experiment that birthed the premise of Jones's 2016 album, *Day Breaks*. And he presented his own works, including *In My Mind* and the *Fats Waller Dance Party*, a funk-inflected take on 1930s swing, made in partnership with the bassist and singer Meshell Ndegeocello. A project called *Finding a Line*, first commissioned by SFJAZZ, had the Bandwagon collaborating with skateboarders on the Kennedy Center plaza. (A special skate ramp was built for the occasion.) Moran's influence on the institution was substantive, and not just with respect to jazz programming. He was instrumental in the appointment of Q-Tip as the Kennedy Center's first artistic director for hip-hop culture. "We've brought people and types of music to the center that we wouldn't have thought about bringing if it hadn't been for Jason," said Kevin Struthers, the director of jazz programming, in a *Washington Post Magazine* story announcing Moran's second contract renewal, through 2021.[11]

The high-minded aim of an institutionally supported contemporary artist and the ground-level stir of a musician reaching for an audience—those two things can be at odds; but as he entered his early forties, Moran seemed closer than ever to reconciling them within his ongoing practice. He composed the mournful, dignified score for *Selma*, Ava DuVernay's film about the voting-rights marches of 1965; at his instigation, a live screening of the film, with orchestral backing, was held at the Kennedy Center. He also scored DuVernay's documentary *13th*, working with a minimalist, percussive strain of pianism. Moran also collaborated with Kara Walker on a piece originally conceived for the 2017 contemporary-art triennial Prospect New Orleans, creating music for a custom, steam-powered calliope, meant to feel like a ghostly hallucination of the old river boats.

Moran's brand of pan-artistic outreach extended beyond his own projects, becoming a sort of progressive norm. The trumpeter and composer Ambrose Akinmusire is one shining exemplar of this: his 2014 album, *The Imagined Savior Is Far Easier to Paint*, features several original art songs, and addresses a welter of sociopolitical themes from a place of reflective interiority. (When NPR Music's pop critic Ann Powers named it one of the best albums of the year, she noted that "Akinmusire's compositions are like Mark Rothko paintings: large, filling every corner of the frame, yet calm, spacious, their colors connected in subtle gradations.")

Another ruminative horn player, the lyrical cornetist Ron Miles, released a standout 2017 album, *I Am a Man*, inspired not only by that civil rights slogan but also by *Condition Report*, a diptych painting by Glenn Ligon, whose annotative scrawl is reprinted as a poem in the CD booklet. Moran is a part of Miles's soulful, shadowy ensemble on the album, alongside Brian Blade, Bill Frisell, and the bassist Thomas Morgan. Miles himself is the driving intellectual force behind *I Am a Man*— on his website, he linked to an art-historical essay about Ligon, as if to explain his analogous intentions—but there's no question that the project owes some of its fuel to the eloquent example set by Moran.

Along with his Kennedy Center duties, Moran began programming a concert series closer to home in 2016, at the Park Avenue Armory. This was a series he called "Artists Studio," in the ornately restored Veterans Room. He kicked things off with a deep-focus solo piano recital later released as *The Armory Concert*—the auspicious first release on Yes Records, which he formed after ending his long affiliation with Blue Note.

The Armory Concert is a solitary statement, but it reverberates with echoes of collaboration. Most of the tracks are distilled from larger works like *Looks of a Lot*, a suite forged in partnership with the Chicago installation artist Theaster Gates, and originally staged with contributions from the avant-garde saxophonist Ken Vandermark, the bassist and singer Katie Ernst, and a high-school jazz band from the South Side. On the album Moran plays "South Side Digging," a tune from the suite guided by a manic, percussive atonality that gradually melts into gospel reassurances.

As he typically does with pieces from his large-scale works, Moran adapted "South Side Digging" to a jazz-club lexicon as well, including it at the Vanguard during a weeklong run late in 2016. A new iteration of the "Gangsterism" series made an appearance, too. On closing night, the Bandwagon sounded ferocious, almost as if still proving something to itself. Moran was recording the gig for a future release on his label— *Thanksgiving at the Vanguard*, released the following spring. Maybe it was posterity he had in mind when he began the set with a friendly, deceivingly simple disclosure: "We're going to play some music that tells where we are."

————————

Ron Miles, *I Am a Man* (Yellowbird)
Jason Moran, *Black Stars* (Blue Note)
Jason Moran, *Ten* (Blue Note)
Jason Moran, *The Armory Concert* (Yes)
Greg Osby, *Banned in New York* (Blue Note)

7

Learning Jazz

The most influential book in the history of jazz education—some would say the history of jazz—is *The Real Book,* which was published in five editions over the course of three decades before it could legally be sold. A dun-colored, spiral-bound slab of sheet music, marked with chord symbols in a whimsical scrawl, *The Real Book* served as a gateway resource for many thousands of aspiring and working jazz musicians, some of whom never left it behind.

Many established players disparaged it as a crutch, a childish thing to be put away. But its basic utility was undeniable. Neither a bible nor a blasphemy precisely, its reputation lay somewhere in the lumpy middle. And it was ubiquitous: the must-have accessory for any player establishing his or her relationship to the active jazz repertory and modern harmonic vocabulary.

For thirty years it was also contraband, thanks to flagrant copyright violations. You went out and bought *The Real Book* with furtive intention, cash in hand—either from under the counter at a music shop, like pornography, or out of the trunk of a car, like stolen goods. In that regard it was the latest manifestation of a fake book, which had been favored for ages by professionals in the Broadway pit or various other musical trenches. The very name *Real Book* was a winking acknowledgment as well as a shrewd bit of brand differentiation. But the origins of the thing might lead you to believe that realness—an authentication of the intel, if not the intellectual property—was also a motivating aim.

In his 2006 history *The Story of Fake Books: Bootlegging Songs to Musicians*, the musician and archivist Barry Kernfeld traces *The Real Book*'s origins to the 1974–75 academic year at the Berklee College of Music in Boston. Bassist Steve Swallow had recently started teaching there, on a referral from the vibraphonist Gary Burton, in whose band he was playing at the time. Swallow recalls that a couple of students came up with the idea of a better fake book, one that wasn't quite so riddled with sloppy inaccuracies. Clearing the rights was an insurmountable obstacle, so they skipped it, printing the book up at local copy shops.

And *The Real Book* was a runaway success, spreading fast beyond Berklee to become a black-market bestseller. (The identities of the two enterprising students behind the project has remained shrouded in secrecy, protected by Kernfeld and others.) Its story is a reminder of how much looser and more piratical the whole enterprise of jazz education was at the time.

Gary Burton's path through formalized jazz education is also illustrative. A former child prodigy, he ended up devoting more than three decades to a professional career at Berklee, starting out as an instructor and retiring as vice president of the college. He left the place in quite a different condition than when he'd first arrived there, as a student, in 1960.

Recalling that era from a distance of many years, he painted a scrappy picture. "There were only two schools in America where you were welcome as a jazz player: Berklee, which wasn't even accredited at the time, and the University of North Texas, which was a big-band place. But that was it, in the whole country."

There had in fact been a few other early stirrings of jazz education—notably the Lenox School of Jazz, a summer program at the Music Inn in Lenox, Massachusetts. Though it only lasted from 1957 to 1960, this program was remembered by all involved in terms befitting an Eden. The faculty was spearheaded by John Lewis of the Modern Jazz Quartet, and included a handful of other leading modernists—like Dizzy

Gillespie and the composer and theorist George Russell—who mingled freely with the students, in an atmosphere more closely resembling a salon than a formal school. Because some of the leading jazz critics of the day attended as auditors, the Lenox School of Jazz garnered an outsize reputation. In 1959, the year that Atlantic Records subsidized Ornette Coleman's tuition, Martin Williams reported back with "A Letter From Lenox, Mass." for *The Jazz Review,* declaring that "what Ornette Coleman is doing on alto will affect the whole character of jazz music profoundly and pervasively."[1]

Still, the Lenox School of Jazz was a three-week intensive, not a fully functioning institution, and it was over by the time Burton applied to Berklee, sight unseen. He was stunned to discover that the school inhabited a brownstone, with fewer than two hundred students. "Jazz education exploded during the next decade," he said. "By the seventies there were two thousand jazz programs in schools around the country, and it kept growing."[2]

The Real Book played a role in this expansion of jazz education, because it democratized a vast amount of information, especially in the realm of harmony. At times, the result was a myopic distortion: on certain songbook standards, the book might defer to the pastel chord substitutions of a widely admired interpreter like Bill Evans, rather than the original architecture of the song. A tune by someone like Thelonious Monk might be pockmarked with incorrect chords, shaped mainly by guesswork. The most accurate transcriptions were for contemporary pieces procured directly from the source: Swallow, for one, gave the book's compilers access to his lead sheets. So did his partner, pianist and composer Carla Bley. Guitarist Pat Metheny, then in the process of refining the songs for *Bright Size Life,* his groundbreaking debut album, provided a couple of pieces that had yet to be titled.

And so, because of an accident of place and time, this small circle of musical contemporaries had a disproportionate representation among the book's four hundred compositions, which made up a new canon. A handful of Swallow's tunes, like "Hullo Bolinas" and "Falling Grace," became staples of the jazz literature partly on the basis of their inclusion. In similar fashion, when Metheny released *Bright Size Life* on ECM in 1976, any attentive young musician would easily have figured

out that the graceful, diatonic title track was listed in *The Real Book* as
"Exercise #3."

Metheny, who had so named that piece because it was a teaching
exercise he used at Berklee, told Kernfeld that he regarded *The Real
Book* as both a time capsule and a catalyst.

> This was a fertile period where suddenly there were many young
> musicians who felt very comfortable with a vast array of harmonic
> vocabularies (from standards to Joe Henderson and beyond) and
> were at home with modern rhythmic styles as well as even things
> that looked to the rock music of the time as sources of material.
> In this sense I feel *The Real Book* has had an enormous impact.
> It has certainly caused a few generations of players now to have
> to develop skills that were rare at that time—only the very best
> players of that era would be able to go pretty much from start to
> finish in that book and be able to generally deal with the intrinsic
> musical requirements that such a book would demand. Nowadays,
> it is pretty common, and in fact, sort of required.[3]

As successive editions of *The Real Book* were published in the 1980s
and '90s, some compositions were added and others removed, while a
handful of corrections were made. In 1994 Swallow released an album
called *Real Book*, with a tan cover emblazed by the familiar lettering and
even a faded coffee ring. (The liner notes included lead sheets for each
of its ten tracks.)

Then the series went legit: the Hal Leonard Corporation, a leading music publishing and distribution company, began securing the
rights to almost all of the songs. In 2004, Hal Leonard published *The
Real Book—Volume I*, billing it as the first legitimate resource of its kind,
while attempting to preserve the outlaw copy-shop charm of its pre-
decessors. (Though it was "Volume I," the cover bore a stamp reading "Sixth Edition.") The lead sheets featured a familiar typeface and
hand-drawn notation. "You won't even notice the difference," read an
advertising spiel.

To the extent that *The Real Book* amounted to a clandestine literature for the self-motivated young jazz musician, Jamey Aebersold's
Play-A-Longs represented a do-it-yourself training regimen. Aeber-

sold was a midwestern music educator in his late twenties when, in 1967, he first published *How to Play Jazz and Improvise*—a play-along album and method book designed to demystify the fundamentals of jazz harmony. The recording featured a rhythm section (with Aebersold on piano) sketching out a series of common musical scenarios, like "Cycle of Dominant Seventh Chords." A player could solo over these tracks, using what's known as the chord-scale approach as a strategy for navigating harmonic progressions.

Aebersold originally conceived *How to Play Jazz and Improvise* as a practical aid for hobbyist musicians, especially those with no access to a peer group or a scene. "I had no intention of doing Volume 2, let alone Volume 133,"[4] he later marveled. But he was quick to realize that there was not only a commercial demand for the series but also a pedagogical vacuum that it helped to fill. As the Play-A-Long series took off—known in musician circles by a shorthand, as "Aebersolds"—their level of professionalism rose accordingly. Volume Six, a Charlie Parker immersion first published in 1976, features an all-star rhythm team with Kenny Barron on piano, Ron Carter on bass, and Ben Riley on drums. Later installments came similarly stacked. (Barron, an impeccable bebop paragon, played on more than half a dozen of them.)

The appeal of the Aebersolds was obvious: even for a fledgling jazz musician who *wasn't* stranded in the hinterlands, there was something both wildly aspirational and warmly self-affirming about the practice of sitting in with giants (without risk of humiliation, and with the substantial benefit of a pause button). There was something missing, of course: actual human interaction, the real-time flow of information that gives jazz its lifeblood. As with *The Real Book,* there was also a potential downside in overreliance on the training wheels. But as Aebersold always hastened to point out, his Play-A-Longs were designed to give any interested party the keys to jazz improvisation, at least on a fundamental level. No other product, not even *The Real Book,* better encapsulates the mass commercialization of jazz instruction.

That is, unless you count as a product the many jazz camps, workshops, and retreats around the globe. Before the proliferation of programs at institutions of higher learning, jazz instruction flourished in this vein. The composer and arranger Stan Kenton, whose postwar big band was a laboratory of what he called "progressive jazz," established the first Stan Kenton Jazz Camp in 1959, under the auspices of the National Stage Band Camp. As that affiliation implies, it was an intensive for big bands, with substantial emphasis on the mechanics of ensemble work. But there were so few other options at the time that Kenton's program, rooted as it was in preprofessional practical knowledge, was an instant magnet. Burton attended the inaugural Stan Kenton Jazz Camp at sixteen, after seeing an ad in *DownBeat.* (It was at a Kenton camp that he first met Keith Jarrett, his equal in precocity.)

By 1967 Kenton had splintered off from the National Stage Band Camp, rebranding his event the Stan Kenton Band Clinic, whose name had an intentionally serious ring. Other summer jazz camps were cropping up by then, some more focused than others. The Stanford Jazz Workshop, still a gold standard, was founded in California in 1972. The Jamey Aebersold Summer Jazz Workshop, a one-week program at the University of Louisville, began in 1977. Aebersold, who had been among the small number of attendees at the Lenox School of Jazz, understood the value of a focused environment with hands-on instruction, even if his core teaching philosophy could make jazz feel more like a craft than an art.

The composer and conductor David Baker—another veteran of the Lenox School of Jazz, where he had a formative experience studying with George Russell—took his insight in another direction. After joining the music faculty at his alma mater, Indiana University, in 1966, he directed the jazz program there for forty-five years. His example set a high standard, and not just among the many students he instructed: in 1979 he published *David Baker's Jazz Pedagogy: A Comprehensive Method of Jazz Education for Teacher and Student,* a book combining functional utility with philosophical reflection. (Chapter One, "Myths," amounts to a corrective overture.) *Jazz Pedagogy* became a bedrock resource, and Baker was hailed, long before his death in 2016, at eighty-four, as one of the most important figures in the history of jazz education.

Jazz's place in the conservatory expanded and deepened over the course of his half-century career. What was once an exotic pursuit in the academy became a booming industry, and an essential part of the picture. Whereas jazz musicians of a bygone era could support themselves entirely through record sales and tour revenues, the prevailing model now involves an institutional perch and a teaching gig. The implications for the art form aren't clear and simple, but one result of this shift is a boost in overall proficiency, because of the level of available instruction. Not every fine jazz instructor has to be an accomplished artist, and many accomplished artists make poor pedagogues. But when a notable musician turns out to be an excellent teacher besides, the benefit is large.

Meanwhile, the effects of the Internet, and the increasing fluidity of cultural transmission in general, have produced new generations of players with a world of information at their instant command. The more easily distracted young musicians in their midst might disappear down a rabbit hole and never reemerge. The more sophisticated might enact a new version of the process that Metheny identified— developing competencies, proficiencies, and perspectives that a prior generation would never have dreamed of grasping at that age.

An extreme case in point is Joey Alexander, the pianist who became a media sensation when he released his debut album, *My Favorite Things*, at eleven years of age. He was an undeniable child prodigy, reason enough for the hoopla. What wasn't noted often enough was the remarkable fact of his development in isolation. Joey grew up in Bali, Indonesia, many miles from anything resembling a thriving jazz scene. His father, a jazz fan and amateur musician who had studied in New York, introduced him to some recordings, and encouraged his talent. But the sheer availability of information on the Internet—recordings, instructional videos, performance footage—served as a hothouse incubator.

The web was also useful in spreading the word: Joey was a cherubic ten-year-old when one of his YouTube videos caught the notice of Wynton Marsalis, who arranged for him to be flown to New York to perform in Jazz at Lincoln Center's annual gala. From that moment on, opportunities spilled forth in abundance: Motéma Music made Joey the youngest-ever signing to its roster, and his family moved to New York, supported by a coterie of wealthy patrons. *My Favorite Things* hit number one on *Billboard*'s jazz albums chart and garnered two Grammy nominations, for Best Jazz Instrumental Album and Best Improvised Jazz Solo.

Joey Alexander's talent was exceptional on its face, but within the jazz community it was also the source of some watchful ambivalence. His youthful limitations were easy enough to discern, for a seasoned listener. But the scope of his success gave him no obvious incentive to pursue a formal jazz education, or even a conventional apprenticeship. "I love to play with elders and people before me," he said diplomatically in 2016, a month before turning thirteen. "But you know, I have a different path than other musicians."[5] The open question, for those with a rooting interest, was how much higher Joey could elevate his gift by taking advantage of resources in an institutional setting. Jazz instruction had developed along one track for Aebersold's legions of hobbyists, and along another for the gifted young musicians rocketing toward major careers.

The first music I ever heard by Andy Clausen was a wafting, harmonically layered composition for a group he called the Split Stream Big Band. Clausen, a clean-cut trombonist with an earnest demeanor, was leading his ten-piece ensemble at a colorfully dingy spot called Café Racer, in his hometown of Seattle, Washington. The ranks of the band formed a peer group, including another trombonist, Willem de Koch, and a trumpeter named Riley Mulherkar.

Clausen's writing showed an unforced grasp of advanced large-ensemble compositional techniques, like those of Gil Evans and Maria Schneider. It struck me as startlingly impressive, as did the high level of musicianship in the group. The impression stayed with me, and not only because every member of Clausen's Split Stream Big Band was a teenager, still in high school.

I was poking around Seattle, in the spring of 2010, to report a story about the city's conspicuously healthy jazz scene. Going in, I already knew that educational institutions were an anchor of that scene, as well as an engine pumping out promising young talent year after year. Most of the players in Clausen's band were classmates at Roosevelt High School, near the University District. A few others, including Mulherkar, hailed from Garfield High School, closer to downtown. Both schools were perennial favorites at the Essentially Ellington High School Jazz Band Competition, a popular nationwide program run by Jazz at Lincoln Center in New York; over the previous decade, Roosevelt and Garfield had won first place a combined seven times.

Dropping in on band practice at both schools provided a study in contrasts and a reminder of best practices. Each program took its jazz division seriously—"The big band programs here are kind of like high-school football in Texas," said one local musician, a Garfield alum—and the students were focused even as they jostled and joked their way through rehearsals. At Roosevelt, Scott Brown led the band with a careful attunement to the details, often pausing to tinker with the mechanics of a tricky passage. Clarence Acox, the veteran bandleader at Garfield, exuded a more booming authority, like a wrestling coach.

For young musicians in Seattle, this was all part of a visible, accessible pathway to the music. "My babysitters were in the Garfield High School jazz ensemble," Mulherkar told me. "I would watch them play and I knew I wanted to do that, from when I was really, really little." Before reaching Garfield High, he passed through nearby Washington Middle School, encountering a legendary jazz educator named Robert Knatt. "He was like a drill sergeant," Mulherkar said admiringly. "He was on everyone's case about learning their scales. He would yell at you, scare you to death, but he motivated people more than anyone I've ever seen."[6]

The Essentially Ellington Competition was held a month after my Seattle visit, at Frederick P. Rose Hall in Manhattan. Garfield and Roosevelt were two of thirteen bands in the running, each of which played several Duke Ellington charts for a panel of judges that included Marsalis. At one point, in between Garfield's performance and the announcement of the three schools moving on to the finals, Mulherkar slipped away to audition up the street at the Juilliard School.

Later that evening the three finalists performed, Garfield among them. During a piece called "The Shepherd," Marsalis joined as a featured soloist, and Mulherkar stood beside him, trading smartly coiled barbs and plunger-muted whinnies. The young man's composure earned him a stagy glare from Marsalis, some encouraging hollers from the hall, and finally a standing ovation. He received the Ella Fitzgerald Outstanding Soloist Award, the highest individual honor in the competition, and Garfield took first prize. (Clausen won a nod for outstanding trombone.)

Mulherkar and Clausen both attended Juilliard, receiving some of the most intensive classroom tutelage available to a young jazz musician. They also fell into life in New York, connecting with a range of musicians on the scene. But when I next heard from them, they were playing music with two more old high-school pals: Zubin Hensler, a trumpeter, and Willem de Koch, the trombonist I'd seen at Café Racer.

These four musicians had formed an improvising brass quartet called the Westerlies. Their debut album—*Wish the Children Would Come on Home*, released on Songlines in 2014—featured a dozen deftly reframed compositions by a former mentor back home, the keyboardist and composer Wayne Horvitz. (He'd moved to Seattle in 1988, after leaving his initial mark at the Knitting Factory.) A track called "The Band with Muddy," from the *Otis Spann Suite*, was a tour de force of dynamics and breath control, with Mulherkar nailing a perilous series of pirouettes originally scored for flute or violins. Another piece, "Waltz from *Woman of Tokyo*," had the trombones creating a hypnotic phase effect, in an echo of postminimalist pianism.

The Westerlies didn't sound like a jazz ensemble per se, but neither did they resemble a conventional brass quartet. Their arrangements, all by group members, were technically demanding and daringly inventive—and their original compositions, captured on a self-titled double album in 2016, showed a highly sophisticated group mind. They played the Newport Jazz Festival that year, on the smallest stage but to a packed house, and the roughly hourlong performance was burbling and kinetic, with a youthful spirit of possibility. During an episodic invention called "So So Shy," by Hensler, a riveting, smeary solo by Mulherkar was backed by an odd textural effect: the others had wrapped aluminum foil around the bells of their horns. (This was novel, but done with such expressive musical effect that it didn't scan as novelty.)

By 2017, the Westerlies had expanded their profile through savvy collaboration. The prominent Malian guitarist and vocalist Vieux Farka Touré had already featured the group on a track of his album *Touristes*. Now Dave Douglas tapped the ensemble for an album called *Little Giant Still Life*, inspired by the American artist Stuart Davis and also featuring the drummer Anwar Marshall. The Westerlies also went on tour with the prominent indie-folk band Fleet Foxes, playing backing arrangements as well as an opening set. The entrance music for Fleet Foxes during the tour was "A Nearer Sun," a Mulherkar composition with the bucolic solemnity of an Aaron Copland prelude.

To some extent the trajectories of Clausen and Mulherkar, from the moment I first heard them in a Seattle coffee shop, feel exceptional: there isn't another group in improvised music that sounds precisely like the Westerlies, for one thing. And yet their experience cycling through the jazz educational system—and their shrewdly selective actions *around* that system—illuminate a contemporary reality. Jazz education was integral to their foundation, in a way that might have seemed more unusual a generation or two ago. They're shining products of a formalized training arc that has taken years to lock into place, and years more to allow for such permissive liberties.

When Clausen and Mulherkar both enrolled at Juilliard in 2010, its Jazz Studies department wasn't yet a decade old. It had been designed as an elite preprofessional program, with a student body of just eighteen musicians, and a hands-on faculty of notable jazz musicians, such as the pianist Frank Kimbrough. By contrast, Miles Davis went to Juilliard in the 1940s—partly as a concession to his parents and partly to be close to the action in New York at the time. He later characterized the classical program at Juilliard as valuable in certain technical and compositional respects, but otherwise stifling: "The shit they was talking about was too white for me."[7]

The school wasn't really all that different when Marsalis dropped out of Juilliard in the late seventies, though he was more receptive to the premise of European classical instruction. Marsalis later became the director of Jazz Studies at Juilliard—in the summer of 2014, just after Clausen and Mulherkar graduated with their bachelor's degrees.

During the first major boom in conservatory jazz programs, in the 1970s and '80s, a common complaint among older musicians was that the schools merely turned out imitators: eager young players with basic proficiency and some solid book learning but nothing resembling an original voice. The implicit (or, at times, explicit) comparison was to a more heroic jazz generation that willed itself into being, learning the music as an indomitably creative folk art. (To wit, the indelible first line of Clark Terry's autobiography: "I made my first trumpet with scraps from a junkyard.")[8]

There was some truth in this critique, which had a lot to do with methods of instruction. It also reflected the ways in which a school can be an echo chamber, the sort of place where a consensus is unwittingly formed. At one point in the seventies, it was common to hear skeptics complaining about "Coltrane clones," in the same way that the fifties produced a proliferation of wannabe Charlie Parkers. By the eighties, the frame of reference had largely shifted—to Michael Brecker, the ingenious, astonishingly proficient tenor and soprano saxophonist who sheathed Coltrane's style in a layer of Teflon. Sticking with the tenor saxophone as a case study, you could have ducked into almost any jazz school in the nineties and heard an emulation of either Chris Potter, who embodies the next step after Brecker, or Mark Turner, whose innovation set different parameters: a sleeker line, a lighter sound, a more labyrinthine path, a more introspective tone.

Turner's influence in the academy turned out to be nearly overwhelming, as some students of his style have observed—none more insightfully than the saxophonist Kevin Sun, in an article titled "Every Single Tree in the Forest: Mark Turner as Seen by His Peers, Part One." Sun includes several amusing vignettes, including one from Boston circa the fall of 1998, involving a young man who bought an album from the Tower Records at the corner of Newbury Street and Massachusetts Avenue.

> The next day, the same young man, a Berklee freshman saxophonist from Houston named Walter Smith III, starts picking out melodies by ear from his new acquisition: *In This World*, Mark Turner's second release for Warner Brothers. A few hours later, Smith steps out into the hall to clear his ears. He pauses for a moment when he realizes he is still hearing fragments of songs from the album in his head, and then realizes the sounds aren't in his head; they're seeping out from practice rooms throughout the entire floor.[9]

Kurt Rosenwinkel, one of Turner's closest peers at Berklee and beyond, offered a similar testimonial in the same publication: "A lot of people used to gather outside his practice room at various times and just listen to him. He would be in there ten hours a day, usually."[10]

There's no question that Turner's style has reverberated farther, as a result of obsessive emulation in the conservatory, than it would have simply out in the world. (This is no slight to his originality, his industriousness, or his genius, all of which are secure.) Melissa Aldana, a tenor saxophonist born in 1988, not long after Turner himself arrived at Berklee, asserted that "Mark is as important to my generation as Michael Brecker or Coltrane or Sonny Rollins or Coleman Hawkins were to generations before me."[11]

What's different about Aldana's generation, to state the obvious, is that the entire spectrum of those influences, from Hawkins to Turner, is available as a resource. Today's aspiring player has a choice of school programs, method and theory books, videos, and transcriptions. This profusion of information—compounded by the endless epiphanies and distractions of the Internet—produces quite a different formative landscape than the one that faced jazz musicians in an earlier age.

Bill Pierce, chair of the woodwinds department at Berklee, is one of many musicians I've heard describe this situation with a resigned ambivalence. "You can learn every Coltrane solo there is without ever listening to a record," he told me in his office in Boston. "I'm not saying that's a good thing. But it's there. The musicianship, on a purely technical level, is accessible to anyone who wants to pursue it."[12]

Pierce had his most formative professional experience with Art Blakey and the Jazz Messengers, in the same world-beating edition that showcased a young Wynton Marsalis. The Jazz Messengers famously set a gold standard for apprenticeship in the music, earning a reputation as the ultimate finishing school. The guildlike process by which young musicians absorb lessons from their elders, upheld by Blakey and the singer Betty Carter, among others, was seen as a key path to success.

Then came the 1990s, and the deaths of Blakey, Carter, and Miles Davis, among other mentor-bandleaders. Due to market forces, fewer jazz musicians were finding it possible to keep a working band on payroll. But the jazz ecology abhors a vacuum, and there are still bright young musicians in need of counsel. "The apprenticeship model doesn't exist in the way that it once did," Pierce told me at Berklee. "So it's being incubated in institutions."[13]

Conservatories like the New School for Jazz and Contemporary

Music now take pains to encourage a mentorship dynamic among their faculty, an effort that hasn't gone unnoticed by those deciding where to apply or which scholarship to accept. Most serious high-school musicians study the faculty at the prospective college music programs: "That's my highest priority, who's the faculty there," a senior at Houston's High School for the Performing and Visual Arts told me in the school library one afternoon.

In Seattle, musicians as gifted as the Westerlies could be trusted to find their way to the independent sage Wayne Horvitz—but had they stayed put rather than heading east, they might have also discovered mentors at the Cornish College of the Arts, which has a deep connection to the avant-garde, or the University of Washington, whose Jazz Studies department is headed by Cuong Vu, a trumpeter, electronic musician, and composer who grew up in Seattle and returned after carving out a career in and beyond New York's downtown scene.

A fascinating wrinkle in this system was the eventual inclusion of some mentors from outside the usual framework for jazz education. Ethan Iverson, a true jazz autodidact, joined the faculty at the New England Conservatory in 2016, formalizing a process of instruction that he'd been carrying out, much more informally, in salonlike master classes. And Vijay Iyer, whose entire mentorship experience occurred outside the conservatory, brought a specific perspective to the table when he became the director of the Banff International Workshop in Jazz and Creative Music in Canada, and then a tenured professor at Harvard, in partnership with the NEC.

"There's a lot about music, especially improvisational music, that you learn in the course of performance and nowhere else," Iyer said. "Before this hardened into a tradition—which is pretty recent, when you think about it—there was a sense of people creating their own reality. And if you access the right people, that's still the case."[14]

"The reason for this book is quite simple," wrote Marshall Stearns in *The Story of Jazz*. "More people in the United States listen to and enjoy jazz or near-jazz than any other music. Jazz is of tremendous importance for its quantity alone." Stearns, a professor of English at Hunter

College, penned this passage in June of 1956, a few weeks before chairing a panel called "Jazz as Communication" at the Newport Jazz Festival. The panel preceded by a day Duke Ellington's *Diminuendo and Crescendo in Blue,* an amen chorus for the professor's claim. More than half a century later, his words testify to a vanished culture, as impossible to recapture as the fresh jolt of Paul Gonsalves's twenty-seven-chorus tenor solo. But *The Story of Jazz* remains relevant, part of the founding literature of an interdisciplinary field of academic jazz studies, which has had many implications for a music no longer served by popular appeal.

Stearns didn't invent jazz studies, but he probably coined the phrase when he incorporated his vast personal holdings—recordings, writings, and other artifacts—into an Institute of Jazz Studies in 1952. For the next fifteen years, Stearns and the institute cohabited in a large apartment off Washington Square that served variously as library, museum, and salon. A thousand miles away, similar stirrings were afoot at the Archive of New Orleans Jazz, founded in 1958 by Tulane professor William Ransom Hogan and tended by William Russell. A lapsed composer of the percussive avant-garde, Russell served as curator until 1965, when the archive shifted from Hogan's history department to the Tulane Libraries. Up north the following year, Stearns arranged for the transfer of his Institute of Jazz Studies to the Newark campus of Rutgers. The IJS and the Hogan Archive became, each in its own way, compulsory resources for jazz scholars, many of whom have their own university affiliations.

But until the last quarter of the twentieth century, the best that a jazz-loving faculty member could hope for from a university was that it sanctioned extracurricular interests, as Hunter did with Stearns. Aficionados went about the business of discography, biography, and history, but the closest thing to an academic discourse happened in the field of criticism—where, in the late fifties, Nat Hentoff and Martin Williams co-founded *The Jazz Review.* Touting jazz as serious art, their journal employed formalist close-reading practices adapted from the New Criticism; Williams had an MA in English from Penn. He and a few others, like Third Stream exponent Gunther Schuller, canonized some jazz performances solely on the basis of thematic coherence. This

model set the tone for the jazz criticism to follow. Its detractors, like
Eric Hobsbawm, argued for a jazz that was ephemeral and emotional,
and inseparable from social context. But Hobsbawm, a leader of the
British Communist Party's Historians Group, sometimes seemed more
interested in politics than in music. He published his midcentury jazz
writing pseudonymously (as "Francis Newton"), jazz being a greater
academic liability than communism.

Not surprisingly, institutional acceptance of jazz studies was concur-
rent with the music's rise in cultural stature. Jazz at Lincoln Center took
baby steps in 1987; the following year saw the first jazz-related panel
at a meeting of the Modern Language Association. Krin Gabbard, the
comp-lit professor behind that incursion, represented a new group of
jazz scholars from an array of academic disciplines. Gabbard tapped
this far-flung community for a pair of anthologies published in 1995 by
Duke University Press. *Representing Jazz* and *Jazz Among the Discourses*
introduced essays by the likes of ethnomusicologist Ronald Radano, art
historian Mona Hadler, and poet-theorist Nathaniel Mackey. "Relying
on various poststructuralisms as well as on discourses developed by
cultural historians and literary theorists," Gabbard wrote, "many of the
contributors have broken new ground by placing the music much more
securely within specific cultural moments."

The movement gained momentum at Columbia, where the Ralph
Ellison scholar Robert O'Meally was advancing Ellison's notion of a
"jazz-shaped" American landscape. Building on an interdepartmental
collaboration with musicologist Mark Tucker, O'Meally secured Ford
Foundation funding for a Jazz Study Group, which met on campus at
least twice a year. In 1998 he edited a pointedly interdisciplinary anthology called *The Jazz Cadence of American Culture*. The following year he
founded the Center for Jazz Studies, making the unorthodox argument
for jazz as "indispensable equipment for living in our time." The project
gradually won over a skeptical university community with the popularity of its classes, concerts, and staff. George Lewis, the composer,
computer-music specialist, trombonist, and AACM historian, became
the chair of composition in Columbia's Music Department, establishing a space for crosstalk between humanities types in the jazz studies
realm and heavy-duty composition students, some of whom, like saxo-

phonist Steve Lehman and drummer Tyshawn Sorey, were also notable improviser-bandleaders.

In 2004, after much negotiation, Columbia admitted jazz into its core curriculum. This coincided with the publication of a second essay collection, *Uptown Conversation: The New Jazz Studies*. Co-edited by O'Meally, Farah Griffin, and the English professor Brent Hayes Edwards, it consisted of more scholarship from the Jazz Study Group, suggesting the maturation of a field. At a university lecture around that time, university provost Alan Brinkley introduced O'Meally by praising Columbia's jazz studies program as "one of the academic jewels of the university—precisely because it has no real counterpart anywhere else."

If that was technically true at the time, it wasn't true for long: the new jazz studies were already cropping up across the board. By now the proliferation looks like a status quo, but the field is young enough that most of its heavy hitters are still in their prime. Among them are Ingrid Monson, the Quincy Jones Professor of African American Music at Harvard; John Szwed, who has applied his anthropological training to authoritative biographies of Sun Ra, Billie Holiday, and Miles Davis; Edwards, who authored a brilliant work of literary criticism called *Epistrophies: Jazz and the Literary Imagination;* and Gabbard, who in 2016 published *Better Git It in Your Soul: An Interpretive Biography of Charles Mingus,* devoting a substantial portion of the book to Mingus's voluminous writing.

Robin D. G. Kelley, who also applied what you could call a jazz-studies methodology to his perceptive and exhaustive 2009 biography *Thelonious Monk: The Life and Times of an American Original,* suggests that these interdisciplinary and contextual approaches are in some ways a reversion to form. "There's a lot that's new in the new jazz studies," he told me. "But there's also a lot that's not so new." As examples, he cited longstanding work by the pianist-composer Randy Weston, the drummer Max Roach, and the poet-critic Amiri Baraka. O'Meally, offering a similar disclaimer, included Jackson Pollock, Albert Murray, Jack Kerouac, and Alvin Ailey.

It's worth noting that Stearns was thinking contextually, too—*The Story of Jazz* delved into anthropology and social history—and that he wrote the definitive study *Jazz Dance,* along with his wife, Jean. (Note too that the 1956 Newport panel included poet Langston Hughes.) The vision that he prophesied may have turned out a little differently in the particulars, but not in the essence. And because an influential subset of jazz artists were paying attention, the new jazz studies found meaningful traction where it really counted, in the new jazz.

————————

Ornette Coleman, *The Lenox Jazz School Concert* (Free Factory)
Pat Metheny, *Bright Size Life* (ECM)
Steve Swallow, *Real Book* (XtraWatt)
Mark Turner, *In This World* (Warner Bros.)
The Westerlies, *The Westerlies* (Songlines)

8

Infiltrate and Ambush

The concert began in a state of rippling composure: Vijay Iyer at a Steinway, his tolling chords and arpeggios carried aloft in the evening air. When his sextet landed on the downbeat, completing a phrase initiated at the piano, it was with a sharp sensory jolt. The band was lashing into "Far from Over," the title track of an album due out months later on ECM Records. This performance effectively served as the public debut of the music, to an outdoor festival audience of roughly a thousand, and many more tuned in to a live stream on the web.

Iyer chose not to make this stand at a marquee jazz festival, though his sextet headlined its share of those around the album's release later that summer. Instead, he was putting the finishing flourish on the Ojai Music Festival, a prestigious event of classical pedigree. Established in the late 1940s, this annual convocation—in scenic Ojai, California, framed by the rugged Topatopa Mountains—has long upheld a tradition of rotating music directors, including composers like Aaron Copland, Pierre Boulez, even Igor Stravinsky. In 2017 that privilege went to Iyer, who took the opportunity to expand the frame, bringing in not only ensembles like the Brentano String Quartet but also an array of mentors and peers at the interstices of orchestral composition, collective improvisation, and what you might call experimental jazz, though he'd probably prefer the less idiomatic term "creative music."

The Ojai Music Festival leadership, then marshaled by artistic director Tom Morris, had seen in Iyer a persuasive avatar of the ever-increasing dialogue among an array of new musics—some of which traditionally fell under a "classical" header, forming the heart of the Ojai enterprise, and some of which fell under a "jazz" header and usually found their foothold somewhere else. "He's an exceptional figure in his breadth," said Morris of Iyer, speaking in an administrative office during the festival. "His deep and vocal advocacy of a borderless music world is also what's happening today—and I suspect he's leading part of that change."[1]

As if to confirm this impression, Iyer's festival programming felt pointed, wide-open, and supercharged. He naturally performed in a handful of concerts himself, notably with several configurations of the International Contemporary Ensemble. He presided over the world premiere of *Trouble,* a violin concerto he'd composed for Jennifer Koh. He played with an all-star quartet of Indian descent: the vocalist Aruna Sairam, the tabla master Zakir Hussain, and the alto saxophonist Rudresh Mahanthappa. He also played a riveting duo set with one of his mentors, the trumpeter Wadada Leo Smith, drawing from an acclaimed recent album.

Other festival offerings conveyed Iyer's perspective without the need for his presence. A collective called the Trio, comprising three additional mentors—Muhal Richard Abrams, Roscoe Mitchell, and George Lewis—performed an hourlong concert free of any premeditated impulse, let alone a score. Bach and Stravinsky shared airspace with new chamber works by the flutists Nicole Mitchell and Claire Chase. Another irrepressible force, Jen Shyu, presented *Solo Rites: Seven Breaths,* a mesmerizing performance piece featuring her pliable voice, a series of choreographic movements, and a small array of folk instruments.

The brilliant drummer and composer Tyshawn Sorey, a member of Iyer's sextet, was almost ubiquitous: playing a rumbling duet with Chase, expanding on a theme by Edgard Varèse; leading an improvisational "conduction" of chamber musicians, in the style of Butch Morris; manning an orchestral percussion rig in Iyer's hybridist work *Emergence;* performing *The Inner Spectrum of Variables,* his own unclassifiable suite.

On some level Iyer saw his stewardship of the programming at Ojai as an invitation to stir things up, and not just in musical terms. "It's an overwhelmingly white audience, and wealthy," he had told *Rolling Stone India* a few weeks before load-in. "So this is a chance to infiltrate and ambush into that space with a lot of different ideas and different perspectives on music that they may not have been aware of or willing to pay attention to."[2]

But "infiltrate and ambush"—terms of covert action with subversive intent—amount to a distortion of Iyer's larger project, at Ojai and beyond. He doesn't quite have an iconoclast's compulsion for chaos. And yet his empowerment by elite institutions presented what he saw as a moral imperative, a responsibility to speak for the margin. It hadn't been long since he was bouncing around in those hinterlands himself.

If there was ever a hinge on which Iyer's career tilted toward cultural prominence, it came in late summer of 2013, when he was in possession of two big secrets. The first was that he would be joining the music faculty at Harvard, in a tenured position as its first jazz artist in residence, beginning the following term. The second was his selection for a coveted MacArthur Fellowship, the so-called genius grant. As a pianist and composer with an academic background and a working foundation in the avant-garde, Iyer had already been the recipient of vaulting critical acclaim. But the combination of these two announcements would catapult him to an exceedingly rare tier of prominence. Because of who he was, or what he represented, it would also strike some in the jazz world as a needling provocation.

Even aside from the news, Iyer was at a pivotal moment in his career. After almost twenty years of making albums on an assortment of small independent labels, he had been signed to ECM, an august German operation whose roster includes revered new-music composers like Arvo Pärt and Meredith Monk as well as heralded improvisers like Keith Jarrett. As he held on to his secrets, Iyer was getting ready to record his label debut, *Mutations,* whose centerpiece was an inquisitive ten-part suite for string quartet, piano, and electronics. There had been all sorts of issues with the availability of the classical players, bringing a frantic air to his preparations, but the recording session turned out beautifully. The string quartet brought a singing resonance to Iyer's writing, and he played piano while running the sampler and software behind the electronic manipulation that lurks at the heart of the piece.

Mutations was just being mixed when the big news broke: Iyer was one of twenty-four individuals, the only improviser and composer across a range of disciplines, to be honored as a 2013 MacArthur Fellow. Congratulations began to pour in.

Then came the startling backlash, from an assortment of jazz musicians who regarded Iyer as an unqualified outlier, someone who hadn't met the right criteria or paid the appropriate dues. This grousing unfolded in the nebulous public-private zone of social media, notably on the Facebook wall of the guitarist Kurt Rosenwinkel, who carped that Iyer had been the beneficiary of an opportunistic and credulous media. "Well I guess I will be one who says it: Vijay Iyer is not a great pianist," he wrote, voicing what he called a counterbalance to the hype. "No touch, no tone, no melody, nothing exceptional in any way. Sorry, I'm not hating I'm just de-glorifying. It's just not true."

This was the first salvo in what quickly became a hail of darts, a comment-thread denunciation of Iyer not only in terms of his fitness for the MacArthur but also his basic validity and competency as a jazz musician. The ugliness intensified, producing ripostes from those who defended Iyer, retrenchments and counterattacks from the opposition, and stunned silence from the pianist himself, followed by a diplomatic and above-the-fray response.

Behind the scenes, Iyer engaged with a few of his dissenters, yielding tenuous but conciliatory dialogue. He did some private seething. But he also had the distraction of another pressing commitment: having just finished *Mutations,* he was now gearing up for the world premiere of a large-format commission for a twenty-person ensemble, at Montclair State University in New Jersey. Iyer had titled this piece *Open City,* after the acclaimed first novel by the Nigerian-American writer Teju Cole, who read excerpts from the book as part of the performance.

Iyer's collaborative assembly for *Open City* further included one of his mentors, Steve Coleman, and one of his recent students, the flutist Elena Pinderhughes. Also in the ranks were Ambrose Akinmusire and Jonathan Finlayson, progressive postbop trumpeters of similar experience; Okkyung Lee and Mat Maneri, probing improvisers on, respectively, cello and viola; and Hafez Modirzadeh, a tenor saxophonist and ethnomusicologist with a theory of convergence between Western and Persian musical dialects. Himanshu Suri, the rapper best known for his role in the mischievous, provocative hip-hop group Das Racist, joined Cole in punctuating the music with spoken word.

Open City was riff-based but mysterious in its development, an elaborative bloom of rhythmic feints and spontaneous interjections. Iyer later characterized it as "this beautiful expression of family and community,"[3] the manifestation of a creative peer group spanning multiple generations, backgrounds, and approaches. "It was just what I needed at that moment," he said, referring to the dustup around him. "Because what I was hearing from certain corners was being completely contradicted by what was happening in my midst."

The fractious dispute over Iyer's place and pedigree in the jazz lineage was a momentary distraction as far as the public discourse was concerned. It might even have become an obscure footnote to his achievement, except for the fact that its animating tension—the policing of acceptable artistic or social practices, based on a grid of bias and presumption—forms an important subtext in Iyer's output. This policing, which goes arm-in-arm with a less antagonistic tendency toward pigeonholing and exceptionalism, had often kept Iyer at arm's length from "the jazz tradition," even in the midst of overwhelming acclaim from the jazz establishment. The irony is that his work preempts such narrow-minded perceptions.

> With *Mutations,* and with all of my music, I am interested in probing this loose constellation of concepts: change, stasis, repetition, evolution, attraction, repulsion, composition, improvisation, noise, technology, race, ethnicity, hybridity.
>
> —VIJAY IYER, program notes, January 2005

Mutations had its premiere eight years before Iyer recorded it, at Merkin Concert Hall, one block north of Lincoln Center. The string quartet was Ethel, and the performance hummed with a carefully layered unrest. After a mournfully elegant first movement, the second movement opened with the strings in a unison glissando, sliding up the pitch scale like a slo-mo air-raid siren. Later, in the ninth, there was a recurrence of that sound in sampled form, which confronted the string players with digital echoes of their own recent actions. Elsewhere the suite deployed the strings in a contrapuntal web or a tensile hush, drawing from twentieth-century classical modernism and post-minimalism as well as experimental electronic music. Iyer divided his physical attentions between a grand piano and his laptop, plugged into a console. When he improvised, as in the rhythmically brittle fourth movement, his playing was confident and clear.

The suite was emphatically a new-music composition, but unimaginable without a process derived from jazz. Its score combined precise compositional notation with what Iyer called "structural improvisations," melodic scraps that served as signposts or motifs. In a slippery way, *Mutations* tied together a range of ideas Iyer had put forth in the program notes: evolution and genetics, Western notions of the mutant "other," technology as an alien intermediary, noise as a musical tool.

These concepts resurfaced in the concert's second half, which began with a solo medley: "Somewhere," by Leonard Bernstein, into "Imagine," by John Lennon. Iyer's articulation at the piano was circumfluent, at once percussive and flowing, and his sonic manipulation of the instrument—sustaining some notes, damping others—emphasized both its machinelike attributes and the breadth of its expressive potential.

Iyer devoted the rest of the concert to a brief set with his working rhythm team: Stephan Crump on bass and Marcus Gilmore on drums. They drew from a powerfully realized album, *Reimagining,* which also featured Rudresh Mahanthappa. Among the pieces in the trio set were "Cardio," a slanted workout driven by Gilmore's stop-and-start funk rhythms, with a chromatic bustle of pianism for a melody; "Inertia," which took the opposite tack, with solemn chimes in a languid tempo; and "Composites," whose churning asymmetries of pulse created the feeling of tidal variation, an inexorable but volatile pattern of surge and swell.

Another highlight of this performance was "Historicity," a piece with an ominous, ringing melody lashed to a destabilized beat, like a snippet of James Brown funk that had been liquefied and pressure-sprayed. Four years later, "Historicity" would be the title track of the 2009 trio album that turned Iyer into a soaring critical favorite, topping year-end-lists in *DownBeat,* the Village Voice Jazz Critics' Poll, and *The New York Times.*

The acclaim around *Historicity* had a lot to do with the unique combustion properties of Iyer's trio, which involved his furiously dynamic pianism alongside Crump's roving center of gravity and Gilmore's magical propulsion—his capacity for pairing a floating, semiabstract feeling with heavy undertow. As the title implied, it was concerned with a historical matrix, all the ways in which the past and the present are in a state of perpetual dialogue. This was a fruitful line of inquiry for a trio indebted to pianistic precursors including Cecil Taylor, Geri Allen, and Randy Weston and rhythm ninjas like Gilmore's grandfather the magisterial drummer Roy Haynes.

The album was also graspable by way of its link to an established literature. As Iyer had done selectively in the past—notably with "Imagine" on *Reimagining* and an earlier tune called "Habeas Corpus," based on the harmonic blueprint of the standard "Body and Soul"—he presented *Historicity* as a series of reinvented themes. Bernstein's "Somewhere" was one of these. So was Ronnie Foster's "Mystic Brew," a 1972 jazz-funk tune known in hip-hop circles as the core sample for a classic single by A Tribe Called Quest. Even more out of the box was Iyer's ingenious acoustic translation of "Galang," an anthem by the riotously energetic rapper, producer, and songwriter M.I.A. (Born in London of Sri Lankan heritage, she was an Internet star turned underground heroine, a geopolitical radical with dance-pop flair.)

Then, too, *Historicity* had one theme apiece by a pair of important figures from the jazz avant-garde: the multireedist Julius Hemphill ("Dogon A.D.") and the pianist Andrew Hill ("Smokestack"). And Iyer's strategy with all of the album's covers seemed to carry an implicit air of critique. In the liner notes, he referred to this process as "versioning," evoking a term from the otherwise unrelated words of software development and Jamaican dub music.

Some listeners needed a little time to absorb *Historicity.* Many had caught up by the time Iyer's trio made a follow-up, *Accelerando,* which encapsulated his knack for making prickly experimentalism feel approachable, intuitive, even stylish. Released in 2012, *Accelerando* featured a similar ratio of vibrantly redrawn covers to kinetic originals. As

before, there were moments when Crump provided an essential ful-
crum while Gilmore and Iyer circled one another like praying mantises
in combat.

Pulse once again proved an unstable compound in the music, in
exhilarating ways. On "Actions Speak," Gilmore's lightly jagged funk
complemented a swarming repetition by Iyer. "The Star of a Story,"
a 1977 album track by the disco group Heatwave, took on an artfully
smudged beat, with a jackhammering hi-hat and ride cymbal framing
the woozy imprecision of kick drum and snare. And if that description evoked the style of a far-out electronic producer like Flying Lotus,
that was only fitting: the album also had a cover of one of his tunes,
"Mmmhmm," adapted to an acoustic-trio palette.

As for "Accelerando," the title track, originally part of a suite composed for a modern dance company, it featured Iyer tracing a series of
arpeggios with the lurching, tumbling cadence of a heavy gear turned
by hand. This was a device that his trio had already employed on *Historicity,* in the title track and a song called "Helix." But it received a
purer distillation here, imparting a feeling both disorienting and easily
understood in visceral terms.

So it was no surprise that *Accelerando* received even wider acclaim
than its predecessor, though few could have predicted the scale of the
victory: in the 2012 *DownBeat* Critics Poll, it swept most of the major categories, winning top Jazz Album and securing Iyer top honors as Jazz
Artist, Pianist, and Rising Star Composer and the trio honors as best
Jazz Group. The forces that made Iyer a pacesetter, one of the more
important figures on the vanguard of postmillennial jazz, were already
hard at work.

Iyer was born in Albany, New York, in 1971, and grew up in Rochester.
His parents were part of a wave of educated South Asians who came to
the United States around the time of the Immigration and Nationality
Amendments of 1965, which made exceptions for professionals in technical fields; his father earned a PhD in pharmacology. Iyer was raised
in an assimilationist fashion, though he encountered acute reminders
of his difference.

He began taking classical violin lessons at age three. By six he had gravitated toward the piano, which turned into an autodidactic obsession. Jazz entered the picture in high school. "When I heard Thelonious Monk, it was a revelation," he said. "Something about it just seemed so close to home for me—maybe partially as a self-taught pianist. Because of the way I was dealing with the piano, it wasn't on any formal terms. Well, the formal terms were my body and its interaction with the instrument."

The role of the body in music perception would eventually be the subject of Iyer's doctoral dissertation, which he developed at the University of California, Berkeley after an undergraduate degree in physics at Yale. Originally intending to pursue graduate studies in physics, Iyer switched to an interdisciplinary PhD in music and cognitive science after crossing paths with a pair of mentors. The first was David Wessel, chair of the university's Center for New Music and Audio Technologies and a groundbreaking researcher in the field of music perception and cognition. The second was George Lewis, the trombonist, composer, and longtime pillar of the Association for the Advancement of Creative Musicians as well as a pioneer in computer music.

Iyer's dissertation, which he defended in 1998, was titled "Microstructures of Feel, Macrostructures of Sound: Embodied Cognition in West African and African-American Musics." Drawing on a wide range of ethnomusicological and cognitive research, the work proposed what Iyer called a "body-based view of music cognition"—in short, an understanding of music perception in physical rather than abstract terms, especially as it relates to rhythm. "In the sensorimotor perspective, a perceived beat is literally an imagined movement,"[4] he wrote. "It seems to involve the same neural facilities as motor activity, most notably motor-sequence planning. Hence, the act of listening to music involves the same mental processes that generate bodily motion."

This was a subject of more than strictly academic interest for Iyer. Among other things, it helped frame his personal interface with the piano, as he explained in conversation:

What are the rhythm domains that are involved in music? They're all the rhythmic domains that our bodies are using: breathing, and walking, and talking. There are musical corollaries to all those activities. Then when you think about music in a way that fore-grounds the body, then you get closer to understanding someone like Monk. Not that it explains him entirely. But you see that he just felt at home exploring the instrument with his hands, in the same way, actually, that people like Chopin and Liszt did. It's a body-based view of piano playing.

In his dissertation, Iyer demonstrated how the knotty intervals and rhythmic idiosyncrasies of Monk's melodies, in compositions like "Four in One" and especially "Trinkle, Tinkle," actually adhered to patterns that fell naturally under the pianist's fingers. This insight took root in some of Iyer's own music: his 2001 album *Panoptic Modes* includes at least two explicit extensions of the concept, a polytonal whorl called "Invariants" and a "Trinkle"-ish swinger called "Circular Argument."

Beyond the tactile body-rhythm concept, Iyer's doctoral work, which was well received in the scientific community, pointedly redressed a Eurocentric bias in cognitive studies. He had noticed that the academic literature around music perception was rooted in Western concepts of tonality and form—an approach ill suited to the analysis of rhythmic styles descended from African music, including (but by no means lim-ited to) jazz. "A major reason for this mismatch between tonal-music grammars and most music of the world is not (as is commonly thought) differing levels of musical sophistication or complexity," he wrote, "but rather a major cultural disparity in approaches to rhythmic organiza-tion and musical form." By way of example, he invoked a hypnotic James Brown funk performance of the sort that summons a world of human experience over a single palpitating chord—a musical miracle that by a standard analytic framework would be understood as devoid of meaningful content.

This commonsensical but carefully litigated argument was shaped by Iyer's on-the-ground experience as a jazz musician. For his first couple of years in the Bay Area, he lived across the street from the Bird Kage, a club whose jam session was a draw for local jazz veterans like the trumpeter Robert Porter and the pianist Ed Kelly. Iyer became a fixture at the session, which is how he met Donald Bailey, a hard-boppish drummer who'd worked with the organist Jimmy Smith. Iyer joined Bailey's rehearsal band, which met at his house.

These were musicians from the African-American jazz family, and their acceptance was encouraging to Iyer. But he didn't feel a sense of professional validation until he crossed paths with Steve Coleman, the alto saxophonist and composer behind M-Base, an aesthetic theory that advanced, among other things, a pan-African approach to improvised music. Iyer helped set up Coleman with a Bay Area residency in 1994, and their sustained contact led to a fateful invitation: the following year, Coleman asked Iyer to join his Mystic Rhythm Society on tour in Europe. (One of their Paris concerts was later issued as an album on BMG France: *Myths, Modes and Means.*)

Music making had started pulling Iyer's attentions away from pure academic work, and he didn't fight the current. He fell in with a cadre of musicians under the banner of Asian Improv aRts, a nonprofit that had organized partly after the example of Amiri Baraka's revolutionary Black Arts Movement and its offshoots. Asian Improv aRts released Iyer's debut album, *Memorophilia,* which featured supportive cameos by Coleman and Lewis.

Days after recording that album, in 1995, Iyer met Mahanthappa, who had traveled from Chicago to study with Coleman at the Stanford Jazz Workshop. "We hit it off in every way, very quickly," Mahanthappa recalled. "We had so much in common, just as far as our upbringing. We were both children of immigrant Indian parents, intellectuals who came over. We were both trying to find ways to express Indian-American identity—and I think, even more than that, we were still trying to figure out what Indian-American identity *was*."

Artistic othering has to do with innovation, invention and change, upon which cultural health and diversity depend and thrive. Social othering has to do with power, exclusion and privilege, the centralizing of a norm against which otherness is measured, meted out, marginalized. My focus is the practice of the former by people subjected to the latter.

—NATHANIEL MACKEY, "Other: From Noun to Verb,"[5] 1992

Iyer has described his early interactions with South Asian culture as haphazard, a result of largely unformed coalitions that would later become far more concrete. So, like many second-generation Americans, he began to investigate his own heritage as a young adult. He became engrossed in the rhythmic nuances of Carnatic music, a school of Indian classical music distinct from the more widely known Hindustani style associated with Ravi Shankar. Dominant throughout India's southern states, where Iyer's family had its roots, Carnatic music is governed by a complex system involving seven categories of talas, or cyclical rhythmic patterns, and seventy-two melakarta ragas, or melodic modes.

Rather than attempting to imitate this tradition, which he recognized as an impossibly immersive challenge, Iyer adapted some of its language—notably the transfixing power of cyclical rhythm—for his own purposes. Coleman, who has drawn inspiration from ancient Egyptian and African musics, framed this adaptive process in terms of a diligent creative license: "When you're dealing with traditions that are very old, there are no sonic representations, so you're forced to be creative. I would say the same is true if you're living in this country and your music is informed by something from another culture, like South Indian Carnatic music. They don't play pianos in that music. So if Vijay wants to apply this information to a standard jazz-quartet setup, he's going to have to make a lot of creative adjustments."[6]

Iyer's cultural translation was also inexorably influenced by his experience as a nonwhite American citizen. "I grew up in America," he said. "And this is the reason why I continually invoke people like Randy Weston and Max Roach and Coltrane, Jimi Hendrix and Nina Simone."[7] He continued:

They're people who were trying to make music about their perspective in America as people of color, and also as people with a heritage that needed to be reconstructed. My relationship to America is as much about being brown as it is about being Indian. Maybe more so, in a way. My primary experience growing up wasn't so much being seen as Indian as being seen as foreign and different, having a funny name, being dark-skinned. So this legacy of people speaking truth to power, voices on the margins commenting on the mainstream from the periphery—that's what I relate to the most. That's what resounded to me, people who had this real sustained critical dialogue with America.

Baraka, in his landmark 1963 book *Blues People: Negro Music in White America,* described the white appropriation of black music in linguistic terms, as the mutation of "swing" from verb to noun. Another important African-American poet, Nathaniel Mackey, borrowed and inverted this idea in a 1992 essay called "Other: From Noun to Verb." At the core of Mackey's argument was a pragmatic notion of language as symbolic action. As Mackey explained it, victims of racist or otherwise repressive "social othering" have often found subversive power through the innovative practice of "artistic othering," especially in black poetics and jazz. Mackey's essay was pivotal for Iyer, whose work tackles othering in both senses of the word.

Certainly that was true of Iyer's quartet music, which featured Mahanthappa's alto as an incisive lead voice, a whirring blade of agency and critique. Among the original compositions recorded by the quartet were some with an urgent political thrust, like "Numbers (For Mumia)," which sympathized with the plight of Mumia Abu-Jamal, then America's most famous inmate on death row; "Song for Midwood," named after the section of Brooklyn known as Little Pakistan, which suffered a rash of unjust post-9/11 arrests that led many residents to leave the country; and "Macaca Please," a nod to a racist slur used by a Republican presidential candidate.

The practice of artistic othering found even deeper purchase in Iyer's collaboration with Mike Ladd, a rhythmically nimble poet and performer. Their first project, commissioned by the Asia Society, where it premiered in 2003, was *In What Language?*—a song cycle inspired by the experience of the Iranian artist Jafar Panahi, who was en route between two international film festivals when he got detained at JFK Airport and was deported in handcuffs. Exploring a notion of the modern airport as a liminal space, "a contact zone for those empowered or subjugated by globalization," Iyer and Ladd created a linked series of vignettes, often in the voice of a specific passer-through. Ladd and several other spoken-word artists took turns delivering his scathing, wistfully sad, or wryly comic monologues, against electro-acoustic backing by a band including Iyer, Mahanthappa, and Crump. The project, released on Pi Recordings, was an audacious success—a marriage of political indignation and progressive aesthetics that also happened to be one of the more ambitious by-products of the intersection between jazz and hip-hop, so long as you weren't strict with your understanding of either genre.

Iyer and Ladd connected again, in further partnership with the conceptual artist Ibrahim Quraishi, for *Still Life with Commentator,* a multimedia oratorio commissioned by the Brooklyn Academy of Music's Next Wave Festival in 2006. Featuring a similar balance of electronic textures and troubled lyricism, with ambient shadings of hip-hop and jazz, it was designed to satirize the sensory riot of contemporary media and news culture. This was a ripe target, but the execution fell short, with Ladd saying little that wasn't already known.

Glibness was far less of an issue with the third and most devastating Iyer-Ladd alignment, *Holding It Down: The Veterans' Dreams Project,* about the experiences of minority veterans of the wars in Afghanistan and Iraq. Ladd based much of his material on interviews with these veterans. There was also original poetry by Maurice Decaul and Lynn Hill, who served in different places and capacities but with a similar residue of alienation and ambivalence. One track, "Capacity," began with a ghostly toll of piano chords and a self-critiquing litany by Hill, a former drone operator: "I have a capacity for war / I have a capacity for hate / I have a capacity for insanity / For anger / For lies."

Holding It Down was favorably covered in the national media. But it wasn't the sort of artwork that courts an enthusiastic embrace. "I don't think musicians listened to it,"[8] Iyer said a few months after its release. "And whoever listens to jazz records, they didn't listen to it. It scanned as out of the category. It just kind of didn't register. For a lot of reasons. It's a hard topic to face."

Iyer was sitting at the kitchen table of the East Harlem brownstone where he lives with his wife and daughter. (His wife, Christina Leslie, is a computational biologist at the Memorial Sloan Kettering Cancer Center; their daughter was born two weeks before the premiere of *Mutations I–X,* which Leslie's research informed.) Moments earlier Iyer had been downstairs in his garden-level music room with the Brentano String Quartet, finishing a rehearsal of *Time, Place, Action,* another commissioned suite.

Iyer's lingering grievance over a faint reception for *Holding It Down* was striking, given that his work was once completely overlooked and now covers so much ground. *Mutations* would soon be released, inaugurating his highly visible tenure on ECM. He was about to begin his first semester at Harvard, teaching courses including a graduate seminar called Theorizing Improvisation. To the extent that Iyer had stood between worlds—bridging academic and real-world applications, composition and improvisation, the avant-garde and the mainstream—he was finally in the privileged position to close the distance between them.

But there was still something weighing on him, and it had to do with the terms of the art form to which he'd sworn himself. "It needs to be addressed that there is somehow such a huge set of disconnects, under this umbrella of jazz, that people can operate in complete ignorance of one another," he said. "Being willfully blind to each other."

He recalled an exchange he'd had with one of his detractors during the MacArthur fracas, a seasoned jazz pianist with a more straight-down-the-middle style: "Basically I said, 'What is it that we are calling the jazz tradition? Is it more than a series of exclusions?'"

Early in Iyer's life as a professional musician, while he was in graduate school, he had an experience that clarified the range of available possibilities for artistic expression. He was just starting his involvement with Asian Improv aRts when a prominent member of its constituency, a saxophonist and flutist named Gerald Oshita, died at age fifty. Oshita had done pathfinding work in both improvised and contemporary classical music, often applying a philosophical framework rooted in his Japanese ancestry. Among his notable affiliations was a collective trio with Thomas Buckner, a vocal baritone, and Roscoe Mitchell, a fellow saxophonist and composer. This trio favored a branch of formal abstraction and experimentation directly related to Mitchell's work under the banner of the Association for the Advancement of Creative Musicians.

"So right after Gerald died, in 1992," Iyer recalled, "Roscoe came to the Bay Area and did a solo concert, and it totally changed my life."[9]

This twenty-minute segment that he did as part of a larger program just opened up a whole new world: it really was a person in a meaningful dialogue with his instrument on this inquisitive path: what happens if I create this set of resistances, and what is the most marginal behavior that's going to lead to a productive result? So he sat there and blew air through the horn without making any tones. He created this whole flow and statement out of what would not be seen as music. You couldn't notate it; he didn't even play any notes! Every now and then, a tone would emerge almost by accident. A decade later, I got to be on the stage while he was doing that shit—posing more questions than answers, which I love.

Iyer began to draw connections between the scenes he was exploring and the legacies they represented, which amounted to a much broader conversation than the one happening in the jazz press. Lewis, a dedicated mentor, helped him to make these connections, often providing a historical and theoretical context that he couldn't have sussed out without guidance. He performed with Lewis in various settings, and in 1995 he took part in an orchestral project assembled by Cecil Taylor, one of his paramount piano heroes, for the San Francisco Jazz Festival. By 2001 Iyer was working in Mitchell's quintet, and in the equally exploratory ensemble called the Note Factory. Later there came a working affiliation with another AACM veteran, the trumpeter and composer Wadada Leo Smith, in his Golden Quartet.

The multiplicity of perspectives and approaches in this experimental tradition proved irresistibly attractive and meaningful for Iyer. (When he created a music-publishing company for his own compositions, he called it Multiplicity Music.) Rather than an insurrectionary break from the jazz idiom, he saw it as a vital extension. He found a sly but profound resonance in the use of so-called little instruments—bicycle horns, toy rattles, actual bells and whistles—by Mitchell and other members of the Art Ensemble of Chicago.

"Just letting that become a space for creativity, where it's not about mastery," he said. "It's actually just about play and about relation. So it critiques the notion of virtuosity in very much the same way. It's not just about being this heroic, virtuosic soloist. It's kind of about baring something that no one else will bare, and for that reason you become this kind of conduit."[10]

Along with the groups he led under his own name, Iyer explored this strain of avant-gardism in a collective trio called Fieldwork, initially with a pair of Bay Area colleagues, the drummer Elliot Humberto Kavee and the tenor saxophonist Aaron Stewart. Later the lineup of Fieldwork shifted to include Steve Lehman on alto saxophone and Tyshawn Sorey on drums—two fellow explorers with high-academic credentials, protégés of Lewis in the composition program at Columbia University. Fieldwork's signature, a bristling and constantly interactive negotiation among the improvisers, expressed a transparent debt to the AACM, but also a pointed fascination with electronic music, Carnatic and African musics, and underground hip-hop. Each member of the group composed material suited to its strengths. And while Fieldwork released several strong albums, including *Door* in 2008, its most consequential music was made in workshop settings and concert residencies.

The group made a notable pair of appearances in March of 2016 as part of Relation: A Performance Residency, a nearly monthlong series curated by Iyer at the newly opened Met Breuer museum on Fifth Avenue in New York.

An outgrowth of Iyer's work as artist in residence at the Metropolitan Museum of Art (another major institutional endorsement), the residency amounted to a declaration of creative unity even more sprawling and inclusive than *Open City*. Running every day but Monday, when the museum was closed, it took place in a gallery just beyond the lobby of Marcel Breuer's historic brutalist building, which originally housed the Whitney Museum of American Art. The room had a seating capacity of under seventy-five people, but excellent production values, including a sound technician and a video feed for archival use.

As the title suggested, *"Relation"* was about social connections, and Iyer programmed the series to feature artists both in and just beyond his peer group. But Iyer was there at the piano on most days, despite the demands of his teaching schedule at Harvard. He performed in chamber groupings with most of the artists who'd been involved in *Open City*, including Suri and Cole. He played in duo settings with Mahanthappa and with another brilliant pianist, Craig Taborn, with whom he had worked in Mitchell's Note Factory. He revisited Tirtha, a collaboration with two South Indian musicians, the tabla player Nitin Mitta and the guitarist Prasanna. During the intervals between musical performances, there were often screenings of *Radhe Radhe: Rites of Holi,* a spectacularly colorful film by Prashant Bhargava, featuring Iyer's score—a combined response to the spring festival of Holi and Stravinsky's *Rite of Spring*—as performed by the International Contemporary Ensemble.

At one point in the residency Iyer played a ticketed concert in a proper hall with Wadada Leo Smith, drawing from a new suite commissioned by the Met Breuer. The suite, *A Cosmic Rhythm with Each Stroke,* was related to a second-floor exhibition of works by the Indian modernist artist Nasreen Mohamedi, whose geometric abstraction resonated with the music. It was released as an album on ECM.

Iyer also made several appearances at the Met Breuer with Crump and Gilmore. They had released their third trio album, *Break Stuff,* the previous year—somehow a stronger achievement than either *Historicity* or *Accelerando,* and a reproach to anyone who would file Iyer's music away in some alternative margin rather than at the thrashing heart of the modern jazz discourse. This wasn't just a matter of the album's links to the jazz repertoire—masterly treatments of a Monk tune ("Work"), a Billy Strayhorn ballad ("Blood Count"), and a Coltrane anthem ("Countdown"). It was more a function of flow and intuition, the shared metabolism of a band that pulsed to its own rhythm.

The first trio set at the Met Breuer occurred out of public view, during the evening of the museum's press opening. A party was under way; members and patrons crowded the lobby in cocktail attire. Back in the lobby gallery, there were never more than a dozen people listening, but Iyer and his bandmates attacked the music as hungrily as if playing a sold-out concert, which had become their standard experience around the world.

They played "Dogon A.D.," Hemphill's burst of angular funk, with a terse equipoise. "Hood," an original dedicated to the minimalist techno pioneer Robert Hood, took the shape of a large, looming crescendo made up of quicksilver accentual details. And then there was the new album's title track, originally commissioned by a competing institution, the Museum of Modern Art.

Swirling and incantatory, with a deftly slanted groove, "Break Stuff" conveyed breathless exertion but also a cool reserve. Iyer, calmly stirring up rhythmic eddies at the piano, seemed deeply in his element with it. He'd named the tune with a mind tuned to transgression, but he was also working "in the break,"[11] as his colleagues in academic jazz studies might put it—expressing a desire for reinvention, rooted in African-American revolutionary practice, that ultimately evoked not brokenness but its opposite, a continuum.

Fieldwork, *Door* (Pi)

Vijay Iyer, *Far from Over* (ECM)

Vijay Iyer, *Mutations* (ECM)

Vijay Iyer, *Reimagining* (Savoy)

Tyshawn Sorey, *The Inner Spectrum of Variables* (Pi)

9

Changing Sames

The Soulquarians didn't set out to revolutionize the pulse of modern jazz. Maybe it's an overstatement to imply that they did. But there can be no doubt that the slouchy, loose-jointed, atmospherically humid funk that they alchemized in the studio—specifically, Electric Lady Studios, in Greenwich Village—had a reach well beyond the scope of neo soul, the inexact genre coalescing around them. A considerable number of young jazz artists were paying close attention to what they were doing, at any rate. A few even got in on the ground floor.

What they encountered was something familiar at the root. Black music, in its broadest possible sweep, was a rallying cause for the core members of the Soulquarians: D'Angelo, a R&B singer and pianist oozing every sort of charisma; Questlove, a whip-smart drummer steeped in soul and hip-hop arcana; James Poyser, a thoughtful keyboardist well versed in gospel, funk, and fusion; and J Dilla, a crate-digging producer with the wizardly ability to turn a simple backbeat into something tilted, woozy, or smudged.

This foursome initially convened with the express purpose of creating a follow-up to D'Angelo's 1995 debut album, *Brown Sugar*. There was significance in their choice of Electric Lady Studios, which had been christened by Jimi Hendrix in 1970, later serving as the incubator for classic albums by Stevie Wonder and the Rolling Stones before it fell into a commercial slump. Russell Elevado, a recording engineer with an artisan's fondness for vintage equipment, tipped D'Angelo off to the fact that Electric Lady was still operational, available, and more or less untouched since its heyday. "We were literally blowing dust off of the Fender Rhodes that was in there," he recalled. "I was wiping dust off of the microphones."[1]

For a handful of years straddling the turn of the century, the Soul-quarians treated Electric Lady as a clubhouse—a perpetual hang unburdened by the usual ticking clock of the recording studio. Some-times their work involved more input than output: Questlove and D'Angelo would hunker down to study bootleg videotapes from old Prince and Stevie Wonder tours, like a coaching staff reviewing game film. Sometimes the energy shifted to accommodate a drop-in guest with fresh ideas. Progress was vague, halting, nonlinear. But the creative vibe of these hothouse experiments attracted other works-in-progress: while D'Angelo and company held court in Studio A, the rapper Com-mon began recording *his* new album in Studio B, and others (the rapper Mos Def, for example) followed suit in Studio C. These simultaneous recording projects often shared personnel, a sonic aesthetic, even con-crete musical ideas: a riff or a groove conceived for one artist might be put to better use by another, leading to some tactical horse trading. Still, the overwhelming mood was one of urgent creative independence, a conviction that ran counter to the prevailing commercial mode at the time.

"I think it really is a movement," Elevado told me. "All these people had a vision, and they're finding people of the same vision, at the same time. I think where it stems from is these hip-hop grooves—and it's coming out of the old seventies funk records, and R&B. But I think hip-hop was the one element to fuse these people together."[2]

More than half a century ago, Amiri Baraka wrote a penetrating essay called "The Changing Same (R&B and New Black Music)," for his collection *Black Music.* A reassertion of African diasporic traditions like call and response, and an attack on the dilution brought on by west-ern influence—both the Christianizing and commodifying kinds—it championed the spirit-seeking avant-garde of Pharoah Sanders and Albert Ayler, along with sublimities like "the hard, driving shouting" of James Brown. (Baraka's crosshairs were trained on white bohemians like the Rolling Stones, and on "whitened" black musicians hewing to a conformist middlebrow.) Waving away genre terminologies, Baraka placed ecstatic rhythm and blues on the same discursive plane as jazz's New Thing—an argument that would come to feel uncannily prescient during the Soulquarian age, and in the mutative period that followed:

> And Rhythm and Blues music is "new" as well. It is contemporary and has changed, as jazz has remained the changing same. Fresh Life. R&B has gone through evolution, as its singers have, gotten "modern," taken things from jazz, as jazz has taken things from R&B. New R&B takes things from old blues, gospel, white popular music, instrumentation, harmonies (just as these musics have in turn borrowed) and made these diverse elements its own.[3]

Voodoo is the album that eventually emerged out of D'Angelo's Electric Lady residency. Arriving several weeks into the year 2000, it debuted at number one, driven in large part by the smash success of its third single, "Untitled (How Does It Feel)," a sensuous, Prince-like slow jam. (The accompanying video, depicting the artist's naked body, chiseled and smoldering, had something to do with the song's reception.) Beyond the single, *Voodoo* stood out at once for its principled stand against the prevailing aesthetic of pop-R&B, which had been steadily marching toward digital clarity and precision. This album trafficked instead in murk and sweat, warp and grit. There were throwback energies in the music: not just vintage Prince but also Hendrix, James Brown, and Sly and the Family Stone. The critic Jayson Greene has called it "a murmured album, music made from the implications of other music."[4] On more than one level, that meant jazz.

D'Angelo had literally been a boy wonder on piano in his native Richmond, Virginia, the sort of musician with an incredible ear and natural facility but little patience for formal training. He was thirteen when a classical piano teacher recommended him to the music program at Virginia Commonwealth University, where he auditioned for the jazz pianist and educator Ellis Marsalis. By D'Angelo's own account, he would have studied with the patriarch of the Marsalis clan if not for some cosmic timing: Ellis already had one foot out the door at Virginia Commonwealth, having committed to a position at the University of New Orleans.[5]

Voodoo isn't a jazz album, but it contains discrete elements that could have come from no other musical source. The guitarist Charlie Hunter, who'd made his name in the nineties with a series of new-breed soul-jazz albums on Blue Note, provides the essential glue on several tracks, playing bass as well as guitar parts on his custom eight-stringed axe. One track, "Spanish Joint," incorporates an Afro-Latin vamp that would be right at home in Hunter's playbook. But the coauthor of "Spanish Joint" is actually another jazz artist, the trumpeter Roy Hargrove, whose contribution on the album extends to a number of strategically terse but soulful horn lines.

There was another, deeper, but less obvious sign of jazz influence on the album, and it had to do with the placement of rhythm. *Voodoo* revels in the tension between metronomic clarity and hazy imprecision. On more than a few tracks, the bassist Pino Palladino hangs way behind the beat even as Questlove keeps it locked in place. D'Angelo's vocal phrasing often adds to the sense of displacement, lying so far back that he almost seems to drag. When *Voodoo* was released, a great number of musicians actually found it difficult to listen to, because of the gluey disorientation imparted by these grooves. It all sounded weird, perverted, wrong. But this was a cultural predisposition, informed by the mechanistic tyranny of pop progress. As Palladino once said, speaking to Jason King: "That sort of back phrasing has been going on in jazz for a long time. D'Angelo honed in on that and used the rhythm section to back phrase as opposed to using solo instruments to back phrase. That was a huge jump forward there, in my opinion."[6]

Each of the principal musicians on *Voodoo* traces this revolution in rhythm back to J Dilla. His signature was a sampling style that sought to radically transform, rather than simply appropriate, existing musical source material. Dilla—born James Dewitt Yancey in Detroit in 1974, and also known professionally as Jay Dee—was the rare producer recognized by musicians as a guru, responsible for elevating sampling not only to the level of an art but to the threshold of some sort of black magic. Hip-hop producers had already demonstrated how effective it could be to turn a "break"—a bar or two of drumming, the merest slice of a track—into the foundation of a new song. Dilla took this practice farther, finding samples in places that few others would think to look, and remolding them like putty. The Jay Dee methodology was first articulated on a debut album by the hip-hop group Slum Village, *Fan-Tas-Tic Vol 1,* unofficially released in 1997. One track, "Hoc N Pucky," rested on a two-bar vamp lifted from a recording of Bill Evans's "T.T.T. (Twelve Tone Tune)." (The waft of Fender Rhodes arpeggios on that track, from 1971, come in the midst of a solo; Dilla slows it down so that it feels like something out of a dream.) Elsewhere on the album there are samples from Herbie Hancock, Gil Evans, and Larry Young. A track called "Things U Do (Remix)" puts a head-bobbing groove under a chiming passage from *Duster,* the 1967 proto-fusion album by the Gary Burton Quartet.

But it wasn't just a connoisseur's taste that set Dilla's production apart. He also resisted any movement toward rhythm quantization— the industry standard, then as now, in popular music. He preferred to dial up the variability and wobble that distinguish a groove as human, intriguing in its imperfection. His beats weren't metronomic; they practically breathed.

That first Slum Village album didn't even see a proper release until late February of 2006, a few weeks after J Dilla's tragic death of a rare blood disorder at age thirty-two. But the startling impact of his style hadn't gone unnoticed in his time, in bohemian hip-hop circles. Questlove has recalled that when *Fan-Tas-Tic Vol 1* began to make the rounds in 1997, "it was a messiah moment, in a way, for people like me and D'Angelo and Q-Tip. We had been looking for someone to lead us out of the darkness, to take us across the desert. Most of the time in those cases, you don't know who you're looking for until you see them."[7]

In an almost tactile way, then, *Voodoo* was an attempt to recapture lightning in a bottle. What's striking is the degree to which it succeeded, and with real musicians in a room. There's an odd sensation that you often encounter listening to the album, not unlike absentmindedly reaching the top of a staircase and being startled when there isn't another step. On a track like "The Root," which drapes D'Angelo's multitracked moan and Hunter's guitar arpeggios over a snaking backbeat, that feeling is recursive, throwing you off balance roughly every two bars.

Today's abnormality often becomes tomorrow's norm, and that's what happened with the dark rhythm science of Dilla and *Voodoo*—especially among the generation or two of improvising musicians who were still in training when the album dropped. But before those musicians had the opportunity to implement their lessons, a more direct adaptation of the *Voodoo* vibe would emerge, from a member of his touring band with unimpeachable jazz cred.

The iconic image from the 45th Grammys, held in 2003 at Madison Square Garden in New York, is a wire photograph from just after the ceremony, depicting newcomer Norah Jones with an armload of awards. Jones, then twenty-three, swept five categories, including Album of the Year, Best New Artist, and Record of the Year. She had trained as a jazz pianist—at Booker T. Washington High School for the Performing and Visual Arts in Dallas, and then at the University of North Texas—before finding a niche in the roots-minded but non-purist singer-songwriter hub on Manhattan's Lower East Side. But it took a few years before her identity was firmly in place. (The first time I heard her, in 2001, it was as a soul-styled guest on a Charlie Hunter gig.) Her debut album, *Come Away with Me*, was released on Blue Note, to the consternation of some jazz partisans who augured the early stirrings of a more crossover-minded direction for the label. This wasn't an unreasonable takeaway. To some degree it was even true.

As it happened, another jazz-rooted Booker T. Washington alum won a Grammy in 2003, without making a splash on the red carpet or in the entertainment press. This was Roy Hargrove, who received an award for Best Jazz Instrumental Album—sharing the honor with Herbie Hancock and Michael Brecker, his co-headliners in a postbop dream team called Directions in Music. (The album was *Directions in Music: Live at Massey Hall—Celebrating Miles Davis & John Coltrane*.) Hargrove's win was consistent with his profile: he was a former Young

Lion with a proven track record of boppish expression, and he made perfect sense in a V.S.O.P.-like touring package.

But Hargrove had been branching out from this baseline. In addition to D'Angelo's *Voodoo,* he'd contributed to two other notable albums from the Soulquarians' Electric Lady takeover: *Like Water for Chocolate,* by the rapper Common, and *Mama's Gun,* by the soul singer Erykah Badu (yet another product of Booker T. Washington High). Each of these releases was a critical and commercial success; together with *Things Fall Apart,* a 1999 album by the Roots, they formed the basis for the emergent sub-genre of neo soul.

Hargrove's stature as the most prominent jazz ambassador in these ranks was only bolstered when he joined D'Angelo on a world tour, playing to capacity crowds in cavernous rooms including Radio City Music Hall. The band, a millennial R&B wrecking crew dubbed the Soultronics, augmented core *Voodoo* personnel with a passel of equally heavy musicians. The level of intensity was high, and D'Angelo reliably took it higher—like Sly Stone, like James Brown. A groove might grow hypnotic in its repetition, and then turn on a dime. The horn section could duck into a boppish tangent, intricate and furious, before just as suddenly dropping back. Among musicians, word spread: the Voodoo Tour was hailed as a historic tour even as it was still under way.

Speaking in 2003, Hargrove recalled the tour as a spiritual experience. He went on:

> The level of talent that was in the band was crazy. I mean, as far as the singers went, each one of them had their own individual vibe. You know, that lent itself to what D' was doing just perfectly. That all fit in together like a glove. Like a well-fitted suit—you know, tailored and whatnot. And the rhythm section was ridiculous. And then the horn section was all the jazz guys: me and Frank Lacy, Jacques Schwarz-Bart, Russell Gunn. And so, man, you could imagine what was going on behind the scenes when we weren't playing—the kind of interaction because of all the different worlds. You had, like, straight-up church cats. And then you had some guys that were more pop. And then you had jazz. And it was all mixed together, the different vibes. I don't think everybody

really realized what it was when it was going on. But I could see that it was very, very special. It was like a revival.[8]

The reverberations of *Voodoo*—and the Voodoo Tour—were still being felt in the music industry at this time, several years later. Along with a Norah Jones sweep, the 2003 Grammys featured the Roots backing Eminem. If you watched the telecast, you saw Badu, in a Dead Prez T-shirt, accepting Best R&B Song for "Love of My Life (An Ode to Hip Hop)," which featured Common and Raphael Saadiq as guests. More to the point, those Grammys included, for the first time, a category titled Urban/Alternative Performance. If it wasn't obvious enough that the nomenclature was code for "neo soul," the list of nominees made it so. Badu and Common were there. So were Saadiq with D'Angelo; Floetry; CeeLo Green; and India.Arie.

A few hours after the ceremony, nearly everyone in that roll call turned up at B.B. King Blues Club & Grill in Times Square. The occasion was an after-party "Grammy jam" hosted by Common and Badu. The house band included Questlove, Poyser, and Meshell Ndegeocello on electric bass. They kept the groove going without pause for several hours, making effortless segues as guests hopped on and off the stage: Musiq Soulchild and Jaguar Wright; Mos Def and Talib Kweli; Jill Scott and Anthony Hamilton; Q-Tip and Bilal; and of course the evening's hosts, a picture-perfect hip-hop couple at the time. Also making a cameo, on just one tune, was Hargrove. He stepped out of the wings looking almost diffident in the spotlight, and soloed for two tantalizing choruses. The crowd, packed tight on the dance floor, literally hollered and screamed for more. He never returned to the stage, though the music kept going past four a.m.

Several days later I met with Hargrove at the Jazz Gallery, the non-profit performance space in lower Manhattan that he'd helped establish in the mid-nineties. We mostly we talked about his forthcoming album, *Hard Groove*, credited to a new entity he called the RH Factor. Inspired in large part by Hargrove's experience helping to create *Voodoo*, it was similarly recorded at Electric Lady, with Elevado and assistant engineer Steve Mandel at the boards.

There had been little structure imposed on the session, which began with Hargrove and a small coterie of associates, including Ndegeo-cello, keyboardist Marc Cary, and drummer Gene Lake. From this baseline, the project expanded to accommodate dozens of other musicians and countless surprises. Although he had notated some songs on sheet music, and arranged certain ideas in preproduction, Hargrove left ample space for his cohorts to fill. Among them were two Soulquarians, Palladino and Poyser. To preserve a spontaneous mood, Hargrove insisted on cutting only first and second takes. And the foundation of almost every track, featuring two drummers and an array of other sonic layers, was recorded with live instruments in real time.

"The whole thing was just one creative night after another," Hargrove recalled. "The entourage started growing, 'cause people were hearing about us down in the studio. Guys were just dropping by." One such drop-in was Anthony Hamilton, whom Hargrove knew from the Voodoo Tour; he delivered an imploring two-part ballad called "Kwah/Home." Another D'Angelo backup singer, Shelby Johnson, applied her luxurious alto to a soul number titled "How I Know." (She wrote lyrics in a studio hallway.) Jacques Schwarz-Bart played tenor saxophone on a number of tracks and contributed an R&B ballad called "Forget Regret," with vocals by Stephanie McKay. Even Steve Coleman, apprised of the session by bassist Reggie Washington, popped in to record an M-Base-inspired funk workout called "Out of Town."

Other visits had been planned in advance. Several days in, Hargrove welcomed a cadre of "Texas cats," who came to the studio straight from the airport, bags in hand. Among them were the funk-fusion pianist Bernard Wright, the rhythm-and-blues guitar veteran Chalmers "Spanky" Alford, and the session-guitar ace Cornell Dupree. This crowd also included the Keith Anderson Trio, whose other members were drummer Jason Thomas and the keyboardist Bobby Sparks.

Anderson, a tenor saxophonist whose relationship with Hargrove dates back to junior high, framed their contribution in regional terms rather than the language of genre. "Texas musicians have a different approach to playing," he said. "It's not from a mechanical standpoint." Sparks, then a musical director for the contemporary gospel star Kirk Franklin, put it this way: "The way we play is not based upon what we see on paper. It's based all on feeling and listening. And that's how Roy plays." The deep and unforced groove of these Dallas-based musicians, until that point an undocumented strand in Hargrove's musical DNA, would come to define much of the album.

But the most eye-catching contributions on *Hard Groove* were cameos by the marquee names of neo soul. On a track called "Poetry," Q-Tip's rapping, sinewy and self-referential, leads to a smartly realized trumpet dialogue (Hargrove, overdubbed), which in turn leads to the gently beat-tripping final section, featuring a lovely metaphysical hook by Badu.

It so happened that Common was upstairs at Electric Lady's Studio B, mixing his album *Electric Circus*, while Hargrove and crew were downstairs in Studio A. The rapper was lured into a recording booth at around five one morning, and he improvised a nimble freestyle, in one take. (It appears on the album as "Common Free Style.")

D'Angelo's cameo vibrates with a different sort of energy. He entered Studio A after midnight one Sunday, as saxophonist Karl Denson was leading about fifteen musicians in an Afrobeat jam. "He comes in and just starts dancing in the control room, 'cause the energy is so happening," recalled Jason Olaine, a coproducer of the album, who was then an A&R executive for Verve. "Then once the cut's done, he goes in and says hi to everybody. It kind of disintegrates into this hang for the next two hours, where everybody's kicking it on couches and kind of discussing what it is they're going to do." Although Hargrove had prepared a Bill Henderson tune for D'Angelo, they ended up playing an impromptu cover of Funkadelic's "I'll Stay." Cut to tape in a couple of takes, it simmers with late-night sensuality and mystique.

While the improvisational spirit of these sessions was familiar to its jazz participants, the logistics were often foreign. "The whole project was very challenging for me," Hargrove admitted. "Usually when we make jazz records I just go in with the cats and we hit. And play like we're playing a set, and then it's done in a couple of days. But this was a lot more involved."

Olaine, who had produced his share of jazz albums, described the looseness of the project in more harrowing terms. "Honestly, I didn't know what Roy was doing half the time," he said. "I was getting gray hair, seeing days tick by and studio hours getting racked up and tape being rolled, and thinking: 'What are we going to get out of this?'"

Hard Groove was an encouraging answer to that question, if not quite a triumphant one. Neither a neo-soul classic nor a new-school fusion gem, it staked out a hybrid middle ground. The undeniable thing about it was its conviction. Hargrove had set out with something other than a commercial motive, and he put an enormous amount of effort into making it come together—to capture a sound, a social energy, a moment in time.

He wasn't alone, within his cohort, in seeking to reconcile his image with his interests. Christian McBride, a lifelong James Brown fanatic, had flirted with funk on his first two albums. His third, *A Family Affair,* released on Verve in 1998, tilted decisively in that direction, with heavy backbeats and wah-wah electric bass solos. (The title track was a Sly Stone anthem.) McBride then lunged toward fusion, full stop, on his 2000 album *Sci-Fi,* and teamed up with Questlove and the keyboardist Uri Caine for an expressly groove-centric project called the Philadelphia Experiment, which released a self-titled album in 2001. By the time the Christian McBride Band recorded a three-CD set called *Live at Tonic* early in 2005, with guests like Charlie Hunter and DJ Logic, the group's explosive mix of jazz-funk and electronic breakbeats felt reasonable. Few questioned the gall of a former Jazz Future evoking actual jazz futurism.

This scenario repeated itself, with variations, across the former Young Lion spectrum. A gifted generation once defined by dutiful conformity was now coming into its own, intent on renegotiating the terms. Nicholas Payton, a New Orleans trumpeter of spectacular instrumental prowess, followed up an album titled *Dear Louis* (Verve, 2001) with another called *Sonic Trance* (Warner Bros., 2003); his band of the same name, infused with electronics and hip-hop swagger, toured widely, working beyond a jazz-club orbit. The saxophonist James Carter, who'd been hailed as a prodigy in the early nineties, formed a group inspired by Ornette Coleman's harmolodic funk bands of the seventies. And Joshua Redman made *Elastic,* a kind of funk-forward organ trio album. He took the trio on tour, making inroads with a thriving jam-band scene.

The gold standard in that circuit was Medeski Martin & Wood, an endlessly resourceful rhythm team with an equal investment in New Orleans funk, à la the Meters; 1960s soul jazz, like Eddie Harris; and farther-out vibrations, via Sun Ra. Formed in the early nineties, driven by an ethos of spontaneous discovery, and beloved by some of the same hippie-groove fanatics who followed Phish and the Grateful Dead, MM&W had shifted well into a jazz-world orbit by the turn of the century: in 1998 it not only signed to Blue Note Records but also made an album on Verve with the guitarist John Scofield, kicking off an association that would yield several more albums and a succession of popular tours.

So there was a ready appetite for the RH Factor when Hargrove turned it into a touring concern. More and more, it resembled an upgraded fusion band, frenetic but tight, with brand-compatible guests. Verve released an EP, *Strength* (2004), and a follow-up album, *Distractions* (2006). What got lost along the way, probably because it was never Hargrove's mission to begin with, was the specific rhythm magic that had coalesced on *Voodoo*.

The Dilla thing, in other words. It would fall to somebody else to carry that forward.

"J Dillalude" is a four-and-a-half-minute collage of chiming harmony and loopy rhythm that can be found on *In My Element*, a 2007 album by pianist Robert Glasper. The track opens with a voice-mail message from Q-Tip. "Yo, you know what I was thinking?" he says. "You guys should play some Dilla joints, like, trio-style. I think it'd be fresh."

The next voice on the track belongs to Glasper, at a club date introducing his trio mates, bassist Vicente Archer and drummer Damion Reid. He's talking while the trio plays a cooled-out, incantatory vamp, piano chords feathered on the upbeat. The listener is trusted to know the allusion: it's the sonic bed of "Thelonious," a track from Common's *Like Water for Chocolate*. J Dilla had produced "Thelonious" by sampling and slowing down a couple of bars from a vintage fusion track by George Duke. Glasper's trio effortlessly re-creates the loop, and then moves on to other millennial touchstones, like De La Soul's "Stakes Is High" (which Dilla built on a sample of "Swahililand," by Ahmad Jamal) and Slum Village's "Fall in Love" (for which he sampled "Diana in the Autumn Wind," by Gap Mangione).

There's a bit of flexing in "J Dillalude," as if Glasper were waving a flag. But the track doesn't feel out of place on *In My Element*, because he intersperses other interludes and fade-outs that point toward the same coordinates. A rustling waltz called "Of Dreams to Come" finishes with a coda of hypnotic chords and breakbeats; something similar happens at the close of "Beatrice," the Sam Rivers ballad. And "F.T.B." is a track whose lilting melody and skittering beat feel like a Dilla homage even without a telltale source to point to.

Glasper had arrived in New York City from Houston in 1997, to attend the New School. (In Houston, he'd attended the High School for the Performing and Visual Arts, the same institution that produced Jason Moran.) On the first day of his freshman year, Glasper met a vocalist from Philadelphia named Bilal Oliver. They fast became friends, circulating the same handful of scenes. This was the late nineties, so they logged time at Electric Lady Studios during the *Voodoo* sessions, and were present for portions of *Like Water for Chocolate*. Though a few years younger than the Soulquarians, they were obvious kindred spirits.

And when Bilal made his debut album, *1st Born Second*, Glasper was an integral part of the process. He was there when Dilla created the humid, disjointed fever dream of bass and drums on a track called "Reminisce," which featured verses by Mos Def and Common.

"We watched him make that beat," Glasper recalled. "He knew what the song sounded like in his head. The bass line alone is from four different albums. It's three or four notes of four different bass lines."

Glasper grew familiar with Dilla's brand of sorcery, recognizing in it a creative impulse closely related to jazz: "He was an extremely melodic producer. I'd watch him make beats and it would kill me, the stuff he would use. And the way he built his beats had a jazz spine, because it felt like a live drummer messing around. Like, he would just take four bars from the middle of a drum solo, and that's the beat."[9]

This imagination and execution were enough to mark J Dilla as a visionary, but Glasper also knew him as a real-time improviser. There were informal, closed-door jam sessions where he'd be playing Fender Rhodes piano, with Bilal singing freestyle and Dilla tapping beats on an MPC, the hands-on drum machine and sampler manufactured by Akai.

·   ·   ·

Glasper radiates a garrulous, slangy charisma along with his untroubled self-assurance. When I first met him in person, during the 2005 recording session for *Canvas,* his Blue Note debut, I noticed how loose and jocular he was between takes, and how quickly he snapped into focus when it was time to play. Already he was straddling two worlds, backing Q-Tip or Mos Def one night and leading his postbop trio the next. He had joined the RH Factor on its first tour. At the time, Glasper professed no intention of merging jazz and hip-hop in his own music: "I keep them separate because they are two separate things," he said. "Every time I play something, I want to be authentic in it. I don't want to sound like I'm playing *at* jazz, or sound like I'm playing *at* hip-hop."[10]

But his hemispheres were already beginning to bleed into one another, defying an either/or dichotomy, on *In My Element.* J Dilla had a lot to do with that. By 2007, one year after the producer's untimely death, it had become fashionable in progressive hip-hop to drop his name, if not his beats, as a signifier of taste. He was a less familiar reference point in jazz, despite some direct connections. The first of many posthumous releases bearing J Dilla's name was *The Shining,* which he'd almost completed before his death; its finishing touches were entrusted to a close friend and fellow Detroit producer, Karriem Riggins, also known as a first-rate jazz drummer. Riggins had been working with Common and others, as a producer and a drummer, even as he kept up notable sideman affiliations with the pianist Mulgrew Miller and the bassist Ray Brown.

While his main outlet was still the acoustic trio, Glasper had been messing around with tricked-out R&B hybridism on the side. He reconnected with a friend from Houston, the virtuoso drummer Chris Dave, and brought in the saxophonist Casey Benjamin, who doubled on vocoder. The last piece of the puzzle was Derrick Hodge, a bassist and composer who had come up around the Philadelphia scene, playing jazz, gospel, and soul. Hodge was a member of the Mulgrew Miller Trio, alongside Riggins; he also worked with the trumpeter Terence Blanchard, in a band full of hyper-proficient young players with no hangups about genre.

The Robert Glasper Experiment grew out of a series of freewheeling underground club gigs, coalescing around the lineup of Glasper, Benjamin, Hodge, and Dave. The band's proficiency and style-blending flexibility made it an instant draw in the bohemian sector of hip-hop and R&B. When the neo-soul singer-songwriter Maxwell made his high-profile return to performing in 2009, the band he took on tour was a modified version of the Robert Glasper Experiment, with Hodge as band director. More than one observer likened the level of musicianship and spirit in Maxwell's arena retinue with that of the Soultronics on the Voodoo Tour.

Glasper released his third Blue Note album around this time, calling it *Double Booked.* The Experiment appeared on the second half, following a first half by the trio. "I wanted to express what was going on with me at that time: touring with Maxwell or Mos Def but playing at the Village Vanguard also, in the same week," Glasper explained.[11] So the title was literal. But it would be reductive to say the album showed two sides of his personality, because Glasper was just as expressive with his hip-hop affinities in the acoustic trio as he was in the Experiment. A trio arrangement of Thelonious Monk's "Think of One," for instance, interpolates the vamp from "Stakes Is High." That ability to emulate a Dilla track without sounding self-conscious or forced—something that had become an issue in certain jazz circles—was still a point of pride for Glasper. "Nobody plays Dilla like us," he told me. "End quote."[12]

But he wasn't just seeking a vehicle for tribute. When he conceived the first full album by the Experiment, he set out to synthesize the full range of music he'd been involved with over the years: state-of-the-art acoustic jazz, underground hip-hop, organic R&B. That album— *Black Radio,* released on Blue Note in early 2012—featured an array of guest vocalists, including the rapper Lupe Fiasco and the singers Lalah Hathaway and Ledisi. The album was made in four days with almost no overdubs, making it all the more impressive how much the music could sound fully produced. A version of "Afro Blue" has Erykah Badu over a head-bobbing groove, a light patter of keyboards, and an ethereal waft of flutes; it could pass for a fresh Dilla production.

Black Radio won the Grammy for Best R&B Album in 2013, upsetting a field that included R. Kelly, one of the genre's biggest stars, and Anthony Hamilton, one of its most admired. The scale of the surprise could be judged by the placement of Glasper and his bandmates in the auditorium: they were seated so far back in Los Angeles's Staples

Center that the camera operator had to swoop around to find them. It took the band a full minute to reach the stage, at which point Glasper was apparently still in shock. "Thank you for allowing us to play real music," he said from the podium, "and to play what we really feel from our heart."

The success of *Black Radio*, in commercial as well as institutional terms, quickly led to a sequel. Glasper stocked *Black Radio 2* with another elite assemblage of talent, including Snoop Dogg, Common, Norah Jones, and Jill Scott. This album yielded a Grammy too. (By then, Chris Dave had left the Experiment for his own groove laboratory, the Drumheadz; his replacement was Mark Colenburg, whom Glasper had recommended to Common years earlier.) The Experiment released a third album, *ArtScience*, in 2016, and on some level it signaled a show of force: there were no guests this time around, as if the band no longer needed the extra shine.

As Glasper gained more visibility, he made a point of speaking out about jazz's failure to reach a broader public. One central problem, as he saw it, is that jazz musicians had grown accustomed to playing more for one another than for the lay listener, boosting the music's complex obscurities at the expense of clarity and emotion. He saw the Experiment as one solution to that problem, especially as its influence began to spread among younger players—something he noticed, traveling around the country to various schools.

"After we won the Grammy, I think it opened a lot of minds, it opened a lot of doors for other people who are doing shit that's not mainstream," he said. "You have to do it like D'Angelo did it. He said fuck it—and *boom*, that became the neo-soul movement. And I think we're the second coming of that. Because neo soul had a nice wave in 2000, all these artists started coming through. I think we're the start of this new sound that is coming from the blood of that era."[13]

One year after Glasper and his crew pulled a dark-horse win for Best R&B Album at the Grammys, something analogous happened in the category of Best R&B Performance. From a nominee pool that included Anthony Hamilton and Tamar Braxton, the winner in 2014 was an upstart jazz-funk band called Snarky Puppy, for a track featuring vocals by Lalah Hathaway.

The track was a cover of "It's Something!"—from an early-eighties album cut by the quiet-storm R&B singer Brenda Russell. And the key to how it won Best R&B Performance probably rested in the last word of the category, "performance." Hathaway, whose father was the transcendent singer-songwriter Donny Hathaway, begins at a low, slow simmer and gradually dials up the intensity through a series of improvised "aah"s, "whoa"s, and "ooh"s. She's scatting, very much like a jazz singer, over a cycle of chords that seems to keep lifting her skyward.

Snarky Puppy had developed an ingenious custom of recording its albums live in a studio setting, with an intimate audience wearing headphones patched into the board mix. The band made a point of filming these sessions and posting the videos online—partly as a means of self-promotion and partly to prove that no tricks or shortcuts were involved. Hathaway's performance of "Something," from the album *Family Dinner, Volume One,* took place in an ornate 1920s auditorium, but with the audience seated onstage, around the band.

Watching this footage, as some Grammy voters presumably did, it's impossible to miss how in tune the musicians are with Hathaway's dynamics and phrasing. And when, after more than six minutes of steady buildup, she flips into her head voice and sings a split-tone multiphonic chord, you see members of the band reacting with awestruck glee. She repeats this otherworldly vocal flourish, slotting her "chord" into the harmonic progression of the song, and this time the musicians lose all composure: laughing and hooting in disbelief, jumping up and down. It's a moment of extravagant vocal command, teed up perfectly by the band. (It probably changed the industry perception of Hathaway, who won Grammys in each of the next two years, including another for Best R&B Performance, backed by the Robert Glasper Experiment.)

There were many in the jazz world who had never heard of Snarky Puppy in 2014, though the band had been on its grind at that point for a decade: crisscrossing the country in vans, sleeping on floors and in sketchy motels, amassing a fan network in ways both newfangled and old-fashioned. The band's raging subcultural success was reminiscent of that moment, around the turn of the century, when jazz musicians were heavily mingling with jam bands—playing to crowds that lived for the spark of improvisation but had no taste for a quiet policy and two-drink minimum.

But Snarky Puppy wasn't really a jam band, a point perhaps best articulated by Charlie Hunter, who played with his share of them in the early 2000s. "Almost all of them were not really ready as musicians, but their business sense was unbelievable," he said. "I was telling my friends at the time: 'You know what? This is a drag, to be here and have to listen to this every night. But I tell you, one day, someone who can really play music is going to figure this out.'"[14] By his estimation, Snarky Puppy had been the band to finally answer that call.

The band's origins suggest a fortuitous alignment of formal training and casual application. Michael League was a bassist struggling through the rigorous jazz program at the University of North Texas when he got nine friends together to play a regular session. Their early gigs were at coffee shops and the basement of a pizza place. League was already writing fusionesque music with a foundation in groove, but he made a crucial leap forward under the wing of an unlikely mentor: the keyboardist Bernard Wright, one of Hargrove's "Texas cats."

A former session ace turned crossover R&B artist who had moved from New York to Dallas, Wright played a regular gig at Riverwalk Fellowship Church, in Haltom City, a suburb of Fort Worth. Through a contact made at a jam session, League started playing there too, initially taken aback both by the high level of play and the intensity of connection with the congregation.

"It was basically Roy Hargrove's RH Factor," League recalled of the Riverwalk Fellowship band personnel. Eventually he brought some of his North Texas colleagues into the fold, playing several services a week. "So that's where the web kind of expanded, and where the music went from white jazz-school stuff to something much groovier, much funkier, much more communicative with the audience. Less nerdy."[15]

Snarky Puppy developed a brawny but hair-trigger-responsive style, and a high bar for group cohesion. The question of where its music fell on the jazz spectrum was, at best, a tertiary concern. But the sound of the group owed plenty to the jazz tradition, especially if your idea of that tradition extended to, say, Weather Report. A League composition like "Lingus" suggests a contraption made up of whirring parts, arranged in a way that feels like clockwork but allows for stretching out at strategic junctures. The video for "Lingus," from the 2014 album *We Like It Here*, became a must-see in musician circles precisely because of a blazing and harmonically venturesome synthesizer solo by Cory Henry. The band's chief drummer, Robert "Sput" Searight, was also a regular source of wonderment, with a diehard following in both hip-hop circles and music schools. League's core achievement was in forming a flexible framework that could accommodate this level of virtuosity without becoming simply a fireworks show.

Whether the band "belonged" to jazz or not, the jazz establishment put up relatively little resistance to Snarky Puppy. This may have been a result of market forces: it was voted Jazz Group of the Year in the 2015 DownBeat Readers Poll. It appeared on the magazine's cover the following year, a few months before playing the main stage at the Newport Jazz Festival. For his part, League expressed no pretensions about the band's music, instead describing it, accurately, in terms of catchiness and groove. (The best comparison wasn't to Weather Report, in fact, so much as to a hook-laden band like the Crusaders.)

"Did I think we would ever win a Grammy?" League said during a conversation over coffee in 2016. "Of course not. Did I think we would ever sell four thousand tickets? I never expected or thought of that, but I planned for it, always. It's like, if you don't plan for it, it won't happen. You don't have to expect it or feel like you deserve it, or even want it. But be ready."

At that moment, the coffee shop playlist landed on something familiar: "Playa Playa," the opening track from D'Angelo's *Voodoo*. League chuckled. "It's going to be difficult for me to speak while this is playing," he said.[16]

Even more than most successful jam bands, Snarky Puppy mobilized its influence—starting a label imprint, GroundUP, to release its own music as well as solo albums by band members and efforts by friends like Hunter and the singer-songwriter Becca Stevens. League produced a series of albums for the label, including one by the folksinger David Crosby, who'd become a passionate fan of Snarky Puppy after watching their videos on YouTube. Beginning in 2017, the band also presented a GroundUP Music Festival, taking over a patch of Miami Beach for several days with a lineup that included jazz musicians like Terence

Blanchard and John Medeski. Among the artists in the 2018 edition were Glasper, Joshua Redman, and the electronic-meets-analog entity known as Mark Guiliana's Beat Music: jazz players laying in the pocket, in a way that felt free of cynical compromise but expressly concerned with making bodies move.

Mark Guiliana's Beat Music is a prime example of the new rhythm genius finding expression among improvisers in the new century. Guiliana, a jazz-trained drummer who combines an aerial view with a microscopic attention to detail, formed Beat Music with the idea of exploring ideas from progressive electronic music: in interviews, he liked to cite the trippy UK beatmakers Squarepusher and Aphex Twin in the same breath as the jazz drummer Tony Williams. Much like Chris Dave, Guiliana became a cult hero, the sort of player that other drummers, in whatever genre, couldn't stop obsessing over. He was also similarly in demand as a collaborator; he had a regular hookup with the keyboardist Jason Lindner, and Brad Mehldau sought him out for a duo project, Mehliana, eventually releasing an album by that name.

To the extent that there was an intrepid new wave of fusion at ground level, its creative locus had little to do with Snarky Puppy. One of the driving forces was Kneebody, another band that originally came together through a conservatory connection but built momentum through word of mouth. Most of the band—trumpeter Shane Endsley, keyboardist Adam Benjamin, multireedist Ben Wendel, and bassist Kaveh Rastegar—first met at the Eastman School of Music in the late nineties. Kneebody officially came together later, in Los Angeles, with the addition of drummer and producer Nate Wood. The band created its own niche with a convergence of strategies pulled from indie rock, hip-hop, electropop, and chamber music. (As with the West Coast Get Down, members of Kneebody held a range of sideman affiliations.) The band's following, like its music, couldn't be pinned down to one scene. But if you had to point to the musical lineage best suited to accommodate the music of Kneebody, it would be fusion.

A separate but related movement was taking shape during the early 2000s at the 55 Bar, a narrow, garden-level Prohibition-era dive in Greenwich Village, next door to the Stonewall Inn. The signature vibe in the room was an aggressive but consonant progressivism, often but not always rock-infused. The Robert Glasper Experiment played some of its early, freewheeling shows at the 55 Bar. The jazz-rock guitarists Mike Stern, Leni Stern, and Wayne Krantz held regular court there, packing the place with awestruck young admirers. So did David Binney, an alto saxophonist and composer with a taste for incendiary catharsis and a working quartet featuring Jacob Sacks on keyboards, Thomas Morgan on bass, and Dan Weiss on drums.

Chris Potter, the dauntingly proficient saxophonist, had been drawing closer to rock and funk since the early 2000s, when he established an affiliation with Steely Dan. The band's first studio album in two decades, *Two Against Nature,* featured him knocking out the sort of tersely bracketed eight-bar solos that were commonplace in the big-band era but had all but disappeared in modern jazz. (It won Album of the Year at the Grammys in 2001.) Potter had begun thinking about how to apply postbop flexibilities to a fusion setting, and to that end he formed a band with Craig Taborn on Fender Rhodes piano, Adam Rogers on electric guitar, and Nate Smith on drums.

Potter called this band Underground, a nod to the 55 Bar, where it found its purpose and its audience. (The cover of its first, self-titled album, released in 2006, features a photograph of Potter sitting in a corner of the club, his tenor saxophone on the tabletop beside him.) While the rhythmic drive of this music relied on a straight eighth-note cadence, like a rock band, the internal dynamics reflected a state-of-the-art jazz sensibility. The band put equal weight on power and precision, with each member of the group making constant micro-adjustments to the output of the others. In its ability to work up a rhythmic vamp to heroic scale, the band was working with strategies epitomized not by fusion groups so much as by the John Coltrane Quartet.

There were, of course, more direct and recent influences on the band's style. David Binney's storm-surge aesthetic was one. Another was an experimental unit led for the previous several years by Tim Berne—a brilliant, bass-less foursome called Science Friction, which also relied on the slashing interplay between Taborn's electric keyboards, an assertive drummer (Tom Rainey), and a fiery electric guitarist (Marc Ducret). When I first heard Underground, it struck me that

Potter had adapted Berne's formula to a situation with more science and less friction. But these emulative aspects of the band wore off, as Underground came into its own.

Potter wasn't the only postbop tenor terror pivoting toward back-beats and distortion. Donny McCaslin, who had replaced Potter in the Dave Douglas Quintet, was beginning to develop his own music in this vein. McCaslin was no stranger to fusion, having toured for several years with Steps Ahead. But it was the exhortation of Binney, a close collaborator, that tilted McCaslin's hand. He formed a group with Lindner, Guiliana, and the electric bassist Tim Lefebvre, whose many sideman appointments included a spot in Wayne Krantz's trio. The Donny McCaslin Quartet joined the David Binney Quartet and Chris Potter's Underground as defining forces in a tightly knit jazz-rock boomlet in New York.

The sound of this scene was carried far and wide by a fortuitous association. One night in 2014, David Bowie, acting on a tip from Maria Schneider, went to the 55 Bar to hear the Donny McCaslin Quartet. Bowie, the chameleonic rock legend, was so impressed by the vaulting energy of the band that he designed his next album, *Blackstar*, around it. According to Tony Visconti, Bowie's longtime producer, the band's intense combustion served as an aspirational model: to prepare for the recording session, they listened to albums by the Donny McCaslin Quartet as well as Mark Guiliana's Beat Music. ("And we watched their YouTube videos," Visconti said. "We were spying on them. David said to me, 'Really listen a lot to this, and get in your mind how they work.'")[17]

Though it wasn't obvious in the music, Bowie had also been inspired by Kendrick Lamar's *To Pimp a Butterfly*—mainly in the way that it defied the conventions of a hip-hop album, making use of a furious live energy from its musicians. Eager to capture a similar energy, he recorded *Blackstar* with almost the entire band playing in one room. (McCaslin tracked his solos in an isolation booth.) Bowie stood among the musicians on the studio floor, belting the songs live even though those vocal takes, riddled with sound bleed, would have to be scrapped. That commitment was striking to all of the musicians—especially after it emerged that Bowie was gravely sick during the making of the album. Released just a few days before his death of liver cancer, it was hailed as a valedictory triumph. McCaslin and his band, meanwhile, gained something deeper than notoriety: they were the handpicked acolytes, to be forever enshrined as "Bowie's last band."

The new rhythm science in jazz—postfusion, post-Dilla, more or less postmodern—wasn't just a posture to strike on the bandstand. It was also a production model. And one thing that began to change, in clear and salutary ways, was the artistic intention that jazz musicians were bringing to the sound of their recordings. At the extreme end of this spectrum sat Flying Lotus, an electronic producer, DJ, rapper, and filmmaker from Los Angeles. A linchpin and lodestar among postmillennial Afrofuturists—soul-forward, syncretic, irreverent but earnest—he emerged in the electronic-music underground, eventually breaking through to the indie mainstream. His third album, *Cosmogramma*, released in 2010 on the British label Warp, met with near-universal acclaim, not only for its audacious atmospheric canvas but also for its tether to an organic experimental tradition. Flying Lotus, born Steven Ellison, was in fact carrying on a supercharged family legacy: his great-aunt was Alice Coltrane, who had directly inspired *Cosmogramma*. Her oldest son, Ellison's cousin Ravi Coltrane, even played tenor saxophone on a couple of tracks, including one titled "Arkestry," a nod to the Sun Ra Arkestra.

Flying Lotus was tangentially dialed into the upstart Los Angeles jazz scene: one of his closest collaborators was Thundercat, the electric bass phenom and falsetto specialist affiliated with the West Coast Get Down. *Until the Quiet Comes*, the album that followed *Cosmogramma*, finds a place of prominence for Thundercat, along with guest spots for Erykah Badu and Thom Yorke of Radiohead. A track called "DMT Song" features Thundercat's vocals drifting through an ethereal dreamscape. One of the song's credited composers, along with Flying Lotus and Thundercat, was the prepossessing twenty-two-year-old jazz pianist Austin Peralta, who died two months after the album's release in 2012, of viral pneumonia aggravated by substance abuse.

The shock of Peralta's death forms an unspoken backdrop to *You're Dead!*, which Flying Lotus released two years later. (Actually, not entirely unspoken: a track called "The Boys Who Died in Their Sleep" is offered in elegiac tribute.) A forty-minute fantasia of psychedelic fusions, *You're Dead!* boldly blends programming with live musicians, producing a sensation of human convergence. Herbie Hancock turns up as a guest eminence, rippling dark arpeggios on a Fender Rhodes. And Kamasi Washington, who had yet to release *The Epic,* makes a strong impression: his tenor saxophone is prominent on several tracks, sonically focused and rhythmically sure.

Flying Lotus had intended *You're Dead!* as a jazz statement, in a manner of speaking. This wasn't merely a matter of surface texture, or contingent on those cameos. He saw the album as an insubordinate push against reigning orthodoxies in the music, especially those still mired in conservationism. He revered the brash mid-1970s fusion of George Duke and Miles Davis, and thought it could be brought into useful contact with contemporary forces. "Just as an outsider looking in," he said, "I saw an opportunity to make something I hadn't really heard before."[18]

A similar motivation drove myriad other projects with a foothold in groove. The smarter of these amounted to much more than horn solos over a backbeat. For a coalition of artists—like the trumpeters Maurice Brown, Keyon Harrold, and Takuya Kuroda; the vocalists José James and Taylor McFerrin; and the producers Raydar Ellis and BIGYUKI— contemporary hip-hop, R&B, and soul vibrated on the same cosmic frequencies as state-of-the-art jazz.

In New York City, the multifaceted organization Revive Music, founded in 2006 by an enterprising Berklee graduate named Meghan Stabile, became a vital conduit for this aesthetic. Revive Music booked and presented concerts, solidifying the center of a scene that could otherwise feel slippery and diffuse. The organization also generated its own enthusiastic coverage in an online zine, at revive-music.com. There was something insular and boosterish about the whole Revive Music circle, but it established a crucial bond with young crossover audiences, and formalized a genuine convergence between various strains of black music. The Revive Big Band, led by the trumpeter Igmar Thomas, served as a house exemplar for the cause. And while Stabile's organization operated on a modest scale, its reach was resounding: in 2015, a compilation album called *Revive Music Presents: Supreme Sonacy Vol. 1* was released in partnership with Blue Note Records.

There were analogous stirrings in other scenes. Across the Atlantic, an organization called Jazz Re:freshed, which began as a live weekly series in London's Notting Hill neighborhood, suggested something like a UK answer to Revive Music. (Its stable of artists included stylish hybridists like the saxophonist Nubya Garcia and the keyboardist and producer Kaidi Tatham.) And more than a few American musicians outside the New York circuit worked in this mode, on record and in performance. Sometimes they worked in stages: recording an improvised jam, splicing the results into a coherent track, and then re-creating the edit on the bandstand.

Two of the best jazz albums of 2016 made use of this recursive funhouse logic, both released on the Chicago label International Anthem. One was *In the Moment,* which the drummer Makaya McCraven had stitched together from some fifty hours of tape, gathered over the course of a yearlong club residency. The music on the album is groove-forward and humid, with an almost tactile sound mix. Discrete compositional elements burble up and fade out, one into the next: what feels like an ambient hip-hop track might take an unexpected turn into a postbop side alley. The core musicians on the album are McCraven's bandmates in the Marquis Hill Blacktet, whose leader, an incisive trumpeter, had won first prize in the Thelonious Monk International Jazz Competition. One track, "Lonely," uses Hill's boppish phraseology as a head fake, moving on to a bobbing vamp over which Jeff Parker etches a cool, contrarian guitar solo.

Parker, a longtime member of the influential Chicago postrock band Tortoise, made the other standout album in this vein, *The New Breed.* It came from a small trove of old home recordings and beat-centric tracks that he'd rediscovered after moving to Los Angeles. He fleshed out some of these scraps into compositions, and then convened a band: the multireedist Josh Johnson, the drummer Jamire Williams, and the bassist Paul Bryan, who also engineered, mixed, and helped produce the sessions. The result is a sort of farm-to-table instrumental hip-hop album—reminiscent of a producer sampling 1970s soul-jazz, but with a live band playing the samples while keeping a boom-bap idea in mind. In addition to electric guitar, Parker is credited as playing Wurlitzer electric piano, Mellotron, Korg synthesizer, and assorted samplers on the album, along with drum programming. But the results are soulful and seamless.

These albums—and their successors, like *Highly Rare,* which McCraven released on limited-edition cassette and vinyl in 2017—threw open a door that had first been unlocked in the original J Dilla era. And no one was more ahead of that curve than Karriem Riggins, who wasn't just a friend of Dilla's but also perhaps his rightful heir.

I first noticed Riggins's producer credit on *Like Water for Chocolate,* from the Electric Lady sessions around the turn of the century. But I took proper measure of his prowess only when Common released his follow-up, *Electric Circus,* in 2002. One of the best tracks is a Riggins production, "The Hustle," which manages to be both woozy and rock-solid in its approach to groove. The album's cover illustration is a *Sgt. Pepper*–style collage featuring a crowd of contributors and patron saints; Riggins is in the lower-right corner, above the black-and-white Parental Advisory logo.

If it was difficult to reconcile this renegade as the same person who apprenticed with Ray Brown, the giant redwood of postwar jazz bassists, Riggins didn't ease the cognitive dissonance. When we spoke in 2012, he had recently logged a sideman credit on *Kisses on the Bottom,* the gold-plated standards album by Sir Paul McCartney. He was also fresh off a three-month stretch on the road with Diana Krall, whom he had originally met through Brown.

What we talked about was his impressive solo debut, *Alone Together,* an instrumental hip-hop album that he produced entirely himself. Riggins had created many of the album's tracks on Krall's tour bus, using portable sampling and sequencing workstations like Akai's MPC 5000 and Native Instruments' Maschine. When I asked, half-joking, whether the music on Krall's tour had influenced his beats, he was quick with a surprising reply: "Most definitely."[19] Many of the ideas on the album, he said, had originated onstage with Krall and her band. One track, "Alto Flute," includes a sample of a wicked bass ostinato by Robert Hurst, tossed off during a sound check and recorded with Riggins's iPhone.

There's no overt trace of swing on *Alone Together,* but that's not to say it isn't swinging. The tracks, which average two minutes but flow seamlessly one into the next, represent a series of meditations on groove. "Esperanza" features an array of twinkling timbres—pizzicato strings, tongue-slurred flute, what sounds like sitar—that come together like delicate clockwork. "A7 Mix" has the annunciatory energy of an early fusion overture. "Double Trouble" layers vibraphone, bass, flutes, and percussion in an ascending array that suggests Tortoise.

What's striking throughout is the human feel behind the mechanized detail, and the surprising amount of melody that slips into the picture. The only moment when Riggins cuts loose on drums is the closer, "J Dilla the Greatest," with polyrhythmic snare and cymbal work that strongly evokes his Detroit drumming lodestar, Elvin Jones.

Riggins released a follow-up to *Alone Together* in 2017, calling it *Head-nod Suite*. This album edges more into straight hip-hop, with an hour's worth of beats that feel like readymades for ambitious rappers. Some tracks chirp, while others ooze; the sonic impression is trippy and fluid. At the center of the album is a succession of four tracks identified as *Cheap Suite*, with samples lifted from eight-bit video games. A track called "Yes Yes Y'all" features a gummy, slowed-down sample of the title phrase over a disjointed beat; it ends with a snippet of Common scatting over a walking bass line, recorded with Riggins's band at the Detroit Jazz Festival.

Riggins re-created those conditions at the 2017 edition of the festival, anchoring a band with Glasper on keyboards and Burniss Earl Travis on bass. Common rapped throughout the set, at one point devising a rousing and site-specific freestyle; in a sense, this was a premonition of August Greene, the hip-hop supergroup that Riggins, Glasper, and Common would unveil early the following year. Still, the high point of the set came in a delirious throwback vein—when Common dug into "The Light," a single from *Like Water for Chocolate*, with Riggins and company expertly nailing the slanted grace, and extending the implications, of a J Dilla groove.

––––––––––

Flying Lotus, *You're Dead!* (Warp)
Robert Glasper Experiment, *Black Radio* (Blue Note)
Roy Hargrove Presents the RH Factor, *Hard Groove* (Verve)
Jeff Parker, *The New Breed* (International Anthem)
REVIVE Music Presents: Supreme Sonacy (Vol. 1) (Blue Note)

10

Exposures

By eleven a.m. Thursday she was writing lyrics on the wall. Slanted blocks of text, all caps, some phrases already crossed out or circled. A wide scroll of butcher paper had been taped to the wall, and the felt tip of her black marker made soft scratchy noises as she scribbled, hurriedly, as if taking notation from an unheard voice.

This was Esperanza Spalding—the irrepressible bassist, singer-songwriter, and composer-bandleader—making her fifth album, *Exposure,* in a Los Angeles recording studio. The entire session was streaming live online, in a multicam feed viewed by as many as a few thousand people at a time; while Spalding wrote her lyrics, a chyron at the bottom of the browser window read 50 HOURS IN. What this meant was that she hadn't left the studio compound in more than two full days, and still had about a day to go. This, of course, was all by purposeful design.

Few jazz musicians have ever been more comfortable in the spotlight than Spalding, and the creation of *Exposure,* in mid-September of 2017, showed how deftly she bends that spotlight to her uses. The project—part marathon recording session, part performance-art Happening, part *Truman Show*-style surveillance ploy—put her in the studio for an uninterrupted seventy-seven hours, ostensibly without so much as a scrap of premeditated material. Spalding's only advance preparation had been to schedule time with her bandmates, along with some featured guests, like the powerhouse vocalist Lalah Hathaway, the keyboardist Robert Glasper, and the violinist and singer-songwriter Andrew Bird. They came and went while Spalding stayed put, musing or tinkering in those ample moments when she wasn't tracking parts.

The unusual constraints of the project led her to approach things differently. She began the recording session not at her bass, laying the foundation of a song, but rather on the microphone, inventing top-line flourishes. She was seated on a greenroom couch, singing wordless hooks and phrases that she then fastidiously multitracked into the contours of a song, like a spider weaving filaments into a web.

Spalding has the animated charisma of a precocious student in a gifted-and-talented program, which may well be the by-product of lived experience. She was a frank, disarming, and weirdly magnetic presence throughout her studio residency, even in the long stretches that amounted to one or another form of drudgery. By three p.m. Pacific Time on Wednesday (30 HOURS IN), she could be seen at a white-lacquered upright piano in what resembled a utility closet, obsessively worrying two or three bars of a serpentine line. She seemed tired. Her hair was tied back, her posture slumped. She kept clearing her throat. That little tendril of melody, spiky with tritone dissonance, was ungainly. She hammered away at that irksome phrase for over an hour.

Other moments during *Exposure* fell closer to a conventional recording session. A visitor checking the stream around hour thirty-nine would have caught Spalding laying instrumental tracks with Glasper, keyboardist Ray Angry, drummer Justin Tyson, and guitarist Matthew Stevens. They were playing the final take of one of her new inventions, a major-key reverie in floating waltz time. She sang instructions, calling audibles, as they played. This action was suitable for a highlight reel; one bootleg video lifted from the stream, seven and a half minutes in duration, quickly racked up more than a hundred thousand views on YouTube.

The larger motivation behind *Exposure* was twofold. On the one hand, it was an experiment in spartan creative focus, and a tribute to the almighty power of a deadline. "There's no editing," Spalding declared in one of the video teasers for the project, posted to social media. "There's no tweaking, fixing, planning, prepping." She seemed excited by this beat-the-buzzer aspect of her self-imposed challenge—convinced that the added pressure could only result in a finer result, a diamond crushed from a lump of coal.

On the other hand, of course, *Exposure* was a canny publicity stunt—a way into the public conversation at a time when one usually had to shout to be heard. A couple of days before the countdown clock began, she performed a spontaneous, hour-long duet with the architect Frank Gehry. The session, streamed on Facebook courtesy of *Architectural Digest*, took place in a light-filled atrium of Gehry's home studio in Los Angeles. While Spalding sang and played, he sketched at an easel. (His charcoal line drawings, conveying a sort of loose, noodly panache, were later auctioned for charity along with a recording of her improvisations.)

So it was a gimmick, yes. But even a viewer predisposed toward cynicism would have had to admit that something audacious was afoot. *Exposure* was the rare peek behind the curtain that managed not to be demystifying, because it rested on a bedrock faith that Spalding was in possession of all the tools—the wit, the stamina, the creative fortitude—to come out looking sharp. It also employed a useful strategy familiar to teachers and magicians alike: show your work.

On her final night in the studio, at 9:05 Pacific Time, Spalding finalized the form of an intimate ballad, alone in the booth with her bass. "Okay, I have the last song," she said, to no one and everyone. She paused. "Let's go ahead and grab this last song," she said to her engineer. "I'll just do it, no click, just bass and voice, so I can get it." Moments later, it was in the can: a love song, flowery but firm, with an elegant melody girded by a disarming clarity of intention. The title, she decided out loud, would be "I Do."

The next day, after she'd stolen a few hours of sleep and recorded some finishing vocal tracks, the production of her new album ended with this very song. Someone popped a bottle and handed her a flute of champagne, at which point she broke the fourth wall one last time.

"It was weird and wonderful," she said of the whole studio experiment. "I had no idea what we were doing, and I didn't even fully understand why, but I felt there was some magic to be conjured in the immediacy of creating, creating without any place to hide."

Then she emerged, blinking, into the daylight. Outside the gate to the studio parking lot, a crowd of strangers, tipped off by her management, had assembled to surprise her with a congratulatory clamor.

The first time "Esperanza Spalding" became a social media trending topic, it was fueled in part by indignant astonishment. This was on the evening of February 13, 2011, when Spalding upset the field to win Best New Artist at the 53rd Annual Grammy Awards. The other nominees in the category were more familiar, in pop-culture terms, by several orders of magnitude. Along with the thump-and-strum folk-rockers Mumford & Sons and Florence + the Machine, they included Drake, then the glummest prom date in hip-hop, and Justin Bieber, a pop-R&B heartthrob inhabiting the body of a child. It was Bieber's hardcore fan base—the Beliebers—who put in the hard work to make Spalding's name go viral, with a generous accompaniment of sputtering invective.

Spalding seemed as surprised as anyone when she walked onstage to accept her honor, in pink platform heels and a citron gown of deconstructed chiffon. "Thank you to the academy for even nominating me in this category," she said on reaching the podium. "Thank you to the incredible community and family of musicians I'm so blessed to be a part of."[1] Her words conveyed not only gracious humility but also a sense of tribal belonging.

For any jazz observer, the moment evoked another recent Grammy memory: Herbie Hancock's dark-horse triumph at the 2008 awards, when *River: The Joni Letters* took home Album of the Year. (The marquee competition in that nominee pool came from *Back to Black,* by Amy Winehouse, and *Graduation,* by Kanye West—each a classic of its kind.) "I'd like to thank the academy for courageously breaking the mold this time," Hancock said after gathering his composure, "and in doing so, honor[ing] the giants upon whose shoulders I stand—some of whom, like Miles Davis, John Coltrane—unquestionably deserved this award in the past."

Hancock was obviously a special case: not just one of the finest pianists of his generation but also a distinguished elder and a crossover pioneer, precisely the sort of guy to earn the trust of the Recording Academy establishment. At the 53rd Grammys, hours before Spalding's coup, he snagged two awards himself, Best Improvised Jazz Solo and Best Pop Collaboration with Vocals, for an all-star event album called *The Imagine Project*.

Spalding stood at a different place on the career continuum in 2011. But like Hancock, she had the benefit of spectacular proficiency, a boundless musical concept, and the ability to reach audiences both highbrow and *hoi polloi*. She was twenty-six, but hardly green. She had performed by request at both the White House and the Nobel Peace Prize ceremony. She'd been the face of a Banana Republic ad campaign. She'd been handpicked by Prince to open a spate of his arena shows. One full year before stepping onto the Grammy stage, she was the subject of a glowing profile in *The New Yorker*—an honor extended to the smallest handful of jazz musicians.

More important than any of this, though, was the regard that Spalding had earned in her field. Born and raised in Portland, Oregon, the second child of a mixed-race single mother, she'd shown early musical promise: her lightbulb moment came at age five, when she saw cellist Yo-Yo Ma perform on an episode of *Mister Rogers' Neighborhood*. She began playing violin in a free community orchestra, the Chamber Music Society of Oregon, and was its concertmaster by age fifteen. Once she took up the bass, discovering an instant communion with the instrument, she worked her way into Portland's close-knit jazz scene; her mentor was a trumpeter named Thara Memory, a taskmaster who pushed her to strive beyond the dimensions of her natural talent.

Spalding attended a private arts high school on scholarship, but dropped out before graduating. She accepted an invitation to study music at Portland State University, where her teachers quickly recognized her gift, recommending that she apply to the Berklee College of Music in Boston. Berklee offered another full scholarship, and she enrolled in 2002.

During her first semester she was placed in an advanced ensemble class led by the saxophonist Joe Lovano. "From the first tune we played together, I felt like she contributed to the music," he later recalled. "She had a beautiful, flowing feel, and she played with a real melodic approach within the bass part, right away. She made me feel like playing."[2] Lovano continued working with Spalding in school ensembles, and then took her out on tour. I first saw her in person on a Lovano gig in 2006, breezily anchoring a quartet alongside the Cuban drummer Francisco Mela, another Berklee discovery, and a veteran pianist, James Weidman. (This personnel would eventually morph—with the addition of a second drummer, Otis Brown III—into the excellent working band Us Five.)

Spalding released the first album under her name in 2006: a springy, cosmopolitan trio outing called *Junjo*, featuring Mela and another proficient Cuban, the pianist Aruán Ortiz. Released on AYVA Musica, a small label in Barcelona, the album served as an official notice of arrival. The bass was at the heart of the enterprise, and while Spalding hadn't yet nailed down the finer points of her intonation, she sounded both rooted and buoyant. She also sang on almost every track—mainly in a wordless patter, deploying her clear, light-gauge vocal timbre as a dynamic frontline instrument. When she did sing lyrics, they were in Spanish—notably on a spare, bass-and-vocal arrangement of "Cantora de Yala," an Argentine folk song by Gustavo "Cuchi" Leguizamón and Manuel Castilla. Like the rest of the album, it radiated freshness, charisma, and a sort of youthful, unguarded enthusiasm.

The drummer Terri Lyne Carrington, a former prodigy herself, joined Berklee's faculty in 2006 and soon encountered Spalding. The first time they played together, Carrington was struck by the ease of their rapport, the way they both instinctively subdivided the beat. And she noticed something else besides: "the fact that she dances on the bass. I was aware of not feeling weighted down by the way she plays. Many bass players, I feel a weight on me. The sound is either really big and huge, or their time feel is kind of like a Mack truck. Not floating."[3]

Whether it was Spalding's instincts as a vocalist or her formative training as a violinist—in both cases, the action occurs well above bass clef—she did approach the bass with a light, bounding step. But it wasn't as if she lacked a fullness of tone, or shrugged off the duties of the low end. She just envisioned her primary role less as a bedrock than as a catalyst. "In the moment, with the band, I'm just trying to play the bass parts that make the music stronger," she said. "And make it more beautiful or more whole-sounding, or create density where there needs to be density, or intensity where there needs to be intensity, or space or an emotion or a color. And the same is true when soloing. It's not about a shape or a pattern. You just are really trying to translate what you're receiving in that moment in the format of sound."[4]

By the time Spalding released her American debut, *Esperanza*, in 2008, her name was familiar to many jazz musicians and close observers of the scene. Notably, the album presented her, first and foremost, as a singer-songwriter. Lyrically speaking, the results could skew a little callow, but the musical foundation was never less than sure. And a few of the songs were outright keepers. "Precious," a soulful, insouciant retort to a lover's unreasonable expectations, was one of these. So too were "I Know You Know," a playful bolt of flirtation over a percolating Afro-Cuban beat, and "Fall In," a dreamy reverie performed with only piano accompaniment, from Leo Genovese.

The crossover success of *Esperanza* was striking enough to inspire some earnest, inevitable rumblings in the press about the new life Spalding was breathing into jazz. (Her first name, of course, means "hope.") While she'd released a thoughtful follow-up to *Esperanza* by the time of the 2011 Grammy Awards, it was more this general idea— extraordinary talent pressed into the service of an enlightened art form—that propelled her into the winner's circle.

With some hindsight, the calculus behind her shocking win looked explicable, almost obvious. According to one plausible theory, Bieber and Drake, a pair of boyish Canadians tilling American R&B soil, split one big voting bloc. Florence + the Machine and Mumford & Sons— two English bands, with a common denominator of yelping catharsis— split another bloc. That left only Spalding and her singular, effervescent prowess. Virtuosity has always played well with the academy, and so has the comforting vision of a brilliant young artist creating what you might inadvisably call Real Music.

In that regard, it was easy to envision Spalding as a spiritual successor to Norah Jones, whose five-category sweep in 2003 had included the Best New Artist award. Jones was another singer-songwriter who'd parlayed her sterling jazz education into a mainstream musical career. And in the years since collecting her first batch of awards, Jones had become part of the Grammy gentry: in 2011 she took the stage for a Dolly Parton tribute, belting out "Jolene" alongside John Mayer and Keith Urban.

Similarly, if you had tuned in to the preshow webcast—the part of the Grammys in which most of the awards are bestowed, with the genial efficiency of a church raffle—you would have seen Esperanza working the stage as cohost, in a tag team with her fellow vocal chameleon Bobby McFerrin. They opened the program by taking a brisk jog through Eddie Harris's "Freedom Jazz Dance" and proceeded to accept dozens of awards on behalf of absentee recipients. "The podium accepts," Spalding said repeatedly, cradling a Grammy in her arms.

But there was also a less obvious precedent to consider. Flashing back to the 26th Annual Grammy Awards, when Herbie Hancock and Wynton Marsalis each clocked their first wins, you could almost envision Spalding as the fulfillment of an unspoken dream—the next-generation by-product of a truce between warring factions. She was "Rockit" and Haydn and "Knozz-Moe-King," all seamlessly combined in one stylish and forward-looking package.

Or maybe she was none of the above, and wouldn't hold still long enough to let such a reductive narrative calcify around her. Maybe the most radical thing about Spalding wasn't her world-beating talent, but the fact that she felt no particular compulsion to fit it into a frame.

She isn't alone in that regard, not even at her echelon of visibility. The same radiant confidence and omnivorous instincts emanate from the pianist and singer Jon Batiste, who in 2015 became the bandleader on *The Late Show with Stephen Colbert*. A network flagship reaching an average of three million viewers, the show typically opens with Batiste out front, his lanky frame in a tailored suit, hyping the audience in the elegant Ed Sullivan Theater. Often you see him with his melodica—a toylike wind instrument that Colbert delights in calling a "face piano." According to age-old late-night custom, there's a brief welcome before the band kicks in with the show's theme, a Batiste original with a staccato hook and a pop-gospel progression. The interstitial music on the show is a stylistic grab bag, but it often bends meaningfully toward jazz.

Batiste is a former prodigy from one of the leading musical families in New Orleans, and he spent the decade before his television gig making a name in New York. His youthful poise at the piano, and his mastery of a jazz language stretching back to ragtime, earned him a glowing reputation from the start. (I first saw him in concert when he was a freshman at Juilliard, making a featured appearance on a Jazz at Lincoln Center concert with Wynton Marsalis.)

Five weeks before making his *Late Show* debut, Batiste and his rangy band, Stay Human, played the main stage at the Newport Jazz Festival. The week before that, they'd done the same at the Newport Folk Festival. Seeing them at work in both settings underscored Batiste's savvy and intuitive connection with an audience. For the Folk Festival, he tailored his set list and delivery to an ideal congruent with that event's north star, the folksinger Pete Seeger. His Jazz Festival set put more emphasis on improvisation, with a high-impact horn section. Both performances ended with a trademark: a euphoric parade through the crowd, with Batiste tootling phrases on his melodica like a Pied Piper of the second line.

"I'm not out to be an ambassador for an art form," Batiste said backstage after his Newport Jazz Festival performance, "because ultimately I feel like your playing does that."[5] He was sharing a couch with his core bandmates, the saxophonist Eddie Barbash and the drummer Joe Saylor, and reflecting on his public profile, which was about to grow exponentially.

While he proudly identifies as a jazz musician, Batiste has few hangups about the sanctity of the style. He prefers to use the term "social music," which makes no claim on any genre. Batiste described it to me as "a declaration," a self-defining banner he could wave. When Stay Human released its first studio album, in 2013, *Social Music* was the obvious title, an accurate descriptor that doubled as a statement of pride and purpose.

New Orleans had something to do with Batiste's deep yet flexible foundation as a musician, and it hardly seems a coincidence that another musician of his scope hails from similar circumstances. The trumpeter Christian Scott was born into a prominent Mardi Gras Indian tribe, and from the age of a preschooler he was masking as a Spy Boy—the scout who struts ahead of the Big Chief and his procession, in a riot of bright plumage, intricate beadwork, and ritual patter. The Spy Boy's main function is to be on the alert for rival tribes. He practices a cherished custom passed down from one generation to the next, but he's also ahead of the pack, looking for trouble.

Scott showed abundant early promise as a jazz musician, much like his uncle Donald Harrison Jr., an alto saxophonist also proudly known as Big Chief of the Congo Nation Afro-New Orleans Cultural Group. Scott would later characterize his precocious musical emergence as the simple fulfillment of a birthright: "I had damn near been bred to be the next guy in the line of New Orleans great trumpet players. That was actually in the bloodline."[6] As he understood it, this was at once a noble calling to embody and a rigid expectation to resist.

Batiste had his social music. Around the same time, Scott—who had adopted two West African surnames to become Christian Scott aTunde Adjuah—was using his own proprietary term, Stretch Music. This was in reference to a style combining postbop sophistication with the atmospheric sweep of art-rock, the loopy pull of electronic music, and the thrust and swagger of hip-hop. All of which combined with a brand-conscious image to turn Scott into a celebrity, the subject of fashion spreads as well as admiring coverage in the rock and hip-hop press.

In 2017 he invoked a checkered centenary—of the first-known jazz recordings, made by the all-white Original Dixieland Jass Band—as the instigating factor for a series of three albums, which he released in staggered fashion as *The Centennial Trilogy,* a sort of righteous rejoinder. The music on these albums—respectively titled *Ruler Rebel, Diaspora,* and *The Emancipation Procrastination*—is fashion-forward, brash but cool, a confluence of plaintive melody and rumbling groove. Along with Scott's bravura trumpet playing and canny atmospherics, the albums showcase several bright young improvisers, like the flutist Elena Pinderhughes and the pianist Lawrence Fields. Some tracks make adaptive use of trap rhythm, a mechanistic hallmark of southern hip-hop. Elsewhere Scott entrusts his two assertive drummers, Corey Fonville and Joe Dyson Jr., with the task of making a rigid beat seem almost to breathe.

The album that qualified Spalding for a nomination at the 2011 Grammys—though again, probably not the driving reason for her presence there—was *Chamber Music Society,* released the previous summer. A taut, elegant expression of lyrical and musical interiority, it advanced her vision of chamber music. This was a concept important mainly for restrictive reasons: she wasn't flirting with funk, or even incorporating electric instruments (beyond the occasional Fender Rhodes piano). Her coproducer was Gil Goldstein, a resourceful arranger and orchestrator who had worked on albums she admired by Joe Lovano.

Spalding established the tone of the album from the top: its overture, "Little Fly," is a string-quartet setting of a poem from William Blake's *Songs of Experience.* What follows is an original composition called "Knowledge of Good and Evil," whose sauntering pace, pizzicato-to-arco transition, and wordless vocal melody all point in the direction of Danilo Pérez's Latin-jazz manifesto *Motherland.* A track named "Chacarera," after the Argentine folk rhythm, has a melody that bobs and whirls like a kite in high wind; it segues into a tango-esque cover of "Wild Is the Wind," a song associated with Nina Simone (whose swooping style is duly evoked).

On another cover, of Antônio Carlos Jobim's "Inútil Paisagem," Spalding sings a duet with the gifted jazz singer Gretchen Parlato, over a background made up entirely of bass, hand percussion, and their voices, one rhythmic obbligato burbling behind the other. And on a delicate art song titled "Apple Blossom," Spalding trades verses with the eminent Brazilian singer-songwriter Milton Nascimento, expressing no evident deference. Singing together on the chorus, an octave apart, they sound like natural partners: embracing a metaphor of changing seasons, the bittersweet fluctuations of romance, a cycle of awakening and renewal.

Spalding's validation from the Recording Academy came just as she was planning a follow-up to *Chamber Music Society.* She'd been thinking about pop music, and the artificial constraints that separated it from so-called art music, like jazz. She considered a couple of her role models, Wayne Shorter and Stevie Wonder—"two really positive examples of how you can play a lot of music and still be 'accessible' to the public at large." But she was bemused by the very notion of "accessibility," a word she bracketed with ironic quotes even as she spoke.

I always say that the problem with jazz "accessibility" is not the content of the music; it's people's ability to *access* it. Meaning, if

you don't already listen to the music or go to concerts, how would
you hear jazz music? How would you? In a movie? If you happen
to be in a city where they have a jazz station? So all of a sudden I
thought, wow, this might actually be possible, to get this music out
on a much larger scale.[7]

So with *Radio Music Society,* Spalding set out to create some music that
might slip past the gatekeepers of an eclectic triple-A (Adult Album
Alternative) format. The end result strayed a good distance from that
aim. As the title suggests, Spalding envisioned this album as the yang to
Chamber Music Society's yin. She brought in a veritable congress of open-
minded jazz musicians, mentors as well as peers.

At the same time, there were aspects of Spalding's process that fell
outside the usual parameters for a jazz album. Her coproducer, and
the album's executive producer, was the rapper Q-Tip. During one of
her band rehearsals in New York, Prince showed up and sat quietly
for several hours. (Later he called with some feedback, including a tip
about "Let Her," one of her songs-in-progress; he thought she was giving away the chorus too soon.)

Radio Music Society includes two emblematic covers: a funk-samba
take on Stevie Wonder's "I Can't Help It," with drifting tenor obbligato
by Lovano; and "Endangered Species," a mid-eighties Wayne Shorter
fusion anthem, featuring Lalah Hathaway as a guest vocalist, singing
new lyrics keyed to a conservationist message. Elsewhere, Spalding
proceeds with those two touchstones clearly in mind, embracing progressive harmonies and roughly equal measures of love songs and social
commentary. "Land of the Free" reflects on the exoneration of a Texas
man, Cornelius Dupree Jr., after thirty years of wrongful imprisonment
for rape and robbery. "Vague Suspicions" is about America's violent
incursions in the Muslim world: "They are faceless numbers in the
headlines we've all read / Drone strike leaves thirteen civilians dead."
And Spalding conceived the album's slow-funk lead single, "Black
Gold," as an exhortation to African-American boys, calling up a proud
cultural legacy predating slavery.

These songs raise questions without pointing fingers, a distinction
Spalding was eager to make. "I don't think I'm taking a stand," she said

when I brought up the subject of protest. "I'm inviting the listener into this dialogue."

But the songs feel better suited to a declaration than to a dialogue, I countered.

"Well, even if something sounds declarative, it's like in a play," she said. "With a song like 'Black Gold,' maybe it is declarative to say: 'Hold your head as high as you can.' But the character from the song is inhabiting a role as a mentor to a young child. So, hmm."

She paused thoughtfully. "Yeah, it's like James Baldwin said: 'The purpose of art is to lay bare the questions that have been hidden by the answers.' I never want to say that I'm declaring the answers. I'm, in my own small way, declaring the questions."[8]

In 2011, Spalding put in a shift on *The Mosaic Project,* an album by Terri Lyne Carrington that managed to be both a crossover bid and a message album. The message, in effect, was solidarity: it's an album made entirely by women—from the stars, like Dee Dee Bridgewater and Nona Hendryx, to the ensemble players, like pianist Helen Sung and bassist Mimi Jones. *The Mosaic Project* won Best Jazz Vocal Album at the Grammys, and seemed to beg for a massive mobilization on tour.

To her credit, Carrington pivoted instead to the formation of a collective trio with Spalding and Geri Allen, whose probing intuition as a pianist, composer, and educator had made her a stealth influence on the scene. The ACS Trio, as this band was called, made the rounds on tour, working with an advanced harmonic language and a liquid sense of groove. It was a true convergence of three imposingly strong artists, but the glowing center was often Spalding, both in her anchoring bass and in the waft of her "ooh"s and "aah"s as she scatted a vocal line. Allen described Spalding's musicianship in a word: "holistic." She clarified:

Everything she has to offer, as a human being, happens when she makes music. She is using the whole picture all the time. All of those things are coming through, and they're not interrupted. It is free and unrestricted, and it's feeding into the moment of spontaneous composition, in a real kind of equal way. Everybody in the

trio is integrating their ideas into every moment, which is thrilling for me.[9]

Spalding thrived in this setting; it could feel like the sort of challenging, nurturing, enlightened situation that best suited her extravagant
talent. It was also unexpectedly liberating to find herself in an all-
female group of peers. Speaking on a 2018 Winter Jazzfest panel about
jazz and gender, moderated by Carrington, Spalding observed that the
routine experience of being the only woman on the bandstand could be
exhausting, if only for self-protective reasons.

> You don't notice that you're bracing. You don't notice that you're
> sending the verbal, behavioral (and so many other -ials) message:
> "I am not accessible to you, in any way, except for the music. You
> can't touch me. You can't kiss me. I don't like you. Don't get near
> me energetically, because it's not that game." And that's some-
> thing that I think male musicians may not encounter as often. And
> believe it or not, that takes a lot of energy to maintain all the time.
> So in the trio context, at first it was weird. I didn't know what was
> going on. But what happened was, I think for the first time we all
> were able to put all of our guard down, and just do what we came
> to do, once we were on the stage. Because there's even something
> about eye contact. Your practice of being the only woman trains
> you, like you have to give eye contact back in a way that's not
> inviting.[10]

These were everyday concerns for Spalding. But she also faced a
more exotic problem: popular culture couldn't seem to get enough of
her. The night before flying to Los Angeles for the 2012 Grammys—one
year after her big win—she stood on a street corner in Greenwich Village and talked about a plan taking shape for another splashy broadcast,
the Academy Awards. The composer Hans Zimmer, who would be its
main musical director, had a notion to form an all-star pit orchestra: a
backing band of A-listers united in a workmanlike setting. Spalding was
tickled by the idea. "The concept is antistardom," she said.

Once the Oscar preparations began in Los Angeles, some hierarchical gravity reasserted itself: Zimmer now wanted Spalding to sing a number during the "In Memoriam" segment, backed by a children's choir. At the appointed moment, she appeared onscreen in a flowing white robe with gold accoutrements to sing a stirring and pitch-perfect version of the Louis Armstrong anthem "What a Wonderful World." (The next morning, she could be found in best-dressed-on-the-red-carpet lists in *Elle* and *Vogue,* wearing an ice-blue gown.)

The intensity of the glare on Spalding goes a way toward explaining the motive of her next move. After the album cycle for *Radio Music Society* was done, she disappeared for a while, returning in unrecognizable form: hair braided, chunky glasses, outfits worthy of a space opera. Her new project was something called *Emily's D+Evolution,* and it came with a backstory involving the pure intentions of childhood role-play. Emily, her middle name, signified a younger self and spirit muse—and also, it seemed clear, a character and a form of cover.

During the public debut of the project, at Le Poisson Rouge in Greenwich Village in 2015, Spalding took the stage holding a small screen in front of her face, and whisked it aside with a flourish. "See this pretty girl," she sang, as if issuing a dare. "Watch this pretty girl flow." The tune, "Good Lava," had a four-on-the-floor drumbeat and a gnarly guitar riff. Spalding was on electric bass, with Matthew Stevens and Justin Tyson working a muscular groove; there were sturdy vocal reinforcements, from Nadia Washington and Corey King. The rest of the show proceeded in this vein: declaratory, theatrical, and funky, with an audacious level of pretension.

When *Emily's D+Evolution* was released as an album the following spring, it was a little easier to wrap your arms around the songs. They reflected a strong set of influences, including vintage Prince and Stevie Wonder, Funkadelic and Steely Dan. Her songs "Earth to Heaven" and "Noble Nobles" had the sophisticated harmony and coltish phrasing of songs from mid-to-late-seventies Joni Mitchell—the era of *Hejira* and *Don Juan's Reckless Daughter,* when Jaco Pastorius was a crucial member of her studio retinue.

What Spalding did with the songs suggested some high-level multitasking: she was Joni and Jaco in the same human form. Another standout song, "Rest in Pleasure," had a floating, Jeff Buckley–ish rock beat and a verse melody with the sort of casual chromatic feints that would cause grave problems for a lot of less nimble singers. The ambition and audacity of the project expanded Spalding's reach, aligning her with an ascendent vogue of Afrofuturism.

But again, she wasn't interested in wheeling away from her jazz foundation. If anything, she was pushing farther: at the 2017 Detroit Jazz Festival, she appeared with Wayne Shorter in a band that also featured Carrington and the pianist Leo Genovese. The music swooped and spiraled; she sang melodic lines almost byzantine in their chromatic complexity. She had been working on an opera with Shorter, and there were elements in this performance that seemed adapted from it. She sounded buoyant and ablaze, bending fearsome, high-modernist complexities into a sleek new shape. She made the music feel miraculous but also matter-of-fact.

Exposure sold out its limited run, and the albums began arriving on subscribers' doorsteps in the final weeks of 2017. Each copy, on CD or vinyl, included a scrap of paper on which Spalding had scrawled her song lyrics during the session; they were presented almost as sacred relics. Several months after its release, copies of the album were selling in online auctions for well over $100. (One sealed LP was listed at $585.)

For anyone who had watched long stretches of the livestream, hearing the album was a bit like seeing a finished jigsaw puzzle after getting acquainted with a scattering of pieces. Spalding, in the spirit of the project, included an occasional nod to her creative process; the opening track, "Swimming Toward the Black Dot," even incorporates the sound of her marker scrawling across the page. Her lyrics often balance ornate metaphor against blunt address, notably on a waltz-time reverie called "Heaven in Pennies," one of the album's more memorable themes. There are also songs of romantic contentment, "I Do" prominent among them. Others get more pointed—like "Colonial Fire," whose title is self-explanatory, and "I Am Telling You," a firm admonition to someone making unwanted sexual advances.

The album also came with a bonus disc labeled "Undeveloped," full of assorted outtakes and castoffs from the studio experiment. But

Spalding had assigned them all track titles, as if to assert that even the ephemera was destined for something other than oblivion, worth naming and preserving. Like so much about *Exposure*, this gesture amounted to an expansion in the guise of a constriction. And like so much about Spalding, it was an expression of wild ambition and unshakable self-confidence couched in the most approachable form, as a gift.

————

Terri Lyne Carrington, *The Mosaic Project* (Concord)
Christian Scott aTunde Adjuah, *The Centennial Trilogy* (Ropeadope)
Esperanza Spalding, *Chamber Music Society* (Heads Up International)
Esperanza Spalding, *Exposure* (Concord)
Esperanza Spalding, *Radio Music Society* (Heads Up International)

11

The Crossroads

Oscar Valdés called out from behind his Batá drums, in a spirit of ritual welcome. He was voicing a traditional chant to Eleguá, the Yoruban orisha of the crossroads, with the hearty, imploring inflection you'd expect to hear in a rumba on the streets of Havana.

Valdés, an eminence among percussionists in Cuba, was in fact performing in the shadow of El Capitolio—but at the Gran Teatro de La Habana, on the proscenium stage of a baroque-revival opera house restored to aristocratic splendor. The occasion was the International Jazz Day All-Star Global Concert, a feat of both musical and diplomatic proportions, co-presented by UNESCO (the United Nations Educational, Scientific and Cultural Organization) and the Thelonious Monk Institute of Jazz. Lights blazed as multiple cameras filmed the action for broadcast, live-streaming to an audience said to be in the millions.

The concert, on April 30, 2017, had a fitting overture in that invocation to Eleguá: a solitary call that led to a collective response, as a twelve-piece band snapped into gear. They played "Manteca," a multicultural anthem that effectively entered the world as a foundational text of Latin jazz.

At the Gran Teatro de La Habana, "Manteca"—composed in 1947 by the Cuban percussionist Chano Pozo and the bebop trumpeter Dizzy Gillespie (with input from Gil Fuller, an arranger in Gillespie's band)—served as a shorthand, ratifying the longstanding musical dialogue between Cuba and the United States and hinting at broader notions of solidarity. The band was stocked with musicians from more than a dozen countries, and some of them took turns firing off compact pyrotechnic displays: first the Russian tenor saxophonist Igor Butman; then a Cuban counterpart, Carlos Miyares; then the American alto saxophonist Antonio Hart. When the action shifted to the trumpet section, the personnel was no less diverse, comprising Till Brönner, from Germany; Takuya Kuroda, from Japan; and Julio Padrón, from Cuba.

This United Nations of musical convergence wasn't just intentional; it was largely the point. The annual event known as International Jazz Day—a brainchild of Herbie Hancock, acting in his dual capacities as a UNESCO goodwill ambassador and chairman of the Thelonious Monk Institute of Jazz—had been conceived to elevate jazz's stature while demonstrating the upside of globalization.[1] (The first edition of the All-Star Global Concert, in 2012, had in fact been held at the United Nations General Assembly Hall in New York.) Along with a gala concert, there were satellite activities in countries around the world—195 in all, according to the official tally in 2017.

Hancock was one of two artistic directors on the concert in Havana. The other was Chucho Valdés, another heralded piano virtuoso, and perhaps the most distinguished jazz musician in Cuba. Half a century earlier, Valdés had been a founding member of the Orquesta Cubana de Música Moderna, a pioneering big band made up of musicians with conservatory training and what was then regarded as a subversive interest in jazz. Out of the Orquesta's ranks came Irakere, an explosive fusion group that enjoyed globetrotting success, beginning in the late 1970s.

One indication of the complicated geopolitics of jazz in Cuba was made manifest in Irakere's shadow legacy at the All-Star Global Concert. The lineup featured a handful of prominent alumni of the band: not just Chucho but also Oscar Valdés, on his Batá drums, and Orlando "Maraca" Valle, on flute. But there were also conspicuous omissions— like trumpeter Arturo Sandoval and multireedist Paquito D'Rivera, who worked together in Irakere's most spectacular front line and later both became defectors and outspoken critics of the Castro regime. They wouldn't have taken part in an International Jazz Day convocation in Cuba even if such an outcome were politically feasible.

Similarly, discretion had led to the exclusion of a whole cadre of important Cuban jazz artists in the United States—expatriate musicians like the saxophonists Yosvany Terry and Román Filiú; drummers Dafnis Prieto and Ignacio Berroa; percussionists Román Díaz and Pedrito Martínez; and pianists Arturo O'Farrill, Elio Villafranca, David Virelles, Aruán Ortiz, Fabian Almazan, Manuel Valera, and Alfredo Rodríguez. Each of these artists (and quite a few others) had established a strong identity in jazz scenes outside their homeland, articulating a vision for Afro-Cuban jazz that tilted toward global cosmopolitanism even as it often reinforced folkloric root systems.

That conscientious yet unforced brand of hybridism echoes a widespread development in jazz in the last few decades, not only among Cuban jazz musicians but also for those who trace their heritage to India, Pakistan, Israel, China, and Iraq (and beyond). The music made by these artists has naturally ranged in scope and tone, but on the whole it speaks to a matter-of-fact polyglot ideal on the ground. Rather than creating the equivalent of a jazz buffet punched up with exotic flavors—à la the well-intentioned Dave Brubeck album *Jazz Impressions of Eurasia,* from 1958—these artists have sought to reconcile their various cultural traditions with jazz practice at the highest levels. It would be reductive to put the result into a kind of subcategory, like "global jazz." Increasingly this syncretic, conversant blend of dialects and syntax describes the very state of the art: jazz itself.

In a tangible sense, jazz had been a polyglot proposition even in its earliest stages, informed not only by the musics of Africa and the Caribbean but also by the pluralism of places where such traditions commingle. (Havana had a formative influence on the music, along with cities like New Orleans, Chicago, and New York.)

"Perhaps no other music is called upon to represent diaspora as often as jazz," the ethnomusicologists Philip V. Bohlman and Goffredo Plastino observe in their useful collection *Jazz Worlds/World Jazz.* "The world charted musically by diaspora, the exile and return of African or South Asian and Rom musicians, appears as an alternative to that mapped by political boundaries. And yet, jazz practices adhere to political boundaries as cultural practice, for example, at the edge of empire or in the musical echoes that resonate between continents."[2]

A state-sanctioned endeavor like International Jazz Day would seem to underscore those political boundaries, if only by adopting the rhetoric of cultural diplomacy. But through the guiding input of Hancock, the event has also advanced the prospect of jazz as a universal, endlessly adaptable art form. Asked to reflect on the concert in Havana while still basking in its glow, Hancock focused less on the precarious advances in Cuban-American relations and more on utopian generalities, hailing its outcome as "a kind of solidarity of the planet that doesn't really happen very often."[3] As in every previous iteration of the concert, the grand finale had been a full-dress version of John Lennon's "Imagine," delivered in the round-robin fashion of a charity pop single.

The song, with its aspirational vision of a world devoid of national borders and rigid doctrines, had become a central facet of Hancock's humanitarian brand. Of course that notion of transcendent unity could easily be disparaged as an earnest oversimplification—especially on the ground in Havana, during the early phase of a United States presidential administration bent on reinforcing every kind of national, ethnic, and demographic division.

Without question, the aims of International Jazz Day had been more in tune with political and diplomatic realities back in 2016, when the All-Star Global Concert had been held on the South Lawn of the White House. One highlight of that concert was a performance featuring Paquito D'Rivera and Chucho Valdés—old confreres, isolated for decades by geopolitics and opinion, but goaded by ceremony to finally (if fleetingly) make music together again.

In his welcoming remarks that evening in 2016, President Barack Obama reiterated the conventional view of jazz as a proud American invention, "perhaps the most honest reflection of who we are as a nation." But where he went next with his address was less predictable, at least for an American head of state. Acknowledging that jazz had long ago reached a global audience, making adaptations in every corner of the world, he offered the assessment that "it speaks to something universal about our humanity—the restlessness that stirs in every soul, the desire to create with no boundaries."[4]

In my humble way, I'm the U.S.A.

—LOUIS ARMSTRONG, in *The Real Ambassadors*

Jazz and the US State Department had a more goal-oriented relationship in the twentieth century—especially from the mid-1950s through the late seventies, when the federal government routinely sent musicians abroad, often to hotspots where the hand of diplomacy was badly needed. In those years, jazz was charged not with "the desire to create without boundaries" but rather the aim of personifying America's democratic principles and, not infrequently, softening its flaws. This official deployment might amount to a trivial piece of jazz history, if not for its direct effect on jazz's development abroad. In some respects it laid a groundwork for generations of musicians and audiences, while helping to map out a global infrastructure for the art form.

The seeds for jazz's strategic diplomatic use were sown early in 1955, when Willis Conover's radio show *Music USA* debuted on the Voice of America. In its first year, the program reached some thirty million people in eighty countries. (Conover kept it going, broadcasting six nights a week, until shortly before his death in 1996.) *Music USA* was most enthusiastically received in places that restricted freedom of expression, notably the Soviet Union and other countries behind the Iron Curtain, like Czechoslovakia and Poland. To listeners in these locales, the program was seen as a beacon of freedom, and Conover—with his plummy announcer's voice and careful, instructive elocution—as its benevolent emissary. Jazz, as a model of improvised accord, mirrored the expression of individuals in a free society. And while Conover largely refrained from editorializing on the air, his own judgment on the matter was clear: he characterized jazz as "structurally parallel to the American political system."

At the same time that the Voice of America was establishing a new pipeline for jazz in Europe, Louis Armstrong traveled there on a major concert tour. As chronicled on a live album released just afterward, Armstrong and His All-Stars met with wild enthusiasm. A foreign correspondent for *The New York Times,* taking in the clamor around the tour, issued a declaration: "America's secret weapon is a blue note in a minor key. Right now its most effective ambassador is Louis (Satchmo) Armstrong."[5] (This remarkable statement probably had at least something to do with the title of that live album, *Ambassador Satch.*)

The definitive text on this curious turn in American foreign diplomacy is Penny M. Von Eschen's 2004 book *Satchmo Blows Up the World: Jazz Ambassadors Play the Cold War.* Among other things, it illuminates a concerted effort to send musicians to some of the most contested and strategic places abroad. So the first official cultural program had Dizzy Gillespie and his band arriving in Abadan, Iran, to what alto saxophonist Phil Woods later recalled as "the smell of crude oil and the sound of gunfire from nearby Iraq."[6] Von Eschen points out that Iraqi coups broke out during tours by the Dave Brubeck Quartet (in 1958) and the Duke Ellington Orchestra (in 1963). She also observes that Armstrong's tour of the Congo in 1960 occurred during the covert American-backed detainment and torture of Prime Minister Patrice Lumumba.

Race is a crucial subtext in the history of the Jazz Ambassadors program, which US officials brandished as a shield against global criticism of segregationist policies at home. "The glaring contradiction in this strategy," Von Eschen notes, "was that the U.S. promoted black artists as goodwill ambassadors—symbols of the triumph of American democracy—when America was still a Jim Crow nation."[7] Armstrong, Gillespie, Ellington, and many of the other musicians on the tours negotiated this enormous irony with characteristic poise, speaking candidly about their nation's problems and insisting, wherever they played, on reaching "the people." Brubeck and his wife, Iola, later went so far as to lampoon the situation in song: *The Real Ambassadors,* a satirical musical featuring Armstrong, Carmen McRae, and Lambert, Hendricks and Ross. It premiered at the 1962 Monterey Jazz Festival, and was later released as a studio album. Unabashed in its critique, it accurately portrays Armstrong as a public figure grudgingly shrugging off some moral ambivalence. As he puts it, singing Iola Brubeck's lyrics: "Though I represent the government / The government don't represent / Some policies I'm for."

Still, it's no slight to *The Real Ambassadors* to suggest that the best musical by-product of the tours came from extracurricular forays into local scenes. Gillespie first met Lalo Schifrin, a composer, arranger, and future collaborator, after hours at a club in Buenos Aires. (In Rio de Janeiro, he left a strong impression on João Gilberto and Antônio Carlos Jobim.) Brubeck played in Bombay with sitar master Abdul Halim Jaffer Khan, sparking ideas that would later surface on *Jazz Impressions of Eurasia*. Ellington and Billy Strayhorn absorbed the sounds and experiences of one 1963 tour and created their landmark *Far East Suite*. Pianist Randy Weston took a momentous trip to Africa under the auspices of a State Department tour in 1967—sharpening his affinity for Morocco, where he subsequently lived for a time, studying the music of the Gwawa people, which he would later help bring into wider circulation worldwide.[8]

The Jazz Ambassadors tours also exerted a profound influence, direct and diffuse, on innumerable local scenes. Where exposure to the music was scarce, a small but concentrated dose could go a long way. And as proponents of the Hancock Doctrine might put it, jazz's most basic imperative—finding common purpose together, through improvisation—was a process that could be adapted to almost any local custom or inflection.

Tomasz Stańko, the most celebrated jazz trumpeter to emerge from Poland, remembers first seeing Brubeck on a State Department tour in 1958, when he was a teenager and already a regular listener of Conover's show. "As a Polish who was living in a Communist country," Stańko recalled, "jazz was a synonym of Western culture, of freedom, of this different style of life."[9]

Through his own career, which started in a tumultuous free-jazz vein and went on to accommodate all manner of whispery poignancies and postbop flair, Stańko became a leading jazz artist in Europe, an exemplar and a mentor. For a good stretch of the early 2000s, he had a superb Polish band whose rhythm section—led by the pianist Marcin Wasilewski, and previously known as the Simple Acoustic Trio—exemplified the high level of curiosity, refinement, and rapport among a younger generation of jazz musicians in Europe.

There's no way to quantify the effect that official US channels had on Stańko's musical development, except to trust his word that it was profound. And just as a generation of expatriate African-American musicians, in places like Paris and Copenhagen, influenced the development of the music abroad in the 1950s and '60s, the rise of homegrown players like Stańko had a reverberative effect on the larger scene.

Still, even in the twenty-first century there are highly cosmopolitan places where jazz is very much a developing story. Tracking that story can produce valuable insights, shedding light on how the music finds traction in between the cracks—lacking much in the way of a support network, an informed constituency, or any institutional resources.

One afternoon in the fall of 2016, I sat at a table in a cavernous, handsomely appointed nightclub as Chick Corea was addressing a group of Chinese investors. We were on the eastern edge of Tiananmen Square, in the basement of a building constructed as part of the American Legation in 1903. Corea had been flown out for the opening of the Blue Note Beijing, a gleaming addition to a global network of branded entertainment venues. This new Blue Note club, renovated to the tune of $7 million, was the first of several planned for China, joining a flagship location in New York; prominent outposts in Japan and Italy; and more recent franchises in Napa Valley and Honolulu. (It preceded by a year the organization's further expansion into Brazil.)

The club's opening, in the posh Legation Quarter, was also a reminder of the uptick of wealth and spending power in Beijing—though that phenomenon has had more of an impact on the city skyline (and its luxury retail) than on its creative jazz scene. In 2015, Beijing's splashiest jazz club up to that point—Yue Fu, a pet project of the successful nightlife entrepreneur Leon Lee—was forced to close within a year because of insufficient revenue. The talk among local musicians was that the Blue Note Beijing, owned by a Chinese company in a licensing agreement, could all too easily suffer a similar fate.

"It takes time to build the tourist business," Steve Bensusan, president of Blue Note Entertainment, said during a tour of his imposing facilities in Beijing, which include a media command center and a greenroom roughly the size of the entire Blue Note club in New York. "But that's what we're striving for: the international traveler, the business traveler. We also want to expose people to the music. We're making a big splash in the hope that it filters down."[10]

Beyond issues of corporate expansion and new-market penetration, the very fact of this Blue Note club also signaled a new chapter in the evolving story of jazz in Beijing. Corea suggested as much in a preshow press conference, when he issued a friendly word of advice, promptly translated for his audience: "Make a vibe here, where the local musicians and the local audiences can hang out and feel comfortable. That's how you build a club that can live."

The press conference also featured a brief solo piano performance by A Bu, a former child prodigy from Beijing. Sixteen at the time, he was enrolled in the precollege program at Juilliard in New York City, while going out on the odd international tour. (Six months after this encounter, I'd run into him again in Havana, at the All-Star Global Concert.)

Speaking of Beijing's jazz ecology, A Bu was sanguine: "It's growing every day now," he said. But he was careful to add that there was room for improvement, especially in the area of audience development: "Most Chinese, I have to say, they do not know what is jazz."[11]

Beijing is not only the seat of Chinese government but also a prized cradle of national culture, and jazz has always been excluded from any substantial institutional support. The East Asian studies scholar Adiel Portugali has drawn a connection between the music's marginal status and the ideological thrust of the post-Maoist state, as exerted through China's powerful Ministry of Culture. "The delicate subtext of the notion of freedom in jazz," he writes, in a collection called *Jazz and Totalitarianism*, "can raise ideas and associations that oppose the bureaucratic nature of political systems that are inclined towards totalitarian control."[12]

But a small, vibrant scene does exist in Beijing, largely situated in and around the city's hutong neighborhoods, whose narrow alleys and crumbling courtyards date back to the thirteenth-century Yuan dynasty. At the time of my visit, two of Beijing's leading jazz rooms inhabited former *siheyuan*—courtyard—houses: Jianghu Bar, a laid-back hangout on Dong Mian Hua Hutong; and Dusk Dawn Club, more commonly known as DDC, about ten minutes away on foot. Both attracted a stylish young audience with at least a modicum of jazz comprehension, or the willingness to listen and learn.

North of the Forbidden City, in a part of town still crisscrossed by hutongs, sits the East Shore Live Jazz Café, the leading jazz club in Beijing and maybe the most crucial in all of China. It can be found up a narrow flight of stairs, amid a huddle of unpretentious buildings near the Jinding Bridge, on Houhai Lake. From inside the club, large picture windows overlook the lake, whose glassy surface shines by night with the reflection of lights from the other shore.

My first of several visits to the East Shore was on a Saturday night, when the room was packed with local twenty- and thirty-somethings, most of them listening intently. They were there to hear Xu Zhihan, a twenty-two-year-old guitarist, leading a quartet of local jazz stalwarts: Xia Jia on piano, Ji Peng on bass, and Bei Bei on drums. The music was sophisticated and sleek, a startlingly close approximation of what you might hear at, say, Smalls Jazz Club in New York City. (Spike Wilner, the owner of Smalls, had been at the East Shore just a day or two earlier.) At one point the band segued from a Joe Henderson tune, arranged in a lilting odd meter, to an original with a luminous chord progression and an easy-drift groove. Xu Zhihan soloed with low-key poise, hanging behind the beat as he spun variations on the theme. Xia Jia was even more impressive, reeling off piano improvisations at once soulful, harmonically forward, and marked by painterly restraint.

Born and raised in a small western village, Xia Jia moved to Beijing in 1986, at age twelve, to study classical piano at a conservatory. He turned on to jazz in the mid-nineties, during the music's first tentative bloom in China. "At that time it was really hard to find any jazz records," he said, between puffs of a cigarette, in a conversation on the roof deck of the East Shore. One prize acquisition in his collection was the 1989 self-titled debut by the Chick Corea Akoustic Band. "I listened to that one album for such a long time," he said. "Endlessly. Because that's the only thing I had."[13]

When he left China to pursue a degree in jazz studies at the Eastman School of Music in Rochester, New York, Xia Jia became an outlier, and in some respects a pioneer. He was mentored in the program by the veteran jazz pianist and educator Harold Danko, amassing classroom and bandstand experience before returning to China. He brought a wealth of insight back to Beijing, where he reconnected with one of his earlier mentors: Liu Yuan, a trailblazing Chinese jazz artist, and the owner of the East Shore.

Liu Yuan, a slender man in round spectacles and a Panama hat, had the gracious but quietly intense demeanor of a man accustomed to making things happen. We spoke one evening on the East Shore roof deck, with translation from Nathaniel Gao, a Chinese-American alto saxophonist who arrived in Beijing from the States in 2006, the same year that the club opened. A saxophonist himself, Liu Yuan started performing jazz in public in 1986, when few other Chinese musicians were doing so. He'd been trained on his father's instrument, the *suona*, a double-reed horn common in the music of the northern provinces. And he had experience touring internationally with a traditional folk troupe, but his main affiliation was with Cui Jian, a massively popular singer-songwriter known as the Father of Chinese Rock.

China was gradually opening to Western culture in the wake of the cultural revolution, but unlike Shanghai, a port city where trade and commerce have always yielded a vibrant nightlife, the capital city had little infrastructure for live music at the time. For a while the only places to play jazz were a French restaurant and some hotel bars in the embassy district, where foreigners made up most of the clientele.

But in the mid-nineties Liu Yuan began playing at a bar called CD Café, eventually turning it into Beijing's first dedicated jazz club. He was the club's manager and main attraction, working with a small handful of other early adopters like the bassist Huang Yong and the pianist Kong Hongwei, commonly known as Golden Buddha. The first Beijing International Jazz Festival got up and running around this time, focusing much-needed attention and audience interest on the music until it faltered in 2001. A kind of retrenchment followed, with some jazz musicians fretting that any forward momentum in the nineties had been a tantalizing fluke.

But then Liu Yuan, seeking more creative independence, left the CD Café in 2006, and opened the East Shore. "For the last twenty years, with all of these places, I've been trying to maintain a place for real jazz exclusively," he said. "There has been some financial pressure. It's still worth it."[14] He was also part of the committee that agitated for and helped organize a major new event, the Nine Gates International Jazz Festival, which ran annually from 2006 to 2013.

Like most musicians I met in Beijing, Liu Yuan characterized the scene as motivated more by art than by commerce—an explicit contrast to Shanghai, where there's plenty of work but in a less creative vein, and the audiences are likelier to talk over the music. The East Shore, proudly operating without a cover charge, had been set up as a sort of clubhouse, for players as well as fans. As soon as the Blue Note Beijing was up and running across town, marquee American musicians booked there began popping up at the East Shore after hours, to hang out and jam with the locals.

This conferred a certain legitimacy, though Westerners don't exert the level of influence they once did in Beijing. Matt Roberts, an American trombonist who first arrived there as a student in the late eighties, recalls forming one ragtag early group with Chinese musicians playing folk instruments like the *suona* and the *sheng,* a reedy mouth organ. "We just kind of made it up as we went along," Roberts said. "I had about ten cassette tapes, and I kept loaning them out."[15]

The situation was drastically different for a more recent wave of American expats, like Gao, who grew up in Iowa City; the trombonist and composer Terence Hsieh, who was born in Durham, North Carolina, and studied at Oberlin Conservatory; and Anthony Vanacore, a drummer who moved to China to teach music in Hangzhou, before arriving in Beijing. All three are pillars of the Beijing jazz scene, but they work on more or less equal footing with their Chinese counterparts, in a mutual exchange. "What's interesting about Beijing is that you really associate with the local Chinese," Vanacore said, "whereas Shanghai is more Westernized, so a lot of the musicians are foreigners. Here in Beijing there are some phenomenal musicians—guys who have never been abroad, can't really speak much English, and they play incredibly. These guys have had so many barriers to deal with: language, access to the information. They overcame it. It's amazing."[16]

At the same time, some of the most promising developments on the Beijing jazz scene were the direct result of foreign exposure: local musicians who, following Xia Jia's lead a generation later, were seeking out training in Europe or the United States, and bringing their expertise back home. Liu Yuan and Xia Jia both pointed to the fact that some of these talented young players were unknown to them, having headed abroad straight from the outer provinces. In a jazz ecosystem that once felt stiflingly small, this was an encouraging sign.

Xu Zhihan, the guitarist, has a twin brother: Xu Zhitong, who plays drums. When I met them in Beijing, they were both studying jazz at conservatories in Germany, where the tuition and cost of living is cheaper than New York. They spoke broken English with an unusual accent, part German in its inflection, and part Chinese. We sat in a booth at Jianghu Bar with Matt Roberts before he played a gig with his band.

At one point I asked Roberts to explain the difference between the Beijing scene now, as opposed to the early nineties, before Xu Zhihan and Xu Zhitong were born. "Oh, it's very easy," he replied. "You're sitting next to two phenomenal musicians. And when I first arrived, foreign musicians knew how to play jazz and Chinese musicians didn't. It was very one-sided. Now the number of really exceptional Chinese jazz musicians is much, much larger."[17]

The generational transfer of knowledge, which has always been the gold standard in jazz, played out neatly in the story of the twins: Xu Zhihan learned to play jazz guitar by studying with Liu Yue, whose drummer was Xu Zhitong's teacher, Bei Bei. Unlike their elders, they were familiar with jazz, as a mode of expression, from the very start of their musical training. The Internet isn't quite the frictionless experience in China that it is in the West, but their exposure to music via YouTube and various file-sharing services was a far cry from the limitations of an informal lending library of worn cassette tapes.

After our conversation, I heard the first half hour of Roberts's set, which consisted of surefooted arrangements of familiar postbop fare. Then I headed out into the night, walking down Minhua Hutong in the direction of the East Shore. There I heard the Xia Jia Trio, with Ji Peng on bass and Xu Zhitong on drums. They played a mix of smart originals and jazz standards, in a meditative but deeply swinging style. Xia Jia was, as before, the picture of soulful restraint. Xu Zhitong's rhythm foundation had a persuasive undercurrent, even as he occasionally spiked the beat with small but neatly surprising digressions.

The music pulsed with creative freedom—a quality that, in context, would seem to invite a political allegory, one that decades of

State Department policy had been designed to instill. But that jazz-as-democracy narrative reflects a crude binary that every Chinese jazz musician I met took pains to disavow. "Jazz, for me, it's not politicized," said Liu Yuan. "It was just a new method of expression. So in that sense it does represent freedom, on a personal level."

Hsieh, though born and raised in the West, has echoed that ambivalence in a series of perceptive articles about the misattribution of political motive among Chinese musicians. "Some very smart people, academics and such, assume that jazz must be an instigator of democracy in China," he told me. "It's a double standard, not just in jazz but with art in general. The West supports art in China that reflects a revolutionary narrative, or protests against the government. But there are a lot of other ways to frame whatever's happening here."[18]

What has been happening in Beijing, and with jazz in China more broadly, is difficult to capture in a phrase—unless you're content to point out that both the quantity and quality of homegrown musicians has been sharply on the rise. The factors in this change are plentiful, and the situation is rapidly evolving. Long after I left Beijing, I was still thinking about Xia Jia's confident forecast for the city's jazz ecology. "I think in a few years, if you look back at this moment, you will see that it was when everything changed, in some big step," he said. "I can feel that."

When we talk about jazz's reach around the world, it's standard practice to refer to the dissemination of a language. Extending the metaphor, progress can be charted in terms of proficiency—and there's no doubt that many more players around the world meet that criterion than did a generation or two ago. Hancock's assessment is right on the mark in that sense: as a musical lingua franca, jazz has had remarkable, even stunning, success.

But there's also a more mutable connotation in the jazz-as-language metaphor. The English critic Stuart Nicholson conjures it succinctly in his formulation of a global jazz landscape.

Just as the use of the English language in the global context does not always mirror the vocabulary and rules of grammar and syn-

tax and the way English is spoken in Britain or America, there
are jazz styles that have evolved outside the United States that
do not necessarily follow the way that jazz is played inside the
United States. No language, not even the musical "language" of
jazz, remains pure in the globalized world.[19]

Nicholson is far from an objective source here. He first floated the
notion of "glocalized" jazz practice, borrowing a term from corporate
buzz-speak, in his 2005 book *Is Jazz Dead? (Or Has It Moved to a New
Address)*[20]—a work of impassioned advocacy for new European jazz,
framed as a reactionary polemic against the American status quo. With
that agenda-driven argument, Nicholson effectively railed against one
blind spot while trying to package and sell another one. Still, he has a
point when he alludes to the vicissitudes of grammar and syntax. He's
also right to suggest that many jazz musicians outside the United States
have carved out modes of expression beyond a standard framework,
personalizing and hybridizing the music.

Consider the Thelonious Monk International Jazz Competition,
which for more than a quarter century was jazz's most rigorous and
prestigious proficiency test. Every year submissions poured in from
all over the world, often resulting in a dozen or so semifinalists from
a handful of countries. Starting in 2005, the first prize went to some
of these international arrivals, including Melissa Aldana, a suavely
capable tenor saxophonist from Chile; Lage Lund, a cool-tempered,
inventive guitarist from Norway; and Tigran Hamasyan, a precise,
hyperdynamic pianist from Armenia. Each prevailed over a field of
immaculately trained Americans by proving sure mastery of consensus
jazz protocols.

Hamasyan, for example, won the Monk competition in 2006 in part
by finessing the standards "Solar" and "Cherokee." But then he went
on to build a prominent career out of cultural fusions, either with
electronics and high-contrast dynamics or—as on the 2017 album *An
Ancient Observer*—with Armenian folk and Euro-classical references. In
a sense, Hamasyan earned his place at the table with a demonstration of
fluency but secured it with an expression of artistry, accessing a specific
cultural lineage.

And as his example illustrates, a folkloric accent is only one path to that outcome. When the electric guitarist Hedvig Mollestad rips through a jagged squall of distortion, she's drawing from a much more brackish well than the one that gives Tord Gustavsen, a sedate and fastidious pianist, his brand of sustenance. But both artists represent an extension of the Nordic jazz that Nicholson champions. So too does the electroacoustic ensemble Supersilent, which can traverse a spectrum from rippling stillness to crushing heat in a single group improvisation. In short, there are many layers of precedent and possibility—and funding—for an emerging improviser in Oslo. The same is true to varying degrees in Barcelona, and Seoul, and Tel Aviv.

Lionel Loueke, a guitarist from Benin, grew up playing in traditional West African percussion groups while absorbing the strains of Afropop and Brazilian music that he heard at home and around his mother's coastal village. He was seventeen when he first picked up the guitar, and cosmopolitan from the jump: because Benin has no native guitar style, his early influences came from elsewhere on the African continent, like Nigeria, Mali, and the Congo. When he stumbled across a George Benson CD, he was able to draw a parallel from jazz improvisation to the vocalizations of West African griots. In jazz, he also recognized a cousin to the rhythmic nuance that animates most African music.

Loueke left Benin to study music in Ivory Coast in 1990, but it wasn't until relocating to Paris a few years later, to attend the American School of Modern Music, that he had proper exposure to jazz. He was then recruited by the Berklee College of Music, where he formed what would become his longstanding trio with a couple of fellow students: Massimo Biolcati, a bassist with roots in Sweden and Italy, and Ferenc Nemeth, a Hungarian drummer.

Like most jazz musicians, Loueke would have little practical use for a word like "glocalization." But in conversation, he employs the metaphor of local dialect. "Jazz is a language," he said in 2008, shortly before the release of *Karibu*, his Blue Note debut. "I have my accent, I have my way to choose different words. But most important for me is to understand that language."[21]

Loueke's approach as an improviser is buoyant and percolating, with broad fluency in postbop harmony and complex polyrhythm. He also

brings unmistakable perspective from African folk music—not just fin-
gerstyle technique but also vocal-percussive effects, like plosive pops
and palatal clicks. The originality of his hybridized jazz signature was
immediately apparent to Hancock, who heard him during an audition
for the Thelonious Monk Institute of Jazz Performance. Loueke was
not only admitted to the program but also drafted into Hancock's band.

Another leading twenty-first-century jazz artist to embrace the
jazz-as-language idea, in the service of multicultural expression, is
the alto saxophonist and composer Miguel Zenón. Born and raised in
Puerto Rico, he received classical training but was self-taught as a jazz
musician until he, like Loueke, went to Berklee, at nineteen. Zenón
furiously committed himself to learning the music's fundamentals, racing to make up for lost time. When he reconnected with his Puerto
Rican heritage, it was in something like a bloom of self-discovery.

> When I came here, all that I wanted to do was learn how to play
> jazz. That was my goal, and for the first three or four years that I
> spent in this country, going to school and getting immersed, basi-
> cally it was almost like learning a new language for me. Because I
> had never studied jazz formally. But it wasn't until I started think-
> ing about what my music was going to sound like when I asked:
> Who am I? What do I have to give? I started thinking about the
> fact that all this time I had spent studying jazz, I had never done
> that with Puerto Rican music. Even though I grew up with that
> music, I didn't go deep into it. I just felt that it was a responsibility.
> As a Puerto Rican. And I came to appreciate what that meant to
> me, in ways that I probably would have never come to understand
> it if I had stayed in Puerto Rico. I became prouder and more in
> touch with my patriotism and nationalism by *not* being in Puerto
> Rico, and by exploring Puerto Rican–ness through music. From
> the outside.[22]

It helped that one of Zenón's mentors at Berklee was Danilo Pérez,
who was then in the process of pulling together the concept for his
sweeping pan-American statement album, *Motherland*. Zenón already
knew Pérez from the pianist's ambitious earlier albums, like *The Journey*

(1993). He was struck by the fact that this Panamanian musician was so conversant in the jazz mainstream, and not just those varietals with an Afro-Caribbean thrust.

By the time Zenón began first turning heads on the scene, during and after his graduate studies at the Manhattan School of Music, it was obvious he had something special. The first thing to notice about him was his sound: sweet-tart, buoyant, and ripe, with an inflection that could give the impression of earnest emotional transparency. The suggestively vocal quality of his tone was something to which he'd applied conscious effort, willing himself to think of the instrument as an extension of his physical self. And his nimble phrasing was just as striking: Zenón had a dragonfly's speed and lightness, but even in a darting cadence he exuded thoughtful restraint and a resistance to cliché.

His first major turn in the spotlight came by way of a fellow Puerto Rican, the tenor and soprano saxophonist David Sánchez, who was not quite a decade older and then signed to Columbia. Sánchez's album *Melaza,* released in 2000, is a muscular, proudly ethnographic album inspired by the impact of the African slave trade in Puerto Rico. ("Melaza," meaning "molasses," alluded to the by-product of refined sugar cane. Eager to get his larger point across, Sánchez named one track "Against Our Will.") Throughout the album, shrewd arranging strategies fuse Sánchez's earthy tenor with Zenón's flowing alto, often in an urgent unison that splinters into tightly coiled harmony.

If this auspicious major-label exposure left any doubts about Zenón's ambition, he quickly showed his own initiative. He formed the nucleus of a working quartet by drafting a couple of peers from the *Melaza* sessions: the versatile bassist Hans Glawischnig, originally from Austria, and the brilliant drummer Antonio Sánchez, hailing from Mexico. The Venezuelan pianist Luis Perdomo, a classmate of Glawischnig's, completed the band.

Zenón spent a lot of time workshopping his music with these partners, so that by the time he began making albums, it was with a granite surety of purpose. The title of his fine 2002 debut, *Looking Forward,* articulated a direction, while the title of his even stronger 2004 follow-up, *Ceremonial,* implied a process and foundation. What changed in between was mostly his confidence as a composer and bandleader, and the endorsement of Branford Marsalis, who made Zenón one of the earliest signings to his Marsalis Music label. At the 2004 Newport Jazz Festival, Marsalis brought Zenón onstage for one churning tune, without a note of rehearsal. (This attention-grabbing trial by fire had the desired effect.) That same year, Zenón became a founding member of the SFJAZZ Collective, joining a formidable front line that included saxophonist Joshua Redman and trumpeter Nicholas Payton.

As he grew into his career as a solo artist, Zenón organized most of his music around a thematic axis: the folkloric and cultural expressions of his homeland. *Jíbaro*, released in 2005, was his exploration of *música jíbara*, a springy style found in the mountain regions of Puerto Rico, with roots traceable to seventeenth-century Andalusia. With *Esta Plena* (2009), Zenón harnessed the more carnivalesque, drivingly rhythmic style of *plena*. And *Alma Adentro: The Puerto Rican Songbook* (2011) found him presenting a select twentieth-century survey of popular ballads and boleros, with swooning melody and chamber orchestrations. (At that point he had been featured on recent albums of similar purview by the great bassist Charlie Haden.)

Significantly, Zenón also mined the experience of Puerto Ricans in New York, a community marked by both belonging and difference. In 2012 he designed a large-ensemble, multimedia piece, *Identities Are Changeable*, around a series of oral histories and testimonials that he conducted himself. (He borrowed the title of the piece from a remark made by one of his interviewees, Juan Flores, a social theorist whose scholarly book *The Diaspora Strikes Back: Caribeño Tales of Learning and Turning* had partly inspired the project.) An album version of the work occasionally strained under the weight of the premise, putting words and music at odds with each other.

But there were also moments when Zenón used his interviews as building materials. A track called "Through Culture and Tradition" turned the utterance "bomba y plena" into a hooky refrain. "My Home" did something similar with the casually poignant English phrases "spend some time in Puerto Rico" and "back to my homeland." In this sense, a self-conscious view from the outside became something like the reverse—though Zenón, true to form, was generally less interested in the sights than in the seeing.

You might say the same for any number of artists working seriously with cultural hybrids in the twenty-first century, typically along an avant-garde axis. It's true of the Indian-American alto saxophonist Rudresh Mahanthappa, who used music as a portal to his own heritage—notably in 2008, on a spectacularly realized project called *Kinsmen,* with the traditional Carnatic saxophonist Kadri Gopalnath. The same basic intention could be ascribed to Jen Shyu, in her unclassifiable brand of performance art, which features her singing in more than a half-dozen Asian languages and playing stringed instruments like the gayageum, a twelve-stringed Korean zither. So too with the Iraqi-American trumpeter, santur player, vocalist, and composer Amir ElSaffar, in large-ensemble compositions blending state-of-the-art improvisation and the classical Iraqi *maqam.*

A distinct yet related version of the *maqam,* a system of melodic modes prevalent in the Arabic world, animates the multicultural jazz expression of Ibrahim Maalouf, a virtuoso of the four-valved, quarter-tone trumpet. Maalouf was born in Beirut but raised in Paris, where he established a successful career with his brand of expressive fusions. Some of his music has resembled global pop, with simple hooks over a strong, articulated backbeat. But he delivered a complex master class in globalized jazz practice with a transfixing hourlong suite created in tribute to Oum Kalthoum, one of the Arabic world's canonical singers.

During the American premiere of the piece, in 2015, Maalouf played a seventy-five-minute set based almost entirely on an arrangement of "Alf Leila wa Leila," or "One Thousand and One Nights," Kalthoum's best-loved performance. For much of the set, he evoked the swooping charisma of her vocal lines, worrying and finessing his notes in the service of microtonal melody. His band featured the German pianist Frank Woeste along with several marquee Americans: Mark Turner on tenor saxophone, Larry Grenadier on bass, Clarence Penn on drums. They were airtight but flexible, rumbling and shuddering behind him. Often a theme was scored for trumpet and tenor in octaves, or in a chattering counterpoint. Convergence seemed to be the abiding theme.

"There are lots of common points between Arabic music and jazz music," Maalouf said some months later, after *Kalthoum* had been released as an album. "Of course, improvisation is the most important one. But there is one common point that everybody skips, which is Africa. You can find African color with the blue note in jazz. The blue note is actually a quarter tone. It's a note that you lower slightly. This heritage from Africa is a bridge between American culture and Arab culture, when, these days, most people think that those two cultures have nothing to do together, especially with all of what's happening in terms of politics, society, and religion."[23]

The flow of cosmopolitanism in urban centers has always been integral to jazz's evolution, and in the 2010s there was good reason to pay special attention to London. A new crop of stylish, ambitious, bridge-building young musicians was coming to prominence there, partly through the advocacy of the influential BBC radio deejay and record producer Gilles Peterson. The most striking of these was Shabaka Hutchings, a lanky, shyly magnetic tenor saxophonist and clarinetist born in London but mostly raised in Barbados. Hutchings had a creative and popular breakthrough with his imploringly earthy album *Wisdom of Elders*, released on Peterson's Brownswood label in 2016. The album had been recorded in Johannesburg with a cadre of South African musicians, like the trumpeter Mandla Mlangeni and the drummer Tumi Mogorosi. This band, which Hutchings called Shabaka and the Ancestors, made its first stateside appearances at the 2017 NYC Winter Jazz Fest, and the effect was ecstatic and churning.

An associate of Hutchings, the tabla player and electronic artist Sarathy Korwar, released another notable album in roughly the same season—his debut, *Day to Day* (Ninja Tune). Korwar was born in the United States and raised in India before moving to England, where he connected immediately with cosmopolitan London. Partly inspired by his own field research with the Siddi of southern India, who trace their roots to the Bantu people of Africa, Korwar made *Day to Day* a state-of-the-art meditation on cultural migration—a rather pointed theme at a time when Europe and the United States alike were roiled by invective around Middle Eastern refugees and populist ethnonationalism.

Those very issues came into stark relief when some London musicians booked at the 2017 South by Southwest music festival, in Austin, Texas, were denied entry to the United States. Among them was the drummer Yussef Dayes, who had been expecting to appear with the fusionesque bands United Vibrations and Yussef Kamaal. (His visa, like those of his brothers, Ahmed and Kareem, core members of United Vibrations, was suddenly and summarily revoked.) Dayes's case stirred up an international outcry, and London jazz musicians who did make it to Austin—including Hutchings, Korwar, and drummer Moses Boyd—ended their festival showcase in a show of hopeful protest, with a solidarity jam.

Boyd, an anchor of the new British jazz scene, and in some ways a shining embodiment of it, was born and raised in southeast London to parents of Jamaican and Dominican stock. He grew up around a cacophony of West Indian and African music, as well as jazz, garage, dubstep, and grime. All of those elements merge in his music, with the no-nonsense flair of someone accustomed to a high standard for cultural exchange. At South by Southwest, his band Moses Boyd Exodus ended its performance with a rampaging take on its trademark tune, "Rye Lane Shuffle." Rumbling freely on his toms, Boyd was joined by a close partner, Binker Golding, on tenor saxophone.

The groove that emerged was Nigerian Afrobeat by way of a modern jazz metropolis, one with every resource at hand. And on that level Boyd and Golding were simply working under the same presumptions they applied to their improvising duo, Binker and Moses, which won a slew of British awards in 2015 with an album called *Dem Ones* (Gearbox). A follow-up double album on the same label in 2017, *Journey to the Mountain of Forever,* featured a fantastical concept but a similar rugged cohesion, at least on the first disc, which featured the musicians in duologue. The second disc brought in some guests, including Korwar on tabla, Yussef Dayes on drums, and the free-improv lodestar Evan Parker, a hero from a previous generation, on soprano saxophone.

The strength of London's polyglot young jazz cohort had reached undeniable critical mass by early 2018, when Hutchings joined the roster of Impulse!, which had been restarted under the corporate aegis of the Universal Music Group. Hutchings's first move as a major-label artist was to release an album by Sons of Kemet, one of his several working bands. The baseline for Sons of Kemet is rampaging ebullience, with two drummers thrashing carnival rhythms while an apparently inexhaustible tuba player, Theon Cross, maintains a low-end churn.

Hutchings also served as the project coordinator for *We Out Here*, a Brownswood Records compilation conceived as a showcase for the scene. Along with Cross, whose contribution is a lively nod to his southeast London neighborhood, "Brockley," and Boyd, whose track, "The Balance," emulates the hypnotic glow of house music, the sampler includes tracks from the horizon-scanning bands Ezra Collective and Maisha. A persuasive young saxophonist named Nubya Garcia, who like Hutchings had been deeply influenced by a Caribbean heritage, brought presence and charisma to her track, "Once," sounding in no particular hurry to bask in the attention that was suddenly her due.

But London wasn't the only modern jazz city producing compelling work inspired by Diasporic legacies and cultural drift. Back in New York, the Cuban pianist David Virelles turned an interrogation of his heritage—reaching back to ancient expressions of Yoruban religious ritual—into a compelling series of projects and recordings, stretching the scope of possibility for Afro-Cuban jazz.

Virelles, like Zenón and others before him, first demonstrated an advanced fluency in the postbop tradition; by his early thirties, he was the pianist of choice for the saxophonists Ravi Coltrane and Chris Potter. (As a child he'd studied classically in Cuba, where his mother was a symphonic flutist.) Among the elders in his pantheon were Steve Coleman, whom he met in Cuba, and Henry Threadgill, whom he encountered in New York.

After working in a range of settings, Virelles delivered his first great statement with a band he called Continuum, featuring the venerable avant-garde drummer Andrew Cyrille, the revered Afro-Cuban percussionist and vocalist Román Díaz, and the authoritative bassist Ben Street. The group's self-titled debut album, released on Pi Recordings in 2012, presented a swirl of tonal color and intriguing texture, connecting with the pulse of Santería through a prism of modern jazz harmony. The amalgam felt familiar but disorienting, ritualistic but flexible. It wasn't a crowd-pleasing effort, like "Manteca." But it struck a deep chord; that year, Ben Ratliff and I both listed *Continuum* in our top-ten album lists in *The New York Times*.

On a follow-up album, *Mbókò,* released on ECM in 2014, Virelles refined his process without losing any clarity of expression. Drawing inspiration from the Abakuá, a Cuban secret society whose creolized rituals have roots in Nigeria, Virelles reenlisted Díaz on vocals and *biankoméko,* an array of hand drums. The album's subtitle was "Sacred Music for Piano, Two Basses, Drum Set and Biankoméko Abakuá," and the other musicians were bassists Robert Hurst and Thomas Morgan and drummer Marcus Gilmore.

At times the music inverted the standard foreground-and-background arrangement in a jazz ensemble: a track called "The Scribe (Tratado de Mpegó)" gave Díaz the responsibility of advancing a narrative, over a slow, processional cadence and a mysterious toll of chords. Elsewhere the ensemble embraced rhythmic abstraction of the sort you'd associate with the AACM; you could hear "Aberiñán y Aberisún" and draw a connection to an older pianist-composer like Muhal Richard Abrams. "Seven, Through the Divination Horn," with a more focused rhythmic center and a pealing harmonic character, recalls a postbop antecedent like Andrew Hill. But what mattered in the music wasn't the place it inhabited in the so-called jazz lineage. It was the enactment of a process—as culturally specific as the image of Oscar Valdés issuing a chant to Eleguá, but also, like any modern improvisational practice, slippery and free.

———

Ibrahim Maalouf, *Kalthoum* (Impulse!)
Rudresh Mahanthappa, *Kinsmen* (Pi)
Danilo Pérez, *Motherland* (Verve)
Various, *We Out Here* (Brownswood)
Miguel Zenón, *Típico* (Miel)

12

Style Against Style

Mary Halvorson couldn't be seen, and it was a problem. She was settling into the first set of her momentous Village Vanguard debut, in midsummer of 2017. The engagement had been highly touted in the press, and the club was at capacity, humming with the sort of nervous, expectant energy unique to this particular proving ground. Not many female bandleaders had headlined the Vanguard over its unsurpassed reign as a New York institution. Fewer still fit the sort of astringent aesthetic profile that Halvorson had formed over the past decade, as an important new figure in the improvising avant-garde.

The band that she'd brought to the club was an octet, as on her superb recent album *Away with You*. And as on that album, the group's front line comprised some of the most astute composer-improvisers in New York: the trumpeter Jonathan Finlayson, the saxophonists Jon Ira-bagon and Ingrid Laubrock, and the trombonist Jacob Garchik. They formed a phalanx across the Vanguard stage, which was one reason that Halvorson was obscured. "Where is she?" demanded Lorraine Gordon, the club's outspoken nonagenarian owner, troubling the quiet after the first welcoming round of applause. *"I can't see her."*

Halvorson was seated, as usual, with her hollow-body Guild Artist

Award guitar. The dimensions of the instrument, a big box archtop made in 1970, didn't really allow for any other option. And because of the crowded logistics of the bandstand, she was seated behind her horn section, largely inaccessible to any sight line. From a visual standpoint, this was a form of egoless immersion bordering on awkward self-effacement. Gordon repeated her complaint.

Though she heard the remarks, Halvorson didn't acknowledge them from the stage, forging on with the set. The issue was irresolvable, after all. And the music was formidable in both its requirements and its desired effect. On "Spirit Splitter (No. 54)," which opened the set, a featured second guitarist, the pedal steel virtuoso Susan Alcorn, framed a handsome melodic line in a cold, clear beam, while the horns bleated busy annotations. The theme evoked a chamber fanfare, shrewdly hocketed like a medieval motet. When Halvorson made her presence felt, it was with a growl of open intervals from deep within the ensemble stir: you couldn't spot her but you heard her, and felt the unmistakable pull of her design.

Elsewhere in the set, her guitar assumed a more central role. "Away with You," the album's title track, began with a whirling gyre of oblong arpeggios that she traced with staccato flair. Her solo was emblematic, a fluent but wary-seeming set of elaborations that hinged on both her judicious sense of phrase and the physical tactility of her sound. She ended some notes with a wobbly hiccup, and stopped others short, as if biting them off at the ends. Her flinty but resonant tone, produced with a hard attack and just a hint of digital delay, had the spiky, alien beauty of a sea urchin.

Among other things, the improvised music tradition is predicated on an expression of personality. As a listener, you're looking for fluency within a language; you're looking for a spark of spontaneity and maybe truth. But what seals the deal is an instrumental *voice*, one that speaks with an inviolable syntax, cadence, and grain. For all the profusion of bright new talent in our time, artists fulfilling this criterion don't come along as often as you'd think.

Halvorson announced her official arrival in 2008, with her debut as a leader, *Dragon's Head*. Released on the small but stylish avant-garde label Firehouse 12, it was a head-turning trio album featuring the bassist John Hébert and the drummer Ches Smith. There were ten original compositions, spanning a range of structural oddities and off-kilter formal techniques. The lasting takeaway, though, was the decisive jolt of Halvorson's guitar playing. In her graceful deployment of dissonance, her percussive articulation, and her relaxed but assertive cadence, she was already an original in every sense. She seemed to know not only who she was as a musician, but also precisely where she was headed.

Close observers of the experimental improv scene already had some vague familiarity with Halvorson—as one of the younger protégés of Anthony Braxton and as a DIY collaborator of smart iconoclasts like the drummer Weasel Walter and the bassist Trevor Dunn. She had been prominently featured in one of Dunn's bands, Trio Convulsant, alongside Ches Smith. That group's lone studio album, *Sister Phantom Owl Fish*, released on Ipecac in 2004, was a brash, concussive affair informed to no small degree by the doomy churn of underground metal.

Halvorson knew that her bond with Smith would form a flexible spine for her trio. The linchpin was Hébert, whom she first heard in a band led by the postbop avant-gardist Andrew Hill. But the jazz tradition was something that seemed to provoke a studied ambivalence in Halvorson, as if she were preemptively worried about being painted into a corner. "I knew I wanted something sort of based in jazz, but hopefully not with traditional forms and structures," she said of the music on *Dragon's Head*, a few weeks before the album's release. "And not too rigid; I wanted to leave things somewhat open. And I wanted something that had driving energy; that was important to me too. And I felt that both John and Ches could do that."[1]

One thing that drew Halvorson to Hébert's bass playing was the roomy strength of his sound, which she described admiringly with words like "woody" and "hollow." She was concerned with similar properties in her own playing. Producing that sound had been her primordial impulse when she first came into contact with an acoustic guitar in the house, as a child.

I remember instinctively wanting to hit the strings hard, with a really thick pick. That kind of came out of nowhere. So part of it was instinctual: that was how I wanted to play guitar. But also then thinking about it later, having a woody sound like a bass. There are some guitar players that have a more fluid, less pick-oriented sound that I love. But I was sort of taking influence from the upright bass rather than jazz guitar—getting the biggest guitar I could find and having the woodiness of the instrument come across.[2]

This thought was echoed by Smith, whose profile as a sideman at the time extended from the art-rock band Xiu Xiu to Ceramic Dog, a demonically intense trio led by the cult-hero guitar improviser Marc Ribot. "She picks extremely hard, every note," Smith said. "I can relate to that. It's almost like an antagonistic interface with the instrument at times, really aggressive. She's not afraid to really push the limits of the instrument physically. I've played with rock players who play much, much lighter than her."[3]

But there was a delicate quality in Halvorson's playing too, when that's what she intended. The compositions on *Dragon's Head* cover a full dynamic range, in a way that feels entirely natural. Borrowing a practice from Braxton, she gave her compositions numbers as well as titles. The ten tracks on the album come sequenced out of order, but it's possible to trace the evolution of her writing for the trio. The opening track, "Old Nine Two Six Four Two Dies (No. 10)" is in some respects the most sophisticated theme on the album, with a dark chordal path and a loping but determined pulse. The first several compositions she wrote, beginning with "Momentary Lapse (No. 1)," feel a bit more schematic, less tailored to the strengths of the band.

Still, the entire album is an announcement, and a marker. Few debut albums in jazz have landed with a stronger sense of self, or set up a more promising way forward. The cornetist and composer Taylor Ho Bynum, a fellow Braxtonian who had helped bring Halvorson to Firehouse 12 Records, hardly had an objective perspective on the album. But his assessment, delivered in an e-mail, held some key insights worth hanging on to nonetheless:

I think she's made a truly definitive recording. Something that represents the potential of the next generation of musicians: art-

ists who've grown up after the dust has settled on the various aesthetic battles of previous decades; artists who can comfortably
reference rock, or straight-ahead, or avant-jazz, or metal, since
it was all music in their ears growing up. Mary pulls off the feat
of having all of this be a part of her music, yet it remaining iden-
tifiably and uniquely "Halvorson" music. She doesn't sound like
anyone else, and she doesn't sound like she could exist at any time
but the present.[4]

Halvorson grew up in Brookline, Massachusetts, where she studied the
violin for five years, beginning in second grade. A dawning obsession
with Jimi Hendrix led her to the electric guitar: she got a Fender Stra-
tocaster and some tablature books, teaching herself riffs from the classic
rock warhorses. Her first guitar teacher, Issi Rozen, happened to be a
jazz musician, and he imparted some fundamentals of harmony. Her
father also had some jazz records in the house.

There wasn't much of a jazz program at Brookline High School,
though Bynum had also been a student there. (Five years older, he
just missed Halvorson as a student; they first met on a Braxton tour in
2004.) Brookline's proximity to Boston meant access to summer programs at the New England Conservatory and the Berklee College of
Music, where Halvorson learned to deflect sexist appraisals of her talent. "Nobody would take me seriously," she recalled. "They would take
one look at me and say, 'Okay, folk singer.' That was really hard for me,
and I was angry a lot of the time. I did all these summer programs, and
I never encountered another female playing jazz guitar. Ever. So I don't
feel uncomfortable being the only woman in a group, but back then I
would get treated differently."[5]

Even as a teenager, she gravitated toward an experimental ethos:
she saw the Art Ensemble of Chicago in concert, and developed an
obsession with Ornette Coleman. Though her undergraduate major
at Wesleyan was biology, she encountered a life-changing mentor in
Braxton, who urged all of his students to forge their own paths, and
in some cases their own creative lexicons. When Halvorson wrote a
thesis about the Art Ensemble of Chicago, Braxton was her advisor. But
one of the deeper lessons he imparted was the conceptual distinction

between what he called stylists and restructuralists. "A stylist would be somebody that had basically perfected a tradition, and maybe they had their own voice within it but it was definitely confined to a particular style," Halvorson recalled. "Like Wynton Marsalis. And then a restructuralist would be somebody who had come up with their own system and method."[6]

Braxton was a vibrant role model in this respect: a fantastically ambitious conceptualist and composer aligned with the AACM, famous for the abstruse, elusive logic of his creations. He had been a media sensation in the 1970s, when he made a series of frame-exploding musical statements in performance and on record. His compositions utilized proprietary strategies and came with numerical and graphical designations, their titles sometimes resembling notes from a lecture on particle physics. His scale as a composer ran from the unaccompanied soliloquy—he pioneered the interrogative, existential mode for solo saxophone—to a vast sprawl, as in the descriptively titled 1978 album *For Four Orchestras*. At Wesleyan he had presided over more than one generation of musical rule breakers—though his own creative concept had its own set of guidelines, notably an elaborate theoretical framework called the Tri-Centric model.

Halvorson took Braxton's exhortative instruction to heart, though she was still in the formative stage of her musical path. The emphasis on originality was echoed by another important teacher, the experimental guitarist Joe Morris, with whom she took private lessons. And that go-your-own-path ethos stood in stark contrast to the prevailing atmosphere at the New School, where Halvorson transferred in her junior year, in search of more formal training.

She lasted just one year, practicing constantly and bristling against the pressure to conform. But she also met some future collaborators, like the explosive drummer Mike Pride, who introduced her to Trevor Dunn. Even at this stage she gave the impression of someone with a clear bead on her sound. "I remember we played this standards gig, and she came out with these huge, weird intervals," recalled Peter Evans, a trumpeter of audacious instinct and exceptional technique. "Any individual that's pursuing this kind of music, there's going to be this beautiful individual stamp on it, which can only come from this person. Mary always sounded like that, really."[7]

These and other musicians in Halvorson's emerging peer group were serious but not self-serious, well schooled but not overrefined. They drew no distinction between jazz's "inside" and "out," nor between jazz and other musical languages. Evans had studied jazz and classical music at Oberlin; he was already developing a trademark of spontaneous solo recitals that seemed to stretch the limits of human possibility, let alone the delineations of genre. Matana Roberts, a saxophonist who had come up in the Chicago chapter of the AACM, was intently focused on a performance piece called *Coin Coin*, which she envisioned as a living sound assemblage, interweaving genealogy, fugitive slave narratives, superstition, incantation, and folklore.

Halvorson's own constellation of interests included the visionary English multi-instrumentalist Robert Wyatt, formerly of Soft Machine; Deerhoof, a jumpy and exclamatory modern art-rock band; and the heavy-gauge experimental outfits Hella and Orthrelm. But she also had her jazz-world preoccupations: one reference point for her second album—*Saturn Sings*, released on Firehouse 12 in 2010—was the small-group writing of Benny Golson, notably his signature ballad "I Remember Clifford," as arranged for the Jazztet.

Saturn Sings is a quintet album, with Finlayson and Irabagon joining Halvorson's working trio. She released another album by this band in 2012, calling it *Bending Bridges*. Then came an expansion to seven pieces, with the 2013 release *Illusionary Sea*, which signaled a step forward in Halvorson's skills as a composer-arranger. Her indirect inspiration for that album came not only from sources like *Dimensions & Extensions*, a Sam Rivers album with a similar instrumentation, but also recordings by Sam Cooke and the Soul Stirrers, for their use of four-part gospel vocal harmony.

The stubborn integrity of Halvorson's albums, which feel of a piece despite their various quirks, carried her name beyond the avant-garde circle that claimed her. Keith Jarrett once mentioned her as the rare younger improviser who had caused him to sit up and take notice.

"Mary's interesting to me because of who she found," he said. "She found some horn players I never heard of before. Very proficient at the least. But the ideas that are coming out of these guys! I'm sure they probably think they're playing jazz."

He laughed. "I don't think *she* thinks she is."[8]

"I don't enjoy jazz guitar in general," Halvorson said in 2008. "I don't enjoy listening to a lot of it. I don't enjoy the tone. In general I've found its role in jazz to be kind of difficult, and not something I would put on and listen to."[9]

She liked Ben Monder and Kurt Rosenwinkel, two of the instrument's leading miracle workers, each of whom had brought sleek new proficiencies to its modern-jazz dialect. What repelled her was the received wisdom of a boppish fretboard language, though there were some exemptions there too. This was, after all, a matter of taste rather than ideology. And taste is mutable, no less than the historical perceptions around a given work.

One evening in the spring of 2014, Halvorson plugged into an amp at Le Poisson Rouge in Greenwich Village, cleared her throat, and began playing an unusual set. She was the opening act for another guitarist, the well-traveled experimentalist Nels Cline. But whereas he would be leading his longtime band, the Nels Cline Singers, she was onstage with nothing more than a chair, her guitar, and a few standard effects pedals. She was quiet, alert, with an almost classical composure; the air around her grew very still and clear, and so did the mood in the club.

Her first selection was "Sadness," a piece by Ornette Coleman, and she quickly set her own terms of engagement with it: emphatic attack; sparse, deliberative phrasing; a judicious yet jarring pitch-wobble at the tail end of a note, or sometimes the beginning. This was all in keeping with her established style, but the exposure of a solo setting brought an added frisson, intensifying the music's gawky elegance and giving it the lonesome integrity of outsider art.

That impression held through the remainder of the set, which consisted of interesting cover tunes: a slinky and unsettled "Ida Lupino," by Carla Bley; a terse, melancholy "Blood," by the art-rock and free-jazz polymath Annette Peacock; "Platform," by one of Halvorson's peers, the bassist Chris Lightcap, outfitted with gnarly power chords; Thelonious Monk's "Ruby, My Dear," recast as a crooked saloon song. Halvorson varied her approach with each piece, moving along the axis from delicate fingerpicking to furious strumming. She never sounded at a loss for ideas, and her careful sense of pacing kept the set from slipping into monotony.

Sparseness was hardly a new proposition for Halvorson. She had extensive history in a duo with the violinist Jessica Pavone, another Braxton affiliate, with whom she created art songs of dissonant, untutored effect. But the strategies available to Halvorson and Pavone—intuitive counterpoint, prickly call-and-response, chamber miniatures, even a sort of tandem folk singing—were contingent on duologue. As a soloist, Halvorson was more limited. She further circumscribed her options by focusing on the instrument at hand; she wasn't predisposed to build self-referential loops, like Bill Frisell, or elaborate striations of noise, like Cline.

The only touchstone that came easily to mind during Halvorson's performance—maybe a bit too easily, at least during her minor-key elaborations on "Blood"—were the ugly-beauty solo-guitar peregrinations of Marc Ribot, especially on his 2001 album *Saints.* Asked to name her guitar influences in the solo format, Halvorson mentioned Ribot first, followed by Joe Morris and the noise-rock legend Bill Orcutt. There was a kind of punk integrity to her restrictive parameters, which made sense: as it happened, she'd devised her solo-performance ethos as a tour opener for Buzz Osborne, aka King Buzzo, of the Melvins.

Halvorson's album *Meltframe,* which arrived in 2015, was the eventual manifestation of these solo investigations. "Ruby, My Dear" had dropped out of the program, but other songs remained, with notable additions, like Duke Ellington's "Solitude." The album opens with a version of the Oliver Nelson composition "Cascades," which appears on the classic album *The Blues and the Abstract Truth.* Rather than interpret the tune with a postbop pulse, she goes stark—underscoring its original purpose as an étude, while using distortion and halting silence to give it the feeling of something menacing and barbed. McCoy Tyner's ballad "Aisha," best known for its appearance on the John Coltrane album *Olé Coltrane,* comes in for a similar reinvention: Halvorson is reverential with the melody, applying a watery shimmer of delay, but her improvisation edges toward darker territory, briefly flaring into demonic distortion.

Meltframe was heralded as a breakthrough, mainly outside the jazz ecosystem: it received glowing coverage in *Pitchfork* and *Rolling Stone*. It served as a hinge in Halvorson's work, swinging open the door to a more complex articulation of her ideas. "Oddly enough, I think doing the solo record made me think orchestrally," she said. "I was trying to make each song not sound the same. How can I orchestrate these songs and make as wide a palette as possible? So I was in the headspace of thinking about those things when I started writing the octet music."[10]

Away with You, which has a central catalyst in Alcorn's pedal steel, was only one manifestation of Halvorson's capacity for collaboration. From the beginning of her experience as a working musician, well before most people were paying attention, she was forming allegiances with a broad range of improvisers and composers of unplaceable style.

Some were fellow Braxtonians like Bynum, who featured Halvorson on several albums by a chamberlike sextet. "She's completely spoiled me in my own ensembles," he said. "I've always tended towards the Ellington tradition of writing music for specific individuals, and she offers such a powerfully individualistic voice to play with. For a lot of my tunes, I just want to create a canvas for her to do her thing."[11] Bynum also featured Halvorson alongside more than a dozen other improvisers—unconventional virtuosos like the trumpeters Nate Wooley and Stephanie Richards—in a formidable and stylistically roving large ensemble. In 2016 this group released an album whose title reads like a stage direction: *Enter the Plustet.*

Halvorson worked in texture-mad, experimental ensembles led by her own band members, including Smith, Garchik, and Laubrock. She struck a tone of sparse elegance in Secret Keeper, a collaborative duo with the bassist Stephan Crump. In the excellent Tomeka Reid Quartet, which evoked an avant-garde jazz lineage stretching from Eric Dolphy to Abdul Wadud, she served multiple roles at once: chordal scaffold, rhythmic booster, contrapuntal foil for Reid's cello. And in the Hookup, a combo led by the drummer Tomas Fujiwara, Halvorson exercised a slippery license, choosing at any point to mingle with the horn section or hang back with bass and drums.

Together with Fujiwara and the bassist Michael Formanek, she also worked steadily in a collective trio called Thumbscrew, which released its self-titled debut album in 2014. Its guitar-bass-drums format would seem to dictate a conventional hierarchy, but Thumbscrew defied the mold. Pushing toward epiphany, the group explored an ever-shifting alignment of texture while remaining grounded in pulse, a strategy that drew on Halvorson's full creative resources even when she wasn't taking the lead. "Improvisationally she'll find a point of view that I wouldn't have been able to think of on my own," said Formanek, who made Thumbscrew the rhythm foundation of his big band, Ensemble Kolossus. "She's always working on perfecting these different approaches, following these different interval studies and these personal combinations of things. She's kind of ready for any idea."[12]

As if to illustrate that point, Halvorson branched beyond instrumental music for a proudly unclassifiable project called *Code Girl*, featuring the members of Thumbscrew behind a galvanizing front line of Amirtha Kidambi on vocals and Ambrose Akinmusire on trumpet. Commissioned by the Jazz Gallery, where it had its premiere in the summer of 2016, *Code Girl* was conceived as a focused push into songwriting for Halvorson, who took it seriously.

She had long dabbled in writing poetry and lyrics, drawing her earliest inspiration from the likes of Bob Dylan, Joni Mitchell, and Leonard Cohen. Her more recent influences in that vein included Robert Wyatt and Elliott Smith. But the results on *Code Girl* strayed far from any of these reference points, and even farther from anything like a confessional urge.

The title was a nod to Anthony Braxton, whom Halvorson had once heard uttering the phrase while on tour. She'd jotted it in her notebook for possible later use. When Halvorson began mobilizing behind her new project, she latched on to this scrap of free association. "It just seemed to fit," she recalled. "Because at that point I'd written a lot of the lyrics, and they seemed a little bit coded and strange." The multivalence of the term only sharpened its appeal: "It could be like coding a computer, or breaking a code, some kind of a password."

The songs on *Code Girl*, eventually released on an album by that title, do have a coiled and cryptic beauty; they're full of haunting resonances and restive tensions, with a style that borrows from psychedelic folk and art rock as well as new music and avant-garde jazz. Akinmusire moves through the songs with a decisive pliability, equally at home with a crisp melodic line or its tonal opposite, an abstract, smudged-charcoal shading. This plays out not only on several instrumental pieces—like "Thunderhead" and "Off the Record," which employ springy variations on swing rhythm—but also in the elaborative sprawl of the songs with lyrics.

And Kidambi, a powerful singer trained in classical Carnatic methodologies but drawn to uncharted frontiers, proved the ideal messenger for those lyrics. She projects in a voice both clarion and tender, bringing bounce and grace to a melodic framework spiked with chromatic obstacles. She also manages to convey the emotional undercurrent of the lyrics, despite their abstruse designs—the impulse that had led Halvorson to scramble her own signals, applying oblique and nonlinear techniques that belong more to language poetry than conventional song craft. A ballad called "Accurate Hit" features just voice and guitar, evoking an approachable mode of indie-rock intimacy—but the lyrics consist of ominous, disjointed couplets: "original error / terminal insides / searing body." Kidambi imbues them with fearsome presence.

Here and throughout *Code Girl*, Halvorson insists on an expression of complex feeling not only in content but also in form. "It is not predictable my mind," declares Kidambi on the album's calmly unsettled opening track, "My Mind I Find in Time." (Later comes a refrain: "Reconstruction is required in time.") "The Unexpected Natural Phenomenon," an account of a near drowning, begins in dirgelike rubato, builds to a passage of literal screaming, and concludes with a long, thrashing spiral of free improvisation. And on a sci-fi ballad called "Drop the Needle," Kidambi brings deep, declarative intensity to Halvorson's lyrics, which in this case are about the shifting dimensions of the music itself:

> One might drop the needle
> An entire song transcends
> Repeat a twirling hypnotic
> Melody in descending order

Genre, it almost goes without saying, is the least interesting prism through which to assess the songs on *Code Girl.* And yet Halvorson's own expectation for the project was that it might nudge her into an unfamiliar space—something more rigid or repetitive than her usual mode. The results did feel like a stretch, but they were congruent with the rest of her output. What made it personal, in the end, wasn't the incorporation of lyrics so much as the musical signature.

After recording the album, near the close of 2016, Halvorson gave herself a break from composing. "For the first time in my life I felt like I needed to stop for a second," she said. "I feel like the last decade of my life, it's been: 'Okay, next project, write a bunch of music, record an album.' You don't have the time to take a breath and actually take stock in anything. Because I didn't have the next idea, which normally I did, I thought, 'Well great, I'm just going to practice guitar and do the projects that are already happening.'"

One indication of the vitality in Halvorson's peer group, then, is how productive she was over the ensuing year. She performed in duo settings, on separate occasions, with Akinmusire, Crump, Fujiwara, and the harpist Zeena Parkins—and released an album in that format, *Crop Circles,* with the sharply inquisitive pianist Sylvie Courvoisier. She also recorded and toured in a trio led by the drummer Tom Rainey. This was just a small sampling of her collaborative reach, which also extended to the an album titled *Paimon: Book of Angels Volume 32,* a new installment of John Zorn's inexhaustible Masada project. On it, Halvorson leads an ace quartet featuring Fujiwara, her fellow guitarist Miles Okazaki, and the bassist Drew Gress.

Among the other albums she released in 2017 were two standout trio efforts, each released in small-batch form to critical acclaim. The first was *BANGS,* by Jason Moran, with the cornetist Ron Miles—two artists with a profile ostensibly more mainstream than Halvorson's, though that distinction was growing less meaningful all the time. An experiment in form and flow, the album featured compositions from all three musicians, whose stern yet beautiful rapport suggested a sparking of flint and steel.

The second album, released digitally and on limited-edition vinyl, was *New American Songbooks, Volume 1,* an outgrowth of Nate Wooley's online journal *Sound American,* with a mission made plain by its title. It also featured Halvorson with Miles, though the third member came from a different place entirely. He was Greg Saunier, the drummer in Deerhoof, though his energy here skewed more jazz-compatible, in a Paul Motian vein.

Each musician had been asked to bring in a few tunes worth regarding as "standards," whatever they might take that to mean. Halvorson chose some bittersweet songs by Fiona Apple and Elliott Smith. She also arranged "Vignette," a haunting Gary Peacock ballad from *Tales of Another,* an album he'd made in 1977 with Keith Jarrett and Jack DeJohnette, the nascent Standards Trio. She was the picture of fluency on these tunes, but she also delivered a clomp of chords, redolent of Harlem stride piano, on James P. Johnson's "Snowy Morning Blues."

And on "Day Dream," a Duke Ellington–Billy Strayhorn ballad from 1941, Halvorson voiced the melody as an exquisite reverie, slow and serious. She was unerringly, even touchingly faithful to the melody, but her chords flickered like the surface of a faraway mirage.

———————

Mary Halvorson, *Code Girl* (Firehouse 12)
Mary Halvorson Octet, *Away with You* (Firehouse 12)
Mary Halvorson Trio, *Dragon's Head* (Firehouse 12)
Jason Moran, *BANGS* (Yes)
Thumbscrew, *Thumbscrew* (Cuneiform)

Afterword

As long as people have been talking about jazz, they've been talking about where it's going. The conversation rests on presumptions of forward progress and collective striving. But while some musicians have embraced the premise, others refused to play along. A well-meaning interviewer once asked Thelonious Monk where he thought jazz was going, and the pianist replied: "I don't know where it's going. Maybe it's going to hell. You can't make anything go anywhere. It just happens."

Monk's retort, an instant classic, contains the wisdom of intuition. There is no way of prognosticating jazz's future, or even its precise trajectory, because the art form doesn't adhere to a linear axis. The evolutionary thrust in the music is real, but it shouldn't be misconstrued as a motive. Jazz has no inherent locomotive agenda, as some factions would have you believe, nor is it the monolith that some other factions take pains to preserve. The music's ongoing story might best be understood in terms of a climate: volatile, variable, subject to unseen forces outside anyone's direct control.

Here's what we can say, at this stage: the music we call jazz continues to find traction in a range of conditions. Its advances are manifold, proceeding on multiple fronts. It doesn't exist in a vacuum; most improvising musicians maintain a relationship to popular culture, however tenuous or circumscribed. The level of baseline proficiency keeps climbing, and vital new artists keep emerging, often to seize the moment on their own terms. The decentralization of what we used to call "the scene" can be disconcerting, but it's also a boon.

Not to imply that the verities of jazz's past have receded into darkness. Every year brings more attrition among the generation that defined jazz in the postwar era, but their lessons survive—preserved in ever more accessible forms, and carried on by admirers and inheritors. Spend some time in the presence of a swashbuckling artist like Jazzmeia Horn, whose jazz-vocal totems include Betty Carter and Sarah Vaughan, or Aaron Diehl, whose fastidious pianism can evoke John Lewis of the Modern Jazz Quartet—or Riley Mulherkar, whose passions range beyond the Westerlies to the glories of King Oliver, Louis Armstrong, and Dizzy Gillespie—and you leave both inspired and reassured. Young musicians don't come up the way they used to, but the brightest among them will always find a way to access the root traditions of the music.

For another constituency, the vibrant synergies between jazz, hip-hop, electronic music, and R&B amount to a raison d'être—a lifeline to young audiences, and in particular young black audiences, that had seemed almost lost for good. The runaway success of a Robert Glasper or a Kamasi Washington amounts to proof of concept for this crowd, as well as the basis for an inevitable spate of stories about jazz's "new golden age." Among the musicians to watch in this zone are the pianists Kris Bowers and James Francies; the vibraphonists Joel Ross and Warren Wolf; the saxophonists Lakecia Benjamin, Shabaka Hutchings, Logan Richardson, and Nubya Garcia; and the trumpeters Takuya Kuroda and Keyon Harrold. (The list goes on and on.)

Elsewhere, heady potential resides in an ever more advanced articulation of harmony and rhythm, the stuff of complex metrics and intricate maneuvers. The members of Fieldwork—Steve Lehman, Vijay Iyer, Tyshawn Sorey—all helped set the bar for this ascendant strain of experimentation in the music. So too have the pianists Craig Taborn, Matt Mitchell, Kris Davis, and Eve Risser; the vocalists Jen Shyu, Sara Serpa, and Amirtha Kidambi; and the guitarists Miles Okazaki and Liberty Ellman, among many others. The embrace of this cohort by the new-music classical establishment is a form of mutual outreach, and a hopeful turn.

Across every iteration of style, the ascendant currency is an ever greater investment in ideas. To be a successful jazz artist today is to be, on some level, a conceptualist. This isn't just about courting institutional approval, or pursuing grants and commissions—though it's true that many musicians rely on that funding apparatus. As generations of artists have come of age without the promise of a tried-and-true path through the industry, they were forced to start out with the most fundamental questions: Why do this? What's my contribution? What do I want to say, and how best to convey it? These artists, looking to ambitious role models, have set their talent against the odds. For the most disciplined among them, it's a recipe for pure creative possibility, opening up new ways of seeing the music, and not just in the forward view.

The treatment of Thelonious Monk's centenary, in 2017, suggests a case in point. Early in the year there came a glowing artifact direct from the source: the first-ever release of a soundtrack Monk recorded for *Les Liaisons Dangereuses,* the 1959 Roger Vadim film. Musicians took note, savoring rich new documentation of a working band at a moment of great momentum in Monk's career. There also came deluxe reissues of Monk's known output, and an anniversary edition of *Thelonious Monk: The Life and Times of an American Original,* the definitive biography by Robin D. G. Kelley. There was never a better time to draw a clear bead on the dimensions of Monk's genius, and consider its implications.

Jazz culture has grown adept at mobilizing behind a good centennial tribute, and that happened in all the expected ways. Jazz at Lincoln Center held a two-day Monk symposium, and presented a club date by the T. S. Monk Sextet, led by the pianist's son and leading spokesman. A handful of more figurative Monk inheritors released tribute albums, from the teenaged piano phenom Joey Alexander leading his trio, to the composer-arranger John Beasley with the band he calls the MONK'estra. Wadada Leo Smith, the leonine avant-garde hero, recorded a solo trumpet recital of Monk's music, in an air of ascetic solemnity.

But also in the mix were some Monk celebrations that accessed his music and genius in a thrumming present tense. Jason Moran went on tour with his multimedia concert program *In My Mind: Monk at Town Hall, 1959,* an impressionistic homage incorporating found audio, field research, and an affectionate spirit of freedom. And the pianist Ethan Iverson, another diehard Monkophile, spearheaded the programming of a ten-day festival presented by Duke Performances at the Durham Fruit & Produce Company, a fifteen-thousand-square-foot warehouse in downtown Durham, North Carolina.

This event, Monk@100, offered myriad angles on its subject. Iverson led a swinging, old-school rhythm section behind a series of guest saxophonists—Houston Person, Joshua Redman, Melissa Aldana, Ravi Coltrane, Chris Potter—in what amounted to a disquisition on Monk's most steadfast instrumental format. Moran abstracted Monk compositions in a duo with Tyshawn Sorey. A solo piano concert offered those compositions for interpretation by Iverson and four colleagues, including Orrin Evans, his replacement in the Bad Plus. Other creative alignments involved musicians like the pianist Gerald Clayton and the guitarist Bill Frisell.

The profusion of perspectives in the event was not only intentional but instructive, because it honored the spirit of multiplicity that now prevails. There can be no way of knowing whether Monk would have approved of Monk@100, but he probably would have appreciated the notion that no single view of his work reigns supreme.

And as is often true of jazz, the historical thrust of the programming only sharpened a focus on the present moment and its endless possibilities. Progress is almost beside the point. The music will flow and fluctuate, keep going. And where to? Anywhere. It just happens.

The 129 Essential Albums
of the Twenty-First Century (So Far)

A spectacular range of music has been released under the rubric of jazz since the turn of the century. These are among the best, arranged by year: work your way through the list, and you'll have a good impression of the contemporary state of the art. (No artist appears more than once as a leader, though there's ample overlap in personnel.)

2000

   1. Jim Black's AlasNoAxis, *AlasNoAxis* (Winter & Winter)

   2. Brian Blade Fellowship, *Perceptual* (Blue Note)

   3. Kurt Elling, *Live in Chicago* (Blue Note)

   4. Nils Petter Molvær, *Solid Ether* (ECM)

   5. Danilo Pérez, *Motherland* (Verve)

   6. David Sánchez, *Melaza* (Columbia)

   7. David S. Ware, *Surrendered* (Columbia)

2001

   8. Chicago Underground Quartet, *Chicago Underground Quartet* (Thrill Jockey)

   9. The Claudia Quintet, *The Claudia Quintet* (Blueshift CRI)

  10. Marilyn Crispell / Paul Motian / Gary Peacock, *Amaryllis* (ECM)

  11. Kurt Rosenwinkel, *The Next Step* (Verve)

  12. John Scofield, *Works for Me* (Verve)

  13. Matthew Shipp, *New Orbit* (Thirsty Ear)

2002

14. Ben Allison, *Peace Pipe* (Palmetto)
15. Tim Berne, *Science Friction* (Screwgun)
16. Keith Jarrett Trio, *Always Let Me Go* (ECM)
17. Wayne Shorter Quartet, *Footprints Live!* (Blue Note)
18. Luciana Souza, *Brazilian Duos* (Sunnyside)
19. Tomasz Stańko Quartet, *Soul of Things* (ECM)
20. Cecil Taylor, *The Willisau Concert* (Intakt)
21. Cassandra Wilson, *Belly of the Sun* (Blue Note)

2003

22. The Bad Plus, *These Are the Vistas* (Columbia)
23. David Binney, *South* (ACT)
24. Terence Blanchard, *Bounce* (Blue Note)
25. Jane Ira Bloom, *Chasing Paint* (Arabesque)
26. Fred Hersch Trio, *Live at the Village Vanguard* (Palmetto)
27. Dave Holland Quintet, *Extended Play: Live at Birdland* (ECM)
28. Ahmad Jamal, *In Search of Momentum* (Dreyfus)

2004

29. Geri Allen, *The Life of a Song* (Telarc)
30. Don Byron, *Ivey-Divey* (Blue Note)
31. Frank Kimbrough, *Lullabluebye* (Palmetto)
32. Tony Malaby Trio, *Adobe* (Sunnyside)
33. Medeski Martin & Wood, *End of the World Party (Just in Case)* (Blue Note)
34. Brad Mehldau Trio, *Anything Goes* (Warner Bros.)
35. Mulgrew Miller Trio, *Live at Yoshi's: Volume One* (Maxjazz)

2005

36. Amina Figarova, *September Suite* (Munich)
37. Guillermo Klein, *Una Nave* (Sunnyside)
38. Pat Metheny Group, *The Way Up* (Nonesuch)
39. Paul Motian / Bill Frisell / Joe Lovano, *I Have the Room Above Her* (ECM)
40. Sonny Rollins, *Without a Song: The 9/11 Concert* (Milestone)
41. Jenny Scheinman, *12 Songs* (Cryptogramophone)

42. Cuong Vu, *It's Mostly Residual* (Intoxicate)

43. Miguel Zenón, *Jíbaro* (Marsalis Music)

2006

44. Ornette Coleman, *Sound Grammar* (Sound Grammar)

45. Dave Douglas Quintet, *Meaning and Mystery* (Greenleaf)

46. Andrew Hill, *Time Lines* (Blue Note)

47. Christian McBride, *Live at Tonic* (Ropeadope)

2007

48. Michael Brecker, *Pilgrimage* (Heads Up)

49. The Nels Cline Singers, *Draw Breath* (Cryptogramophone)

50. Robert Glasper, *In My Element* (Blue Note)

51. Herbie Hancock, *River: The Joni Letters* (Verve)

52. Lionel Loueke, *Virgin Forest* (ObliqSound)

53. Wynton Marsalis and the Jazz at Lincoln Center Orchestra, *Congo Square* (Jazz at Lincoln Center)

54. Bill McHenry, *Roses* (Sunnyside)

55. Joshua Redman, *Back East* (Nonesuch)

2008

56. J. D. Allen Trio, *I Am I Am* (Sunnyside)

57. Anat Cohen, *Notes from the Village* (Anzic)

58. Fieldwork, *Door* (Pi)

59. Bill Frisell, *History, Mystery* (Nonesuch)

60. Mary Halvorson Trio, *Dragon's Head* (Firehouse 12)

61. Charles Lloyd, *Rabo de Nube* (ECM)

62. Rudresh Mahanthappa, *Kinsmen* (Pi)

63. Gonzalo Rubalcaba, *Avatar* (Blue Note)

2009

64. Five Peace Band, *Five Peace Band Live* (Concord)

65. Fly, *Sky & Country* (ECM)

66. Vijay Iyer Trio, *Historicity* (ACT)

67. Darius Jones, *Man'ish Boy* (Aum Fidelity)

68. Steve Lehman Octet, *Travail, Transformation and Flow* (Pi)

69. Joe Lovano's Us Five, *Folk Art* (Blue Note)
70. Myra Melford's Be Bread, *The Whole Tree Gone* (Firehouse 12)
71. Trio 3 / Geri Allen, *At This Time* (Intakt)
72. Matt Wilson Quartet, *That's Gonna Leave a Mark* (Palmetto)

2010

73. Steve Coleman and Five Elements, *Harvesting Semblances and Affinities* (Pi)
74. The Cookers, *Warriors* (Jazz Legacy)
75. Kneebody, *You Can Have Your Moment* (Winter & Winter)
76. Chris Lightcap's Bigmouth, *Deluxe* (Clean Feed)
77. Jason Moran, *Ten* (Blue Note)
78. Paradoxical Frog, *Paradoxical Frog* (Clean Feed)

2011

79. Chris Dingman, *Waking Dreams* (Between Worlds)
80. Gilad Hekselman, *Hearts Wide Open* (Le Chant du Monde)
81. Arturo O'Farrill and the Afro Latin Jazz Orchestra, *40 Acres and a Burro* (Zoho)
82. Gretchen Parlato, *The Lost and Found* (ObliqSound)

2012

83. Ravi Coltrane, *Spirit Fiction* (Blue Note)
84. Tom Harrell, *Number Five* (HighNote)
85. Masabumi Kikuchi Trio, *Sunrise* (ECM)
86. Donny McCaslin, *Casting for Gravity* (Greenleaf)
87. Linda Oh, *Initial Here* (Greenleaf)
88. Wadada Leo Smith, *Ten Freedom Summers* (Cuneiform)

2013

89. Darcy James Argue's Secret Society, *Brooklyn Babylon* (New Amsterdam)
90. The New Gary Burton Quartet, *Guided Tour* (Mack Avenue)
91. Ben Monder, *Hydra* (Sunnyside)
92. Gregory Porter, *Liquid Spirit* (Blue Note)
93. Chris Potter, *The Sirens* (ECM)
94. Matana Roberts, *COIN COIN Chapter Two: Mississippi Moonchile* (Constellation)
95. Craig Taborn Trio, *Chants* (ECM)

2014

96. Ambrose Akinmusire, *The Imagined Savior Is Far Easier to Paint* (Blue Note)
97. Flying Lotus, *You're Dead!* (Warp)
98. Billy Hart Quartet, *One Is the Other* (ECM)
99. Hedvig Mollestad Trio, *Enfant Terrible* (Rune Grammofon)
100. Loren Stillman and Bad Touch, *Going Public* (Fresh Sound New Talent)
101. Mark Turner Quartet, *Lathe of Heaven* (ECM)
102. David Virelles, *Mbókò* (ECM)

2015

103. Amir ElSaffar's Two Rivers Ensemble, *Crisis* (Pi)
104. Makaya McCraven, *In the Moment* (International Anthem)
105. Mike Moreno, *Lotus* (World Culture)
106. Mike Reed's People, Places & Things, *A New Kind of Dance* (482)
107. Tomeka Reid Quartet, *Tomeka Reid Quartet* (Thirsty Ear)
108. Maria Schneider Orchestra, *The Thompson Fields* (ArtistShare)
109. Jen Shyu and Jade Tongue, *Sounds and Cries of the World* (Pi)
110. Henry Threadgill's Zooid, *In for a Penny, In for a Pound* (Pi)
111. Kamasi Washington, *The Epic* (Brainfeeder)

2016

112. Melissa Aldana & Crash Trio, *Back Home* (Word of Mouth)
113. Kris Davis, *Duopoly* (Pyroclastic)
114. Jeff Parker, *The New Breed* (International Anthem)
115. Shabaka and the Ancestors, *Wisdom of Elders* (Brownswood)
116. Tyshawn Sorey, *The Inner Spectrum of Variables* (Pi)
117. Esperanza Spalding, *Emily's D+Evolution* (Concord)

2017

118. Jaimie Branch, *Fly or Die* (International Anthem)
119. Nubya Garcia, *Nubya's 5ive* (Jazz Re:freshed)
120. Ron Miles, *I Am a Man* (Yellowbird)
121. Nicole Mitchell, *Mandorla Awakening II: Emerging Worlds* (FPE)
122. Roscoe Mitchell, *Bells for the South Side* (ECM)
123. Cécile McLorin Salvant, *Dreams and Daggers* (Mack Avenue)
124. Christian Scott aTunde Adjuah, *The Centennial Trilogy* (Ropeadope)

2018

125. María Grand, *Magdalena* (Biophilia)

126. Julian Lage, *Modern Lore* (Mack Avenue)

127. Dafnis Prieto Big Band, *Back to the Sunset* (Dafnison)

128. Logan Richardson, *Blues People* (Ropeadope)

129. Dan Weiss, *Starebaby* (Pi)

Acknowledgments

My gratitude goes first to those who made this book a reality, notably Erroll McDonald, an editor of deep insight, impeccable judgment, and just the right amount of patience. Our collaboration, beginning with a conversation in 2013, has been grounded always in possibility, a spirit of inquiry, and a driving enthusiasm for the music.

Alex Jacobs at the Cheney Agency brought his guidance, expertise, and moral support, and Elyse Cheney was a clear-eyed advocate during the project's most formative stage. I'm also indebted to everyone at the MacDowell Colony for a lifesaving residency that brought the book's structure into focus, and created the ideal conditions to write like mad.

So many musicians have been generous with their time and wisdom that it would be impractical to attempt a full accounting here. But I'm appreciative of specific acts of kindness and cooperation by Herbie Hancock, Sonny Rollins, Jack DeJohnette, Fred Hersch, Maria Schneider, Jason Moran, Steve Coleman, Vijay Iyer, Christian McBride, Brad Mehldau, Esperanza Spalding, Mary Halvorson, Darcy James Argue, and Dan Tepfer.

During a dozen years spent covering the music for *The New York Times*, I had the best possible colleague and role model in Ben Ratliff, who has also been a friend, and the support of smart editors including Fletcher Roberts, Sia Michel, Peter Keepnews, and Caryn Ganz.

Some of the material in this book originally appeared in *Jazz Times*, and I'm grateful to my editors there over the years—Evan Haga, Christopher Porter, Lee Mergner—for their unflagging trust and support. Thanks to Robert Christgau, my former editor at *The Village Voice,* for sharpening my critical faculties and for commissioning the essay "Jazz Goes to College," a portion of which has been adapted here. Thanks also to Michael Shapiro, my editor at *Hana Hou!* magazine, for making it possible to report on the jazz scene in Beijing. And I owe a debt of gratitude to everyone at WBGO and NPR Music, especially Amy Niles and Anya Grundman, who brought me aboard.

For their lasting friendship, and for many thought-provoking conversations about the music, thanks to George Wein, Mark Christman, Michael Pereira, Matt Applebaum, Russell Motter, David Adler, and Jody Rosen. George Blaustein, who deserves better placement in this paragraph, provided honest and detailed manuscript feedback at a crucial stage.

Best for last: my deepest love and gratitude to Ashley Lederer—an ever-perceptive first reader and sounding board, and a champion of this book through every twist and turn. My partner in every respect, she made this possible in more ways than I can name.

Notes

1 CHANGE OF THE GUARD

1. Washington on *Charlie Rose,* PBS, March 18, 2016; retrieved from charlierose.com.
2. Eric Sullivan, "Kamasi Washington on the Pressures of Being Called Jazz's Savior," *Esquire,* esquire.com, May 2, 2016.
3. Steve Behrens, "After 19 Hours of Passion Comes the Suspense," *Current,* January 15, 2001; retrieved from current.org.
4. DeJohnette, personal interview, February 3, 2015.
5. Francis Davis, "The 2015 NPR Music Jazz Critics Poll," National Public Radio, npr .org, December 21, 2015.
6. Martin Williams, "Will Charles Lloyd Save Jazz for the Masses?," *New York Times,* September 15, 1968; retrieved from nytimes.com.
7. Albert Goldman, "Jazz—Out in Front Again with All the Old Sidemen," *Life,* 1972.
8. Billy Taylor, "Jazz: America's Classical Music," *The Black Perspective in Music* 14, no. 1 (winter 1986), special issue: Black American Music Symposium 1985, p. 21.
9. Herbie Hancock, with Lisa Dickey, *Possibilities* (New York: Viking, 2015), p. 201.
10. Marsalis, interviewed for Ken Burns's *Jazz,* November 19, 1996; transcript retrieved from pbs.com.
11. "Wynton Marsalis: My Relationship to MLK," CBS News, January 16, 2012; retrieved from cbsnews.com.
12. Bernstein, phone interview, November 9, 2015.
13. David Hajdu, *Heroes and Villains: Essays on Music, Movies, Comics, and Culture* (Cambridge, MA: Da Capo, 2009), p. 220.
14. Will Crutchfield, "Trumpet—Wynton Marsalis," *New York Times,* August 26, 1984; retrieved from nytimes.com.
15. Lundvall interview, *Billboard,* October 7, 2000, p. W-20.
16. Robert Palmer, "Perils Confront the Young Lions of Jazz," *New York Times,* May 22, 1983; retrieved from nytimes.com.

17. Francis Davis, *Bebop and Nothingness: Jazz and Pop at the End of the Century* (New York: Schirmer, 1996), p. xi.
18. Ronald M. Radano, *New Musical Figurations: Anthony Braxton's Cultural Critique* (Chicago: University of Chicago Press, 1994), p. 272.
19. Kamasi Washington, with Josef Woodard, "All the Doors Opened," *DownBeat,* July 2016.
20. Ben Ratliff, "Driving Jazz, with Ease, in Los Angeles," *New York Times,* April 26, 2015.
21. Geoff Dyer, "The Intimacy Behind Jazz's Seminal Image," *New York Times Magazine,* May 14, 2017.
22. Kamasi Washington, phone interview, December 22, 2016.

2 FROM THIS MOMENT ON

1. Mehldau, personal interview, May 6, 2015.
2. John S. Wilson, "Jazz Quintet Featuring 2 Holidays," *New York Times,* November 21, 1985; retrieved from nytimes.com.
3. When Bernstein made his debut album, *Somethin's Burnin',* in 1992, he enlisted the same personnel: Cobb, Mehldau, and the bassist John Webber. Cobb reunited the lineup for a 2015 album, *The Original Mob,* on Smoke Sessions Records.
4. Marsalis, June 1983, quoted in Francis Davis, *Jazz and Its Discontents: A Francis Davis Reader* (New York: Da Capo Press, 2004), p. 212.
5. Greg Tate, "The Real Music," *Vibe,* January 1995.
6. Metheny, personal interview, February 15, 2007.
7. Mehldau, phone interview, October 12, 2004.
8. A. O. Scott, "The Best Mind of His Generation," *New York Times,* September 20, 2008; retrieved from nytimes.com.
9. Book 1, Sonnet 3, which includes the line "Song is reality. Simple, for a god."
10. Mehldau, liner notes, *Live at the Village Vanguard: The Art of the Trio Volume Two* (Nonesuch, 1998).
11. Mehldau, phone interview, February 11, 2010.
12. Tad Hendrickson, "Radiohead: The New Standard Bearers?," *JazzTimes,* October 2004.
13. Mehldau, liner notes, *10 Years Solo Live* (Nonesuch, 2015).
14. "The Jon Brion Show—Feat. Elliott Smith/Brad Mehldau ('00)," YouTube video uploaded by AlRosePromotions, youtube.com/watch?v=PK4okHerWeI.
15. Brion, personal interview, May 18, 2009.

3 UPTOWN DOWNTOWN

1. Zorn, quoted in Ben Ratliff, "Barricades to Storm Whether or Not Any Guards Were on Them," *New York Times,* March 12, 2007; retrieved from nytimes.com.
2. Wynton Marsalis, "What Jazz Is—and Isn't," *New York Times,* July 31, 1988; retrieved from nytimes.com.

3. George Lewis, *A Power Stronger Than Itself: The AACM and American Experimental Music* (Chicago: University of Chicago Press, 2008), p. 442.

4. Murray with Marsalis, ed. Devlin, p. 15.

5. Davis, phone interview, July 26, 2006.

6. Ibid.

7. Jon Pareles, "Lincoln Center Is Adding Jazz to Its Repertory," *New York Times,* January 10, 1991; retrieved from nytimes.com.

8. Whitney Balliett, *Collected Works: A Journal of Jazz 1954–2001* (New York: St. Martin's/ Griffin, 2002), p. 769.

9. Peter Watrous, "Lincoln Center Elevates Status of Jazz," *New York Times,* December 19, 1995; retrieved from nytimes.com.

10. Michael Dorf, Knitting Factory press release; retrieved from michaeldorf.com.

11. John Rockwell, "Music: Zorn and Berne Downtown," *New York Times,* August 22, 1987; retrieved from nytimes.com.

12. Berne, personal interview, April 2, 2012.

13. Jon Pareles, "The Pop Life," *New York Times,* February 18, 1987; retrieved from nytimes.com.

14. Ibid.

15. Zorn, personal interview, May 8, 2013.

16. Alex Ross, "A Night of Klezmer Free Jazz (Don't Let Its Name Scare You)," *New York Times,* October 13, 1994; retrieved from nytimes.com.

17. Douglas, personal interview, August 15, 2012.

18. Michael Dorf, "History of the Knitting Factory," December 1991; retrieved from michaeldorf.com.

19. Peter Watrous, "In a Dialectic of Virtuosos, Musical Opposites Attract," *New York Times,* January 11, 1997; retrieved from nytimes.com.

20. Stanley Crouch, "Putting the White Man in Charge," *Jazz Times,* April 2003.

21. Stanley Crouch, "Opinion: The Problem with Jazz Criticism," *Newsweek,* June 4, 2003.

22. David Hajdu, "The Body Eclectic," *New Republic,* February 9, 2004.

23. Thomas Conrad, joint review of *Strange Liberation* and *The Magic Hour, Jazz Times,* April 2004.

24. Francis Davis, "Trumpets No End," *Village Voice,* August 10, 2004; retrieved from villagevoice.com.

25. Redman, personal interview, January 23, 2013.

26. Zorn, personal interview, March 1, 2017.

4 PLAY THE MOUNTAIN

1. Coleman, phone interview, February 8, 1999.

2. Iyer, quoted in Michael J. West, "Steve Coleman: Vital Information," *Jazz Times,* June 2010.

3. Johannes Völz, "Improvisation, Correlation, and Vibration: An Interview with Steve Coleman," *Critical Studies in Improvisation (Études Critiques en Improvisation)* 2, no. 1 (2006).

4. Coleman, personal interview, April 18, 2015.
5. Ibid.
6. Coleman, phone interview, March 7, 2003.
7. Vijay Iyer, "Steve Coleman, M-Base, and Music Collectivism," 1996.
8. Coleman, phone interview, February 8, 1999.
9. John Moser, "Interviewing Steve Coleman: Despite Accolades, Jazz Saxophone Great Finds Respite in Allentown," *Morning Call*, April 29, 2016; retrieved from mcall.com.
10. Coleman, personal interview, April 18, 2015.
11. Ibid.
12. Ibid.

5 THE NEW ELDERS

1. Pérez, personal interview, September 24, 2010.
2. Herbie Hancock, with Lisa Dickey, *Possibilities* (New York: Viking, 2014), p. 61.
3. Stanley Crouch, *Considering Genius* (New York: Basic Civitas, 2006), p. 252.
4. Peter Watrous, "A Jazz Generation and the Miles Davis Curse," *New York Times*, October 15, 1995; retrieved from nytimes.com.
5. Holland, phone interview, January 19, 2013.
6. Potter, personal interview, January 7, 2013.
7. Shorter, personal interview, December 12, 2012.
8. Ethan Iverson, "Interview with Keith Jarrett," September 2009, ethaniverson.com/interviews/interview-with-keith-jarrett.
9. Ethan Iverson, "1973 1990," summer 2006, dothemath.typepad.com. [page now defunct].
10. Lovano, phone interview, March 9, 2013.
11. Frisell, phone interview, March 11, 2013.
12. Abrams, personal interview, April 28, 2008.
13. Taborn, phone interview, February 22, 2015.

6 GANGSTERISM ON A LOOP

1. Moran, personal interview, October 21, 2015.
2. Ibid.
3. Ibid.
4. "Okwui Enwezor in Conversation with Jason Moran," YouTube video, posted May 1, 2015, youtube.com/watch?v=1j23ZLzw7Rg.
5. Jason Moran, "A Return to Town Hall for Monk," *Guardian*, May 15, 2008; accessed at theguardian.com.
6. Interview by Simon Rentner, *The Checkout*, WBGO 88.3 FM, wbgo.org/checkoutjazz/jason-morans-salute-to-cecil-taylor.
7. Moran, phone interview, March 17, 1999.

8. Gary Giddins, *Weather Bird: Jazz at the Dawn of Its Second Century* (New York: Oxford University Press, 2004), p. 513.

9. Moran, personal interview, June 2003.

10. Ibid.

11. Fred Kaplan, "This Kennedy Center Director Is Making Performance Art out of Jazz. Can He Bring Fans Along?" *Washington Post Magazine*, November 2, 2017; retrieved from washingtonpost.com.

7 LEARNING JAZZ

1. Martin Williams, "A Letter from Lenox, Mass," *The Jazz Review* 2, no. 9 (October 1959), p. 31.

2. Burton, personal interview, July 27, 2013.

3. Metheny, quoted in Barry Kernfeld, *The Story of Fake Books: Bootlegging Songs to Musicians* (Lanham, MD: Scarecrow Press, 2006), p. 138.

4. J. Aebersold, "NEA Jazz Masters: Interview with Jamey Aebersold," published January 7, 2014, at https://www.youtube.com/watch?v=_F9CHF41Apo.

5. Joey Alexander, personal interview, May 13, 2016.

6. Mulherkar, personal interview, April 16, 2010.

7. Miles Davis, with Quincy Troupe, *Miles: The Autobiography* (New York: Simon & Schuster, 1990), p. 52.

8. Clark Terry, with Gwen Terry, *Clark: The Autobiography of Clark Terry* (Berkeley: University of California Press, 2011), p. 1.

9. Kevin Sun, "Every Single Tree in the Forest: Mark Turner as Seen by His Peers, Part One," *Music & Literature*, July 21, 2015; retrieved from musicandliterature.org.

10. "Seventeen Ways of Looking at Mark Turner: Kurt Rosenwinkel," *Music & Literature* no. 8, p. 290.

11. "Seventeen Ways of Looking at Mark Turner: Melissa Aldana," *Music & Literature* no. 8, p. 245.

12. Pierce, personal interview, October 20, 2006.

13. Ibid.

14. Iyer, phone interview, July 12, 2012.

8 INFILTRATE AND AMBUSH

1. Morris, personal interview, June 11, 2017.

2. Urvija Banerji, "American Pianist-Composer Vijay Iyer: 'Critics Are Really Bad at Listening,'" *Rolling Stone India*, May 15, 2017; retrieved from rollingstoneindia.com.

3. Iyer, personal interview, January 16, 2014.

4. Vijay Iyer, "Microstructures of Feel, Macrostructures of Sound: Embodied Cognition in West African and African-American Musics," doctoral dissertation, University of California, Berkeley, 1998; retrieved from vijay-iyer.com/writings.

5. Nathaniel Mackey, "Other: From Noun to Verb," *Representations* no. 39 (summer 1992), p. 51.
6. Coleman, phone interview, February 28, 2005.
7. Iyer, personal interview, February 12, 2005.
8. Iyer, personal interview, January 16, 2014.
9. Iyer, personal interview, February 12, 2005.
10. Iyer, personal interview, June 9, 2017.
11. Fred Moten, *In the Break: The Aesthetics of the Black Radical Tradition* (Minneapolis: University of Minnesota Press, 2003).

9 CHANGING SAMES

1. Elevado, quoted in Chris Williams, "The Soulquarians at Electric Lady: An Oral History," *Red Bull Music Academy Daily,* June 1, 2015.
2. Elevado, phone interview, 2003.
3. LeRoi Jones (Amiri Baraka), "The Changing Same (R&B and New Black Music)," *Black Music* (New York: William Morrow, 1967).
4. Jayson Greene, "Waiting for D'Angelo," *Red Bull Music Academy Daily,* April 28, 2014.
5. Nelson George, "A Conversation with D'Angelo," transcript of interview at Brooklyn Museum, May 21, 2014, redbullmusicacademy.com/lectures/dangelo.
6. Jason King, "The Time Is Out of Joint: Notes on D'Angelo's *Voodoo,*" liner notes for reissue of *Voodoo* (Light in the Attic Records, 2012).
7. Ahmir "Questlove" Thompson, with Ben Greenman, *Mo' Meta Blues: The World According to Questlove* (New York: Grand Central Publishing, 2013), p. 160.
8. Hargrove, personal interview, February 27, 2003.
9. Glasper, personal interview, December 21, 2011.
10. Glasper, personal interview, May 22, 2005.
11. Glasper, personal interview, December 21, 2011.
12. Ibid.
13. Glasper, personal interview, September 23, 2013.
14. Hunter, personal interview, January 28, 2016.
15. League, personal interview, January 28, 2016.
16. Ibid.
17. Visconti, phone interview, December 30, 2015.
18. Steven Ellison (Flying Lotus), phone interview, September 30, 2014.
19. Riggins, phone interview, September 14, 2012.

10 EXPOSURES

1. "Esperanza Spalding Accepting the Grammy for Best New Artist at the 53rd Grammy Awards," February 13, 2011, YouTube video, youtube.com/watch?v=_XgkH8_A7vc.

2. Lovano, phone interview, February 27, 2012.

3. Carrington, phone interview, February 29, 2012.

4. Spalding, personal interview, February 6, 2012.

5. Jon Batiste, personal interview, August 1, 2015.

6. Christian Scott, personal interview, March 3, 2010.

7. Ibid.

8. Spalding, phone interview, March 2, 2012.

9. Allen, phone interview, February 28, 2012.

10. E. Spalding, "Jazz and Gender: Challenging Inequality and Forging a New Legacy," panel discussion, January 25, 2018, New York City.

11 THE CROSSROADS

1. Hancock, quoted in Larry Rohter, "Where Nations Debate, Harmony of a Jazz Kind," *New York Times,* April 29, 2002; retrieved from nytimes.com.

2. Philip V. Bohlman and Goffredo Plastino, *Jazz Worlds/World Jazz* (Chicago: University of Chicago Press, 2016), p. 5.

3. Hancock, personal interview, April 30, 2017.

4. Remarks delivered by President Barack Obama at the White House Jazz Festival, April 29, 2016; retrieved from obamawhitehouse.archives.gov.

5. Felix Belair Jr., "United States Has Secret Sonic Weapon—Jazz," *New York Times,* November 6, 1955; retrieved from nytimes.com.

6. Penny Von Eschen, *Satchmo Blows Up the World: Jazz Ambassadors Play the Cold War* (Cambridge, MA: Harvard University Press, 2004), p. 31.

7. Ibid., p. 4.

8. Randy Weston, with Willard Jenkins, *African Rhythms: The Autobiography of Randy Weston* (Durham, NC: Duke University Press, 2010), p. 171.

9. Stańko, personal interview, October 17, 2006.

10. Bensusan, personal interview, September 13, 2016.

11. Bu, personal interview, September 13, 2016.

12. Adiel Portugali, "On the Marginality of Contemporary Jazz in China: The Case of Beijing," in Bruce Johnson (ed.), *Jazz and Totalitarianism,* Transnational Studies in Jazz (New York and London: Routledge, 2017), p. 334.

13. Xia, personal interview, September 10, 2016.

14. Liu, personal interview, September 11, 2016.

15. Roberts, personal interview, September 15, 2016.

16. Vanacore, personal interview, September 14, 2016.

17. Roberts, personal interview, September 15, 2016.

18. Hsieh, personal interview, September 10, 2016.

19. Stuart Nicholson, *Jazz and Culture in a Global Age* (Boston: Northeastern University Press, 2014), p. 108.

20. Stuart Nicholson, *Is Jazz Dead? (Or Has It Moved to a New Address)* (Abingdon, UK: Routledge, 2005).

21. Loueke, personal interview, January 22, 2008.

22. Zenón, phone interview, January 25, 2017.

23. Maalouf, phone interview, September 5, 2016.

12 STYLE AGAINST STYLE

1. Halvorson, personal interview, October 8, 2008.

2. Ibid.

3. Smith, phone interview, October 24, 2008.

4. Bynum, e-mail correspondence, October 26, 2008.

5. Halvorson, personal interview, October 8, 2008.

6. Ibid.

7. Evans, personal interview, November 9, 2016.

8. Jarrett, personal interview, October 26, 2016.

9. Halvorson, personal interview, October 8, 2008.

10. Halvorson, personal interview, October 22, 2016.

11. Bynum, e-mail correspondence, October 26, 2008.

12. Formanek, phone interview, October 24, 2016.

Index

A NOTE ABOUT THE AUTHOR

Nate Chinen has been writing about jazz for more than twenty years. An eleven-time winner of the Helen Dance–Robert Palmer Award for Excellence in Writing, presented by the Jazz Journalists Association, he spent a dozen years covering the music for *The New York Times*, and wrote a long-running column for *JazzTimes*. He became the director of editorial content at WBGO in 2017, overseeing digital coverage and contributing a range of jazz programming to NPR Music. He coauthored *Myself Among Others: A Life in Music*, the 2003 autobiography of jazz impresario George Wein, and his work has appeared in *Best Music Writing 2011*, selected by Alex Ross. He lives in Beacon, New York, with his wife and two daughters.

A NOTE ON THE TYPE

This book was set in Janson, a typeface long thought to have been made by the Dutchman Anton Janson, who was a practicing type-founder in Leipzig during the years 1668–1687. However, it has been conclusively demonstrated that these types are actually the work of Nicholas Kis (1650–1702), a Hungarian, who most probably learned his trade from the master Dutch typefounder Dirk Voskens. The type is an excellent example of the influential and sturdy Dutch types that prevailed in England up to the time William Caslon (1692–1766) developed his own incomparable designs from them.

Typeset by Scribe, Philadelphia, Pennsylvania
Printed and bound by Berryville Graphics, Berryville, Virginia
Designed by Maggie Hinders